Travel the Globe

Travel the Globe

Story Times, Activities, and Crafts for Children

Second Edition

Desiree Webber, Dee Ann Corn, Elaine Harrod,
Sandy Shropshire, Shereen Rasor,
and Donna Norvell (in memoriam)

Illustrated by Sandy Shropshire

LIBRARIES UNLIMITED

AN IMPRINT OF ABC-CLIO, LLC
Santa Barbara, California • Denver, Colorado • Oxford, England

Library of Congress Cataloging-in-Publication Data

Webber, Desiree, 1956–
   Travel the globe : story times, activities, and crafts for children / Desiree Webber, Dee Ann Corn, Elaine Harrod,
Sandy Shropshire, Shereen Rasor, and Donna Norvell (in memoriam). — Second edition.
      pages cm
   Includes bibliographical references and indexes.
   ISBN 978-1-61069-124-6 (pbk.) — ISBN 978-1-61069-125-3 (ebook) (print) 1. Multicultural education—
Activity programs—United States. 2. Children's libraries—Activity programs—United States. 3. Ethnology—Study and
teaching (Early childhood)—United States. 4. International education—United States. 5. Storytelling—United States.
6. Children's literature—Bibliography. I. Title.
LC1099.3.T73   2013
370.1170973—dc23   2012030564

ISBN: 978-1-61069-124-6
EISBN: 978-1-61069-125-3

17 16 15 14 13   1 2 3 4 5

This book is also available on the World Wide Web as an eBook.
Visit www.abc-clio.com for details.

Libraries Unlimited
An Imprint of ABC-CLIO, LLC

ABC-CLIO, LLC
130 Cremona Drive, P.O. Box 1911
Santa Barbara, California 93116-1911

This book is printed on acid-free paper ∞

Manufactured in the United States of America

Contents

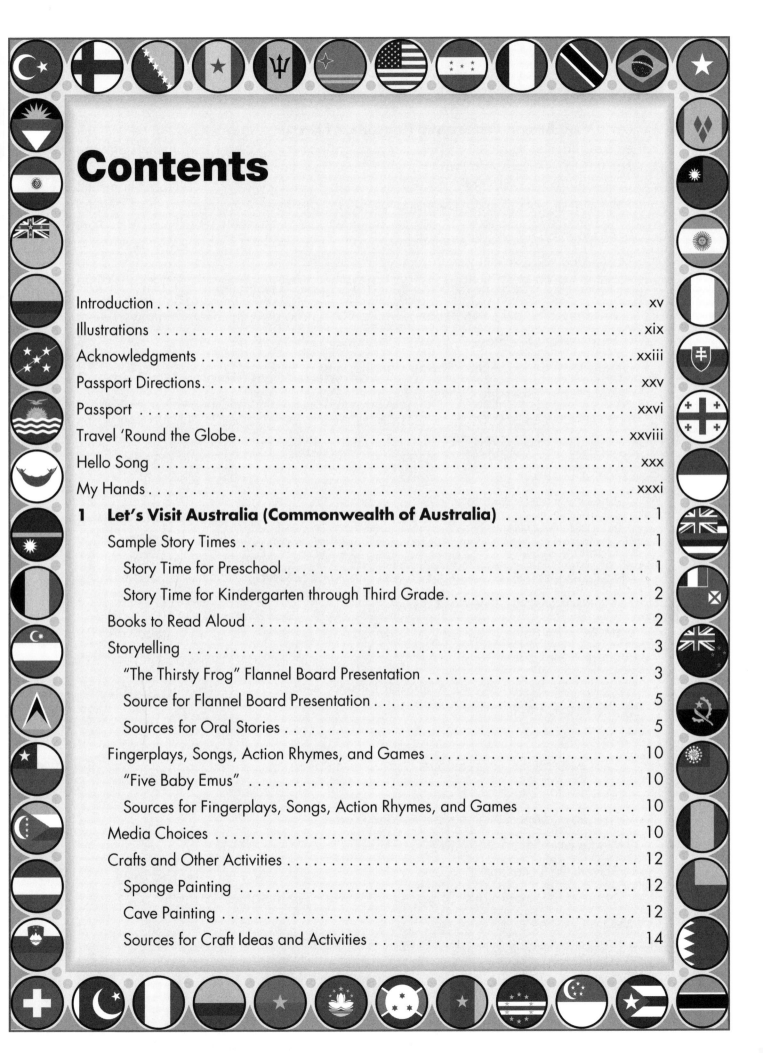

Introduction

It is an exciting undertaking to introduce children to the world and our global neighbors. There are so many wonderful stories, songs, games, crafts, and activities that share information about the varied world in which we live. A "Travel the Globe" story time is a rich, rewarding experience for both the librarian/teacher and young people.

The authors have provided a plethora of ready-to-use materials plus references to related resources. Readers will discover within these pages recommended books to read aloud and stories with patterns for flannel boards and stick puppets. There are also finger-plays with patterns for finger puppets. The readers will also find instructions for simple games and action rhymes to share with young audiences. Children are drawn to crafts. The opportunity to use scissors, tape, glue, glitter, markers, and crayons makes for a fun story time in the eyes of a child. Hands-on activities complete the learning process. Included in every chapter are instructions and patterns for simple, inexpensive craft projects.

Travel the Globe: Story Times, Activities, and Crafts for Children, second edition, assists the busy professional with the materials to present entertaining and educational programming to children in preschool through third grade. This is the second edition of *Travel the Globe*, which was first published in 1998 under the title *Travel the Globe: Multicultural Story Times*. The second edition contains the original flannel boards, puppet stories, and patterns and is updated with new titles to read aloud; new resources for fingerplays, songs, action rhymes and games; along with new media titles and web-based information.

Each chapter focuses on one country, and chapters follow a similar format throughout so that needed information can be easily located. At the beginning of each chapter are two suggested story time outlines: one for preschoolers and one for children in kindergarten through third grade. This is followed by a song for opening each story time, the "Hello Song," along with an action rhyme entitled "My Hands" for closing each story time.

The song sets the mood for the story time and the action rhyme provides closure. In addition, both the song and the action rhyme introduce vocabulary (*hello*, *goodbye*, and *thank you*) from the major language for each country. Presenters may also opt to include a lengthier, more in-depth song for school-age children entitled "Travel 'Round the Globe." The original lyrics and sheet music for "Hello Song" and "Travel 'Round the Globe" follow this introduction.

After the suggested story time outline for each chapter is an annotated bibliography of suggested books to read aloud, followed by at least one oral story using either flannel board characters or simple puppets, such as stick puppets or bag puppets. Patterns and instructions for these visual devices are provided. A section with fingerplays, songs, action rhymes, and games, along with an annotated listing of media, comes next. The last part of the chapter contains crafts, also with patterns and instructions. To make *Travel the Globe* as useful as possible, annotated bibliographies of books or websites with fingerplays, games, action rhymes, oral stories, activities, and crafts are also included in each chapter. This book can be used year after year with fresh, new material introduced in each story time session.

All crafts use low-cost supplies and are simple to prepare and execute. At least two craft projects are included in each chapter. One craft is designed for preschoolers (with suggestions for additional simplification), and one craft is designed for children in kindergarten through third grade. Consider asking parents who bring their children to story time to assist during the craft portion of the program, or recruit volunteers to help.

In the absence of authentic, age-appropriate crafts, literature-based crafts are used. For example, in the chapter on Greece, " 'The Fox and the Grapes' Stick Puppet Theater" is suggested as a craft project. The storyteller may introduce the craft by telling or reading fables attributed to Aesop, a freed Greek slave who lived about 620–560 B.C., and share that the Greeks have a long history of developing and enjoying theater.

The section titled "Books to Read Aloud" contains recently published titles plus perennial classics. With the advent of online booksellers, print-on-demand, and other publishing options, many authors are keeping their titles in print and available for purchase. *Once a Mouse...A Fable Cut in Wood*, by Marcia Brown, was first published in 1961 and named a Caldecott Medal winner. This book remains in print and is a treasure to share when traveling to the Republic of India. These annotated bibliographies of suggested books include titles of merit enjoyed by children in this age group. Children ages 3 to 8 have a wide range of abilities and attention spans. If a book is more appropriate for children in kindergarten through third grade, the authors have noted "Recommended for school-age children" in the annotation. If a title is not available at a nearby public library or media center, pursue it through interlibrary loan.

Travel the Globe provides a selection of books, stories, action rhymes, fingerplays, games, and activities from which a librarian, media specialist, or teacher may plan a program or a single activity. This book also helps media specialists and teachers work together. The media specialist may share a few of the suggested books and stories and then give teachers packets of extending activities (crafts, games, media) for the classroom or gym. The public librarian may pick and choose from the suggested story time outlines to create a 30- to 45-minute story time.

To further enhance the learning process, create an atmosphere for traveling the globe. A sample passport designed for this book follows the introduction. At the beginning of each story time, have children stamp their passports with a decorative rubber stamp. Play music to set the mood. (Suggested titles are included in most chapters.) Bring clothing, toys, dishes, or other artifacts from that country to share with the children. If possible, provide items that young people can touch or handle. Children need as much concrete experience as possible to learn something new. Consider visiting stores or restaurants that have items from the countries the group will be "visiting." Most individuals are eager to share their culture with others.

Whenever possible, show children modern photographs of the people and locales for the countries to be shared. Folktales and other traditional stories may portray lifestyles, clothing, and attitudes that are no longer typical in the modern world. A bibliography of current series titles published on various countries is provided at the back of *Travel the Globe*.

If a series of "Travel the Globe" story times is conducted, the reader may want to conclude his or her travels by returning to the United States. Chapter 13, "Let's Visit the United States of America (Native Americans)," is organized in the same format as the other chapters, with books, stories, action rhymes, media, and activities related to or originating from various Native American tribes in the United States. This is an effective method for tying up the travel theme and ending the series. The children will have completed their passports and can enjoy fond memories to share with parents, siblings and friends.

It is the sincere wish of the authors that our colleagues find this material useful and enjoyable. The authors have a hundred years of combined experience working with children in public library, media center, and classroom settings. The authors have great respect for all cultures and ethnicities. We ask that those who use this resource do so with compassion and consideration for all peoples, beliefs, and customs. Good traveling to all!

Illustrations

Ireland

Italy

Mexico

Russian Federation

United States of America (Native American)

Vietnam

Acknowledgments

For those works that are not acknowledged here, the authors have searched for a known author without success.

"Baby Rattlesnake." From *Baby Rattlesnake*, told by Te Ata, adapted by Lynn Moroney, illustrated by Veg Reisberg (San Francisco: Children's Book Press, 1989). Reprinted by permission of the publisher.

"Billy Beg and the Bull." Retelling based on two variants, found in *Best Stories to Tell to Children* by Sara Cone Bryant (Boston and New York: Houghton Mifflin, 1912), and *In the Chimney Corners: Merry Tales of Irish Folk Lore* by Seumas MacManus (Garden City, NY: Doubleday, 1924).

"The Coyote Scolds His Tail." From *Picture Tales from Mexico* by Dan Storm, illustrated by Mark Storm (Houston, TX: Gulf Publishing, 1995). Reprinted by permission of Mark Storm.

"The Dragon Who Ate the Sun." Based upon information found in *Moon Lore* by Rev. Timothy Harley (London: Swan Sonnenschein, Le Bas & Lowrey, 1885).

"Hello Song." Words and music adapted from "Hello Song" in *Mother Goose Time: Library Programs for Babies and Their Caregivers* by Jane Marino and Dorothy F. Houlihan (New York: H.W. Wilson, 1992). Adapted by permission of the publisher.

"How Jerboa Tricked the Lion." A retelling of "How the Cunning Jerboa Killed the Strong Lion" in *Hausa Superstitions and Customs: An Introduction to the Folk-Lore and the Folk* by Major A. J. N. Tremearne (London: John Bale, Sons & Danielsson, 1913).

"How the Brazilian Beetle Won the Race." A retelling of "How the Brazilian Beetles Got Their Gorgeous Coats" in *Fairy Tales from Brazil* by Elsie Spicer Eells (n.p.: Dodd, Mead, 1917).

"How the Tiger Got His Stripes." A synthesis of four variants, found in *Vietnamese Legends*, adapted from the Vietnamese by George F. Schultz (Rutland, VT: Charles E. Tuttle, 1965); *Once in Vietnam: The Bridge of Reunion, and Other Stories* by Trân Van Diên and Lê Tinh Thông, illustrated by Kim Bang (Lincolnwood, IL: National Textbook, 1983); *Fairy Tales from Vietnam* by Dorothy Lewis Robertson, illustrated by W. T. Mars (New York: Dodd, Mead, 1968); and *Asian-Pacific Folktales and Legends* edited by Jeanette Faurot (New York: Simon & Schuster, 1995).

"Lionbruno." A retelling from *Italian Popular Tales* by Thomas Frederick Crane (Boston and New York: Houghton Mifflin, 1885).

"Mummy Hunt." From *Raising the Roof: Children's Stories and Activities on Houses* by Jan Irving and Robin Currie (Englewood, CO: Teacher Ideas Press, 1991). Reprinted by permission of the Teacher Ideas Press.

"My Hands." Action rhyme reprinted from *Ring a Ring o' Roses*. Reprinted by permission of the publisher, Flint Public Library, Flint, MI.

"The Pearl Thief." A retelling of "No Pearls E'er Placed in His Care" in *Tales and Poems of South India* by Edward Jewitt Robinson (London: T. Woolmer, 1885).

"The Thirsty Frog." A retelling of two variants, found in *The Land of the Kangaroo: Adventures of Two Youths in a Journey through the Great Island Continent* by Thomas W. Knox, illustrated by H. Burgess (Boston: W.A. Wilde, 1896), and *Aboriginal Mythology* by Mudrooroo Nyoongah (London: Thorsons, 1994).

"A Tower for the King." A retelling based on two recorded versions: "Tower to the Moon" from *Folk Tales of Latin America*, adapted by Shirlee P. Newman (Indianapolis, IN: Bobbs-Merrill, 1962), and "El Rey Derrumbao" (The King's Tower) from *Folk-Lore from the Dominican Republic* by Manuel J. Andrade, translated by Julia Contreras (New York: American Folk-Lore Society, G.E. Stechert, 1930).

"What Is an Elephant?" A retelling of "Blind Religion" in *Tales and Poems of South India* by Edward Jewitt Robinson (London: T. Woolmer, 1885).

Passport Directions

The Reading Passport is a fun tool for encouraging children to make believe that they are presenting their personal travel documents at a check station to begin their journey to another country. As the passport agent, welcome the children with the appropriate greeting from the destination country as you stamp their passports inside the grids. (The greetings are found at the beginning of each chapter in the "Hello Song" section.) Encourage children to respond to you with the same greeting. In the same fashion that wearing a colorful shawl or playing ethnic music will influence your young audience, stamping a shamrock for Ireland onto the passport, or a kangaroo sticker for Australia, will produce an immediate connection with a country.

Refer to pages xxvi–xxvii for the Reading Passport and Passport cover art. To create a Reading Passport, photocopy the cover onto 8½- by 11-inch colored paper, then copy the inside of the passport onto the reverse side of the cover. If enlarging capabilities are available, enlarge front and back 30 percent so that the images and words are as large as possible.

Fold the passport in half like a book. Use a calligraphy pen or colorful marker to add each child's names on the blank line of the certificate, which is on the back cover. Print the names of the countries to be visited on the inside of the passport at the bottom of each rectangle. Leave room for the stamp or sticker.

If the *Travel the Globe* program is a weekly library session, the passports may be easily distributed by laying them name side up on a table outside of the story time room. Accompanying adults can help their young children find their own passports prior to the program. If traveling the globe is part of a classroom study unit, the passports may be distributed to the students at their desks.

A final note: The program presenter may add his or her name on the "Travel Agent" line at the end of the final session. In this way, the children will be recognized individually as the presenter signs his or her name with an official flourish, shakes hands, and presents children with their Reading Passports as a memento of their world travels.

READING PASSPORT

Travel the Globe with Books

This is to certify that

_____

has successfully completed
a journey around the
globe with books.

_____

Travel Agent

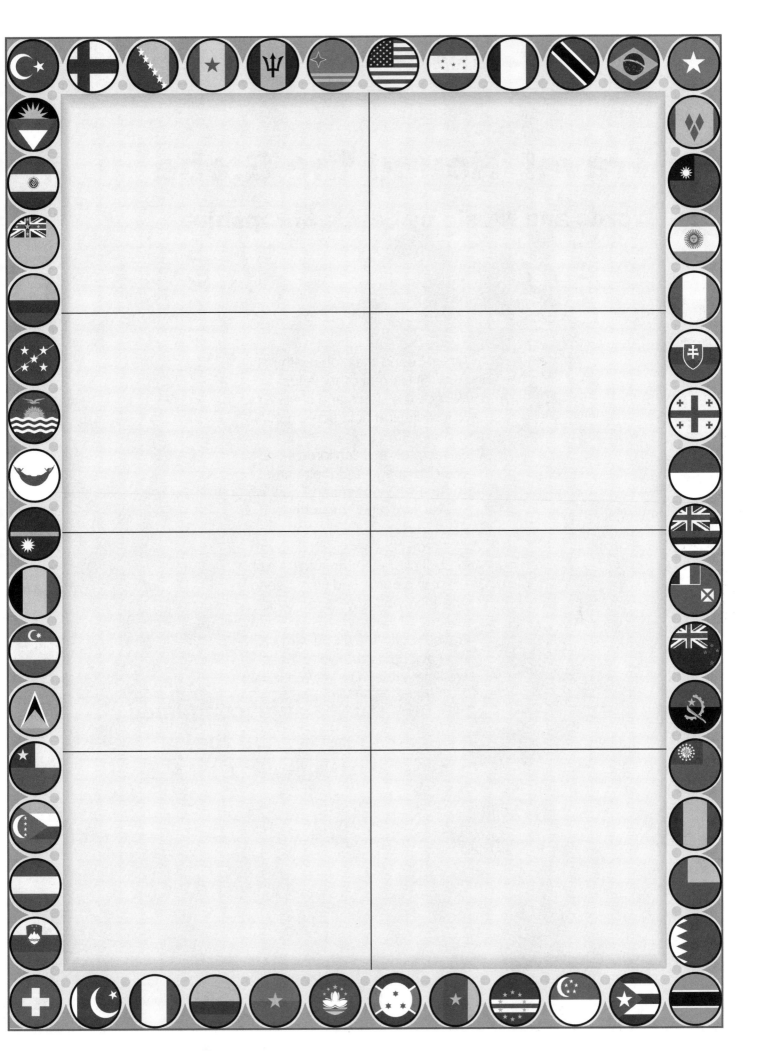

Travel 'Round the Globe

Words and Music by Sandy Shropshire

Travel 'round the globe with us.
We'll learn of other lands.
And we'll see the sights and share a laugh.
We'll smile and hold some hands.

We'll learn of other children's ways:
Their language and their name.
And then we'll understand how we
Are very much the same.

We'll cross the seas and deserts,
And we'll climb the mountains high.
We'll play a game and sing a song,
And then we'll say "good-bye."

Travel 'round the globe with us.
How awesome the world looks!
And we'll never have to leave our seats.
We're traveling with books!

Travel 'Round the Globe

words and music by
S. Shropshire

Giocoso (merrily)

Hello Song

Words and Music Adapted by Sandy Shropshire

Hello ev'rybody,
And how are you? How are you?
Hello ev'rybody,
And how are you today?

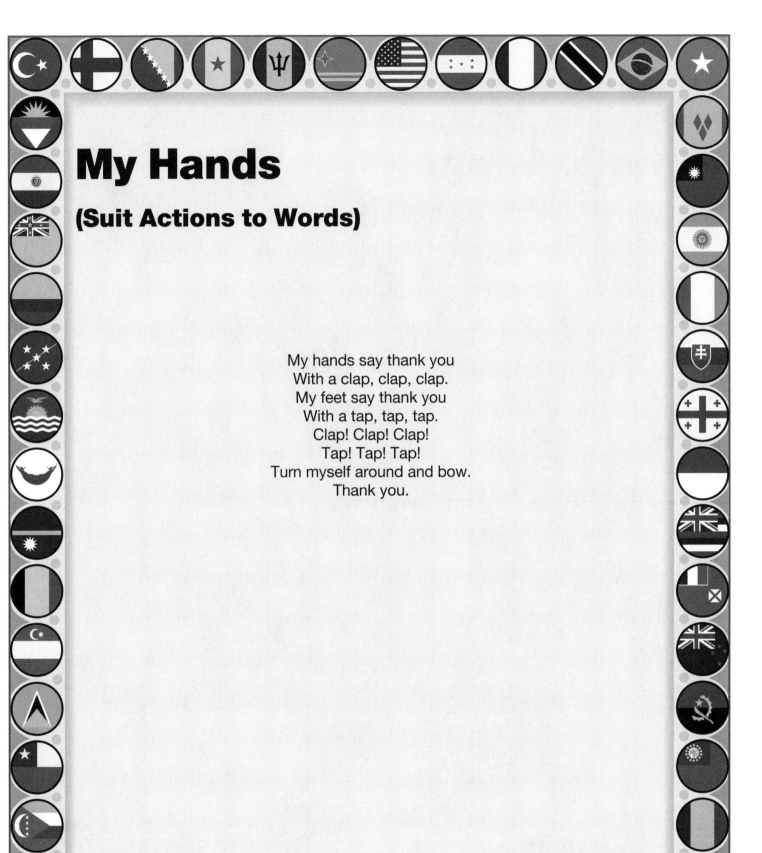

My Hands

(Suit Actions to Words)

My hands say thank you
With a clap, clap, clap.
My feet say thank you
With a tap, tap, tap.
Clap! Clap! Clap!
Tap! Tap! Tap!
Turn myself around and bow.
Thank you.

Chapter 1

Let's Visit

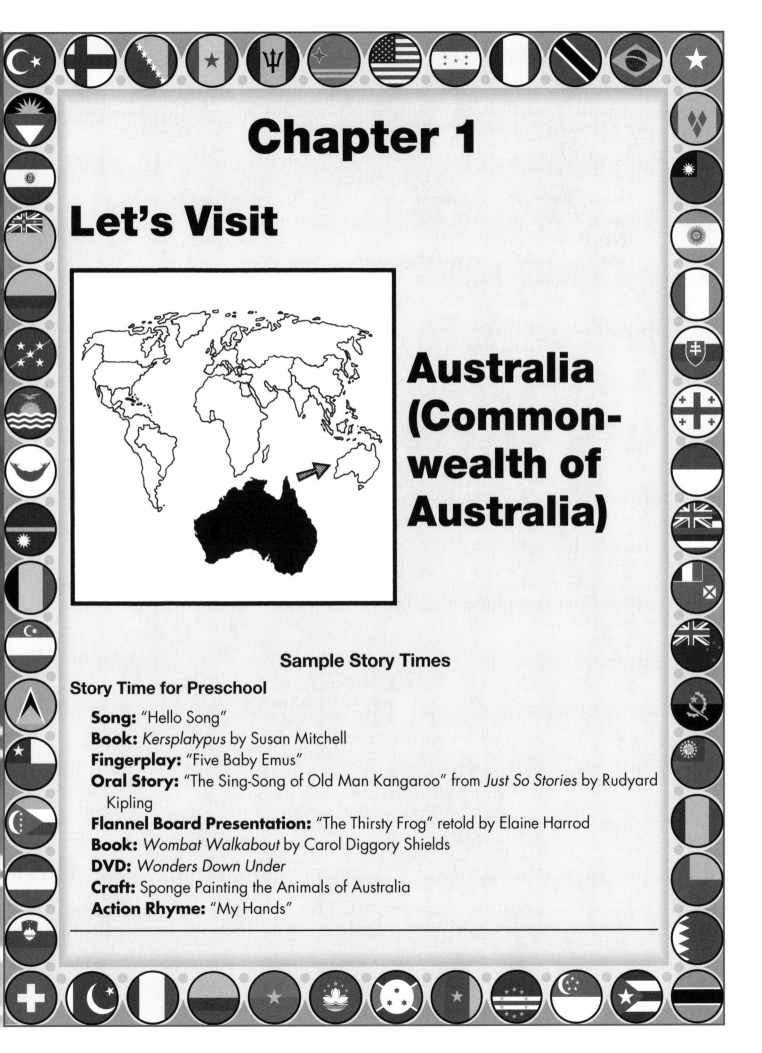

Australia (Commonwealth of Australia)

Sample Story Times

Story Time for Preschool

Song: "Hello Song"

Book: *Kersplatypus* by Susan Mitchell

Fingerplay: "Five Baby Emus"

Oral Story: "The Sing-Song of Old Man Kangaroo" from *Just So Stories* by Rudyard Kipling

Flannel Board Presentation: "The Thirsty Frog" retold by Elaine Harrod

Book: *Wombat Walkabout* by Carol Diggory Shields

DVD: *Wonders Down Under*

Craft: Sponge Painting the Animals of Australia

Action Rhyme: "My Hands"

Story Time for Kindergarten through Third Grade

Song: "Hello Song"
Book: *Over in Australia: Amazing Animals Down Under* by Marianne Berkes
Flannel Board Presentation: "The Thirsty Frog" retold by Elaine Harrod
Book: *Are We There Yet?* by Alison Lester
DVD: *Dermot in Australia*
Craft: A didgeridoo, in *World Crafts* by Greta Speechley
Action Rhyme: "My Hands"

Begin the story time with the "Hello Song." Then sing the song again, substituting the word *hello* with the Australian greeting *g'day mates*. (See p. xxix for the "Hello Song" music.)

Hello Song

Hello ev'rybody,
And how are you? How are you?
Hello ev'rybody,
And how are you today?
G'day mates,
And how are you? How are you?
G'day mates,
And how are you today?

End the story time with the "My Hands" action rhyme, substituting the words *thank you* with the Australian word *ta*, and *goodbye* with *ta ta*. Have children stand up and follow the actions in the rhyme.

My Hands

My hands say ta. *(hold up hands)*
With a clap, clap, clap. *(clap hands)*
My feet say ta. *(point to feet)*
With a tap, tap, tap. *(stamp or tap feet)*
Clap! Clap! Clap! *(clap hands)*
Tap! Tap! Tap! *(stamp or tap feet)*
Turn myself around and bow. *(turn and bow)*
Ta ta. *(wave goodbye)*

Books to Read Aloud

Arnold, Caroline. *A Koala's World*. Minneapolis, MN: Picture Window Books, 2008. (24 pages)
This is one title in the Caroline Arnold's animal series. Although this book is a nonfiction book, it makes for a great read-aloud with its beautiful, large illustrations.

Berkes, Marianne. *Over in Australia: Amazing Animals Down Under*. Illustrated by Jill Dubin. Nevada City, CA: Dawn Publications, 2011. (28 pages)
> The text is written to the tune of "Over in the Meadow" featuring Australian animals.

Blackstone, Stella. *My Granny Went to Market: A Round-the-World Counting Rhyme*. Illustrated by Christopher Corr. Cambridge, MA: Barefoot Books, 2005. (22 pages)
> A granny travels around the world on a magic carpet buying things to take home from her trip. Eight buzzing boomerangs are purchased in Australia. Children will enjoy the maps in the front and back of this counting-format picture book.

French, Jackie. *Diary of a Wombat*. Illustrated by Bruce Whatley. New York, NY: Clarion Books, 2003. (28 pages)
> Fun and expressive illustrations accompany the daily diary entries of a little wombat.

Gibson, Amy. *Around the World on Eighty Legs*. Illustrated by Daniel Salmieri. New York, NY: Scholastic, 2011. (56 pages)
> This book is filled with funny poems about different animals from all over the world. The last 13 poems are specifically about Australian animals. This is a delightful poetry book.

Lester, Alison. *Are We There Yet?* LaJolla, CA: Kane/Miller Book Publishers, 2005. (32 pages)
> This is a story of an Australian family (Mum, Dad, and three children) who spend an educational school term traveling in their camper trailer all around the continent of Australia. The maps in this book will be of great interest to children learning about Australia.

Mitchell, Susan K. *Kersplatypus*. Illustrated by Sherry Rogers. Mt. Pleasant, SC: Sylvan Dell Publishing, 2008. (32 pages)
> The platypus in this story is separated from his mother, and the Blue-Tongued Skink is not kind to him in his search. Readers of this book are given opportunities to talk about social skills, animal classification, and adaptation information. Also visit the following website and click on the book cover for quizzes and other educational activities to go along with this title: www.SylvanDellPublishing.com.

Morgan, Sally and Ezekiel Kwaymullina. *Sam's Bush Journey*. Illustrated by Bronwyn Bancroft. Surry Hills, NSW, Australia: Little Hare Books, 2009. (32 pages)
> Sam is reluctant to enjoy or try to understand more about the Australian land around his grandmother's house. After walking on her land with her and then dreaming about it, Sam starts to have a better appreciation for Australia.

Napoli, Donna Jo and Elena Furrow. *Ready to Dream*. Illustrated by Bronwyn Bancroft. New York: Bloomsbury Children's Books, 2009. (32 pages)
> Ally and her mother go on a trip to Australia, where she meets an Aboriginal artist, and they soon become friends. The two discuss Ally's art, and Ally finds out that even mistakes lead to great discoveries.

Shields, Diggory Carol. *Wombat Walkabout*. Illustrated by Sophie Blackall. New York, NY: Dutton Children's Books, 2009. (32 pages)
> The six little wombats in this story find themselves in a bind with a dingo, but they use their cleverness to survive. The rhyming text makes this book a fun read-aloud.

Storytelling

"The Thirsty Frog" Flannel Board Presentation

"The Thirsty Frog" is a retelling of an Aboriginal myth about a large, greedy frog named Tiddalick. Some believe that the myth of Tiddalick originated from a type of frog called a water-holding frog (*Cyclorana novahollandia*) found in Australia. This frog gorges itself with as much water as it can hold and then burrows into the sand, where it can stay for long periods of time waiting for rain. Desert-dwelling Aborigines have a history of digging for these frogs as a source of water during droughts.

See Figures 1.1 through 1.8. for patterns. Trace the patterns on felt, or photocopy and color them. If photocopying, glue small pieces of felt to the backs of the papers so they will hold to the flannel board. For a tree, use Figures 2.5 and 2.12 from the chapter "Let's Visit Brazil." Before beginning the story, place the tree on the flannel board and place the koala in the tree. Place other figures on the flannel board as they are introduced in the story.

"The Thirsty Frog" retold by Elaine Harrod

Long ago in Australia, there lived a Frog. He lived deep in the sand, where he had burrowed after drinking so much water he could not even hop. After many days and many nights had passed, the frog began to feel very thirsty. So he began to dig his way back to the surface of the earth. *(place the small Frog on the flannel board)*

When the Frog came out of the ground, the other animals were frightened, for they did not know what the Frog wanted. They soon knew why the Frog had come out. He began to drink from the river. The animals watched as he drank and drank. He drank until the river was gone! Then he drank all the rivers dry! Then he drank all the streams and lakes dry! The animals were very concerned.

"Oh no!" the animals cried. "The Frog is even drinking the ocean!" The Frog grew large with water. *(replace the small Frog with the large Frog; place the Platypus on the flannel board)*

The Platypus begged, "Please don't drink all the water in the sea!" But the Frog continued to drink from the ocean, paying no attention to the Platypus. As he drank more and more from the ocean, *(place the Sea Turtle on the flannel board)* a Sea Turtle pleaded, "Frog, if you drink all the water in the sea, my friends and I will have no home." But the Frog had gone so long without water that he did not even hear the pleas of the Sea Turtle.

The animals began gathering around the Frog to beg him not to drink all the water. *(place the Dingo on the flannel board)* The Dingo howled, "Please stop! We will share with yooooooooou, but you don't need all the water. We will die if yooooooooou do not return the water!" But the Frog said nothing. He sat with his mouth tightly closed. He had now drunk every drop of water in the world!

The animals talked to one another, trying to decide what to do. How could they get the water back that the Frog had drunk? *(place the Kookaburra on the flannel board)* The Kookaburra said she had an idea "What if I make my Kookaburra sound? Everyone knows that it sounds like a laugh." All the animals thought this was a great idea, for if they could make the Frog laugh, his mouth would open, and all the water would spill back onto the earth. The Kookaburra began "K-ha-ha-ha, ka ha-ha-ha, ka-ha-ha-ha."

"What is all the noise about?" *(place the Kangaroo on the flannel board)* All the noise had awakened the sleeping Kangaroo. The animals explained what had happened. Kangaroo offered to do a funny hopping dance to try to make the Frog laugh. Kangaroo hopped higher and higher, trying her best to be funny. Before she realized what had happened, she had hopped so high that she landed in a tree and found herself sitting next to a Koala Bear. *(place the Kangaroo in the tree beside the Koala)*

When the Frog saw this, he could not help but grin, and the grin turned into a smile, and the smile turned into a great, roaring laughter. Just as the other animals had hoped, the water spilled out of his mouth and back onto the earth. *(replace the large Frog with the small Frog)*

As for the Kangaroo, the animals had to stand on each other's backs to help her out of the tree. *(following the narrative, place the animals, one on top another, beneath the Kangaroo)* The Dingo stood on the Sea Turtle's back, and then the Platypus stood on the Dingo's back. The Kookaburra stood on the Platypus's back, and then the Frog stood on the Kookaburra's back *(take the Kangaroo out of the tree)* and helped the Kangaroo out of the tree.

On this most unusual day, the Frog became great friends with the other animals. With these newfound friendships, he promised his new friends that he would never drink all the water!

Source for Flannel Board Presentation

MacMillan, Kathy and Christine Kirker. *Storytime Magic: 400 Fingerplays, Flannelboards, and Other Activities.* Chicago, IL: American Library Association, 2009. (pages 31–32)
This book contains the flannel board story, "An Australian Creation Story Flannelboard." There are patterns for the flannel board characters as well as a web page address to print larger sizes of the patterns.

Sources for Oral Stories

Kipling, Rudyard. "The Sing-Song of Old Man Kangaroo." In *Just So Stories: For Little Children.* Illustrated by Barry Moser. New York: Harper Collins, 1996. (pages 41–45)
The humorous tale of Yellow Dog Dingo and how he changes Old Man Kangaroo forever.

Marshall, Vance James. *Stories from the Billabong.* Illustrated by Francis Firebrace. London: Frances Lincoln Children's Books, 2008. (64 pages)
According to the author, these 10 myths and legends are some of the oldest in the world and are favorite oral tales.

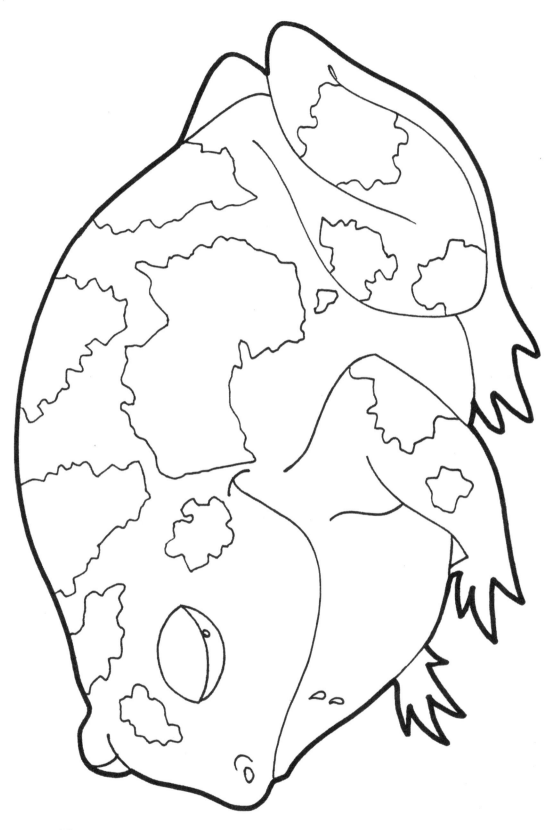

Figure 1.1 **Thirsty Frog**

Figure 1.2 **Kookaburra**   Figure 1.3 **Koala**   Figure 1.4 **Platypus**

Figure 1.5 **Kangaroo** Figure 1.6 **Sea Turtle**

Figure 1.7 **Small Frog**   Figure 1.8 **Dingo**

Fingerplays, Songs, Action Rhymes, and Games

"Five Baby Emus"

For this fingerplay, begin with five emu puppets, one on each finger; bend down a finger each time an emu exits the poem. The storyteller will wear the finger puppets. The children will hold up five fingers and follow along. To make finger puppets, photocopy Figures 1.9 and 1.10 on white tagboard or construction paper. Use markers to color the emus. Laminate and cut out the emus and finger attachments. Tape together the three flaps of each finger attachment. This will fit over the tip of each finger like a thimble. Tape an emu to each finger attachment.

Five Baby Emus
by Elaine Harrod

Five baby emus, wishing they could soar. (five emus)
One went to try and that left four. (remove a puppet)
Four baby emus hungry as can be. (four emus)
One went to eat and that left three. (remove a puppet)
Three baby emus go off to the zoo. (three emus)
Only one ran away and that left two. (remove a puppet)
Two baby emus were looking for some fun. (two emus)
One found a playmate and that left one. (remove a puppet)
One baby emu playing in the sun. (one emu)
Then all were gone and that left none. (remove last puppet)

Sources for Fingerplays, Songs, Action Rhymes, and Games

Putumayo Kids Presents Animal Playground: Playful Tracks from around the World. United States: Putumayo World Music, 2007. Compact disc.
   A fun and upbeat song entitled "Don't Ever Step on a Snake" could be played during a transition time or while the children are creating Australian-inspired art.

Stewart, Georgiana. *Multicultural Bean Bag Fun*. NJ: Kimbo Educational, 2010. Compact disc.
   In song number 11, "Kangaroo Hop," kids pair up with a partner and pass the bean bag back and forth as they pretend to be a kangaroo.

Media Choices

Show a DVD as a transition between storytelling activities and crafts.

Aronson, Billy, John Ten Eyck, and Jonathan Grupper. *Wonders Down Under*. National Geographic, 2005. DVD, 42 min.
   This National Geographic presentation will give children an up-close and personal understanding of the animals of Australia.

Countries around the World: Australia. Wynnewood, PA: Schlessinger, 2007. DVD, 13 min.
   This DVD gives children a great visual tour of Australia and allows them to see the sites of Sydney and listen to Aboriginal people play the didgeridoo.

de Rouvre, Charles-Antoine. *Dermot in Australia*. Wheeling IL: Productions Pixcom, 2009. DVD, 13 min.
   Dermot lives on a sheep ranch in Australia and has a very different life than the average American child.

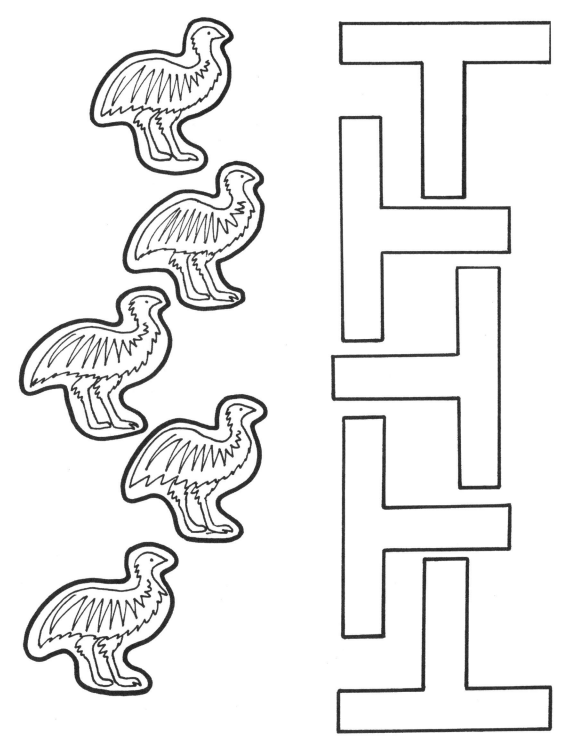

Figure 1.9 **Emu Finger Puppets**   Figure 1.10 **Finger Puppet Attachments**

Crafts and Other Activities

Choose a craft suited for the age level of the group and the time allotted for the story time.

Sponge Painting

Animals of Australia are very unique. Many of the books listed in the "Books to Read Aloud" section would make great read-aloud books to share before introducing the following craft.

Supplies

Sponge sheets	Paintbrush
Scissors	Cookie sheets
Pen	Colored markers and crayons
Tempera paint	White construction paper

Photocopy Figures 1.11 through 1.14 and cut out the patterns. Lay the patterns on the sponge sheets and trace the shapes with a felt-tipped pen. The teacher then uses sharp scissors to cut out several sponges of each animal shape (one for each color so colors won't become mixed). Wet the sponge shapes (they will expand). Pour a small amount of tempera paint, of each color, onto a cookie sheet. Spread the paint using a paintbrush. Have children dip the sponge animals into the paint and press them onto the construction paper. After the paint is dry, have children use crayons and markers to design a background for their Australian scene.

Cave Painting

Some of the most impressive cave paintings in Australia are found in the Northern Territory. Some of these painting are estimated to be more than 5,000 years old. Many Aborigines still create art using techniques developed long ago. Several of the illustrators of the books listed in this chapter are Aborigines. Show some of their art to children before beginning this activity.

Supplies

Butcher paper	Tape
Colored markers, crayons or chalk	

Figure 1.11 **Kangaroo** Figure 1.12 **Goanna Lizard** Figure 1.13 **Platypus** Figure 1.14
Australian Opossum

Sources for Craft Ideas and Activities

Casey, Dawn. *The Barefoot Book of Earth Tales*. Illustrated by Anne Wilson. Cambridge, MA: Barefoot Books, 2009. (95 pages)
   This book contains an Australian folktale and the craft, "Make a Song-Line Painting." Instructions show how to create Aboriginal pictures and the key for creating authentic symbolic art.

French, Jackie. *How to Scratch a Wombat*. Illustrated by Bruce Whatley. New York: Clarion Books, 2009. (86 pages)
   This is an intriguing nonfiction resource for information about wombats written by the author of the picture book *Diary of a Wombat*. Line-drawing illustrations and text about how wombats live are well presented.

Speechley, Greta. *World Crafts*. New York, NY: Gareth Stevens Publishing, 2010. (31 pages)
   Didgeridoos are instruments that have been made by the Aboriginal people of Australia. This book provides instructions for making one.

Chapter 2

Let's Visit

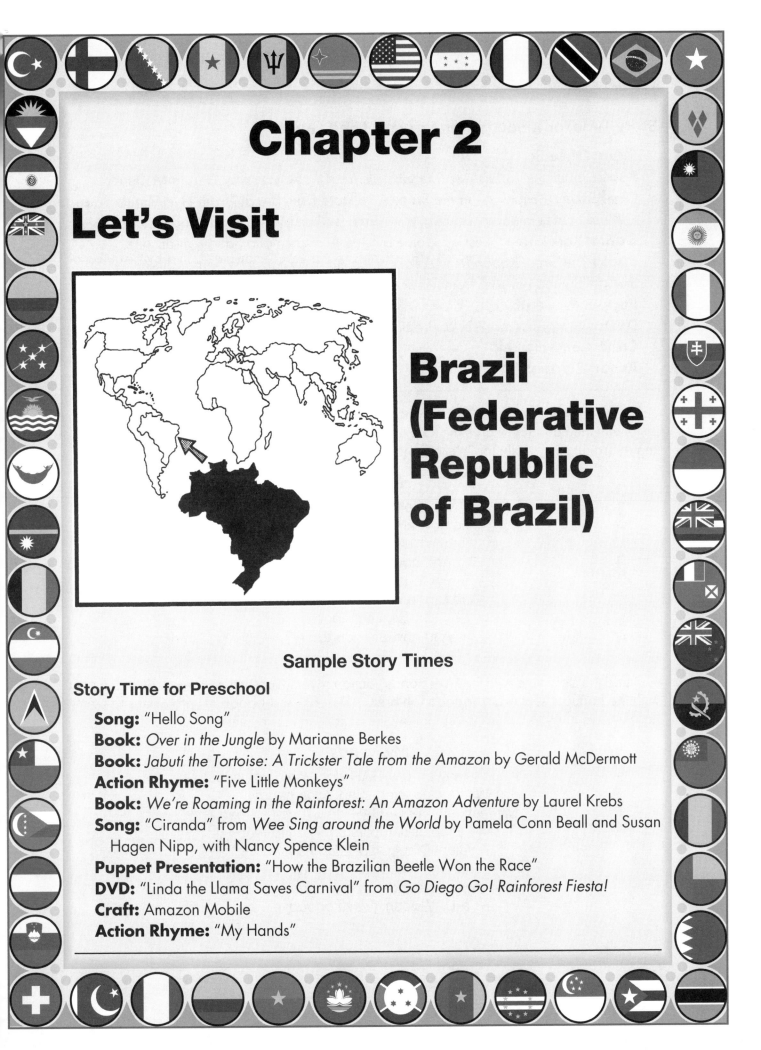

Brazil (Federative Republic of Brazil)

Sample Story Times

Story Time for Preschool

Song: "Hello Song"

Book: *Over in the Jungle* by Marianne Berkes

Book: *Jabutí the Tortoise: A Trickster Tale from the Amazon* by Gerald McDermott

Action Rhyme: "Five Little Monkeys"

Book: *We're Roaming in the Rainforest: An Amazon Adventure* by Laurel Krebs

Song: "Ciranda" from *Wee Sing around the World* by Pamela Conn Beall and Susan Hagen Nipp, with Nancy Spence Klein

Puppet Presentation: "How the Brazilian Beetle Won the Race"

DVD: "Linda the Llama Saves Carnival" from *Go Diego Go! Rainforest Fiesta!*

Craft: Amazon Mobile

Action Rhyme: "My Hands"

Story Time for Kindergarten through Third Grade

Song: "Hello Song"
Book: *Jabutí the Tortoise: A Trickster Tale from the Amazon* by Gerald McDermott
Oral Story: "Monkeys in the Rain: A Folktale from Brazil" from *Five-Minute Tales: More Stories to Read and Tell When Time Is Short* by Margaret Read MacDonald
Game: Kapok Tree Guessing Game by Dee Ann Corn and Sandy Shropshire
Book: *The Great Kapok Tree: A Tale of the Amazon Forest* by Lynne Cherry
Song: "Samba Parade" from *Multicultural Bean Bag Fun* by Georgianna Stewart
Puppet Presentation: "How the Brazilian Beetle Won the Race"
DVD: *Countries of the World: Brazil*
Craft: Carnival Mask
Action Rhyme: "My Hands"

Begin the story time with the "Hello Song." Then sing the song again, substituting the word *hello* with the Portuguese greeting *Olá* [oh-LAH]. (Portuguese is the primary language spoken in Brazil; see p. xxix for "Hello Song" music.)

Hello Song

Hello ev'rybody,
And how are you? How are you?
Hello ev'rybody,
And how are you today?
Oh-LAH ev'rybody,
And how are you? How are you?
Oh-LAH ev'rybody,
And how are you today?

End the story time with the "My Hands" action rhyme, substituting the words *thank you* with the Portuguese word *obrigado* [oh-bre-GAH-doh], and *goodbye* with *adeus* [a-DAY-oosh]. Have children stand up and follow the actions in the rhyme.

My Hands

My hands say oh-bre-GAH-doh. *(hold up hands)*
With a clap, clap, clap. *(clap hands)*
My feet say oh-bre-GAH-doh. *(point to feet)*
With a tap, tap, tap. *(stamp or tap feet)*
Clap! Clap! Clap! *(clap hands)*
Tap! Tap! Tap! *(stamp or tap feet)*
Turn myself around and bow. *(turn and bow)*
a-DAY-oosh. *(wave goodbye)*

Books to Read Aloud

Berkes, Marianne. *Over in the Jungle*. Illustrated by Jeanette Canyon. Nevada City, CA: Dawn Publications, 2004. (26 pages)
>Based on the traditional song "Over in the Meadow," this book introduces different types of animals that can be found in the rainforest. Additional activities can be found at http://dawnpub.com/activities/Jungle-Berkes-Tips.pdf.

Carle, Eric. *"Slowly, Slowly, Slowly," Said the Sloth*. New York: Philomel Books, 2002. (32 pages)
>This simple picture book is great for younger students. It introduces readers to several animals found in the Amazon rainforest as the sloth slowly goes about his day.

Cherry, Lynne. *The Great Kapok Tree: A Tale of the Amazon Forest*. San Diego, CA: Harcourt Brace Jovanovich, 2000. (36 pages)
>A man walks into the Amazon rainforest and begins to chop down a kapok tree that is home to many animals. When the man falls asleep, each animal whispers in his ear a reason not to chop down the tree.

Guiberson, Brenda Z. *Rain, Rain, Rain Forest*. Illustrated by Steve Jenkins. New York: Henry Holt, 2004. (32 pages)
>A beautifully rich and descriptive story that follows some animals that live in the rainforest through the activities of their day.

Haskins, Jim and Kathleen Benson. *Count Your Way through Brazil*. Illustrated by Liz Brenner Dodson. Minneapolis, MN: Carolrhoda Books, 1999. (24 pages)
>Children experience the history and culture of Brazil while learning to count to 10 in Portuguese.

Krebs, Laurie. *We're Roaming in the Rainforest: An Amazon Adventure*. Illustrated by Anne Wilson. Cambridge, MA: Barefoot Books, 2010. (40 pages)
>A picture book that introduces readers to the many animals that make the Amazon rainforest their home.

Maldonado, Cristina Falcón. *1,2,3 Suddenly in Brazil*. Illustrated by Marta Fàbrega. Hauppauge, NY: Barron's Educational Series, 2011. (36 pages)
>Using his magic necklace, Martin travels to Brazil and is introduced to many interesting facts and places. This is a wonderful book for elementary-age children.

McDermott, Gerald. *Jabutí the Tortoise: A Trickster Tale from the Amazon*. New York: Harcourt, 2001. (32 pages)
>This colorfully illustrated story is about Jabutí, the tortoise who wants to play his flute for the King of Heaven. Jealous Vulture tricks Jabutí into riding on his back to heaven.

Witte, Anna. *Parrot Tico Tango*. Cambridge, MA: Barefoot Books, 2004. (24 pages)
>This cumulative tale is about a greedy parrot named Tico Tango who steals fruit from the other animals in the rainforest. With a fun rhyming text, this book is a great read-aloud for your younger readers.

Worth, Bonnie. *If I Ran the Rain Forest: All about Tropical Rain Forests*. Illustrated by Aristides Ruiz. London: Harper Collins Children's, 2008. (45 pages)
>The Cat in the Hat introduces us to the climate, various animals, and the different layers of the Amazon rainforest by using an "umbrella-vator."

Storytelling

"How the Brazilian Beetle Won the Race" Puppet Presentation

"How the Brazilian Beetle Won the Race" is based on a Brazilian folktale that has been passed down from generation to generation. The agouti in the story is a large rodent of Brazil that can run quickly. See Figures 2.1 through 2.3 for patterns. Trace the patterns on thick, brown posterboard, or photocopy them on brown paper, glue them to posterboard, and then cut them out. If possible, use two colors of brown to differentiate between the two stick puppets. Cut carefully outside the heavy black lines. For the beetle's legs, it is best to cut well outside the lines to avoid cutting them too thin. Hot glue (or tape) a paint stick, available at paint supply stores, to the back of each puppet. Lamination can add brightness, and it makes the puppets more durable.

To add the wings to the beetle, make holes where indicated (on wings and body) with an object no larger than an ice pick. Attach wings to the body using brass fasteners. Bend an 18-inch piece of thick florist wire (or any thick, pliable wire) to form a V. Working from the back of the puppet, attach the ends of the wire to the side holes in the wings (see Figure 2.4). Use pliers to crimp the ends if necessary. Adjust the wire so that when holding the puppet by the stick with one hand and moving the V of the wire with the other hand, the wings open and close over the body of the beetle.

Hold both puppets while telling the story. To create a surprise, do not spread the beetle's wings until the end. After the story, share with the group a picture of a Brazilian beetle that shows its myriad of brilliant colors.

"How the Brazilian Beetle Won the Race" retold by Dee Ann Corn

Various beetles from Brazil today are wonderfully colorful insects. In fact, people often make jewelry, such as earrings, necklaces, and pins, from these beetles because they are so beautiful. But some say that the beetle has not always been so beautifully colored. It is said that these beetles were once a dull, brown color. This is the story of how the beetle became so colorful.

There was once a little brown beetle crawling along, enjoying a lovely day. *(raise beetle puppet)* All of a sudden, a large, brown Brazilian rat known as an agouti stopped the beetle in his path and began teasing him. *(raise agouti puppet)*

"Look at the little, slow beetle crawling down the road," said the agouti. "You are so slow it doesn't even look like you are moving at all. Watch how fast I can run." With that, the agouti took off down the road as fast as he could, then turned around and came back. The little brown beetle continued along at his own slow, steady pace down the path.

"I bet you wish you could be like me and run like the wind!" exclaimed the agouti with a large grin. The agouti was extremely proud of himself for his quickness.

The little brown beetle just shyly nodded and smiled, not wanting to draw any more attention to himself. His parents had always taught him never to brag about the things he could do. "You do run like the wind. You should be very proud," the little brown beetle whispered timidly, then continued on his way.

Just then, a beautiful parrot flew down and landed on a tree limb above the little brown beetle and the agouti. "Excuse me, but I was listening to both of you and wondered if you would like to see who truly is the fastest. How would you like to have a race?" asked the beautiful parrot. "I will even give the champion a prize for winning."

The agouti perked up his ears when he heard the word prize. "Prize? What kind of prize would I win, I mean, would the champion win?" The agouti was very confident that he would win the race.

The parrot began to think of prizes that both the little brown beetle and the agouti would like. "I know," said the parrot, "I will give the winner a beautifully colored coat of his choice."

The agouti jumped up and yelled, "I want a coat like the jaguar who lives in the rainforest!" The jaguar was admired throughout the land as being beautiful, graceful, and strong.

The little brown beetle shyly said to the parrot, "I would like to be the color of the gold and green feathers in your tail."

The agouti laughed loudly. He laughed so hard he rolled over in the road. "Why are you even thinking about a prize? You know I'm the fastest runner!"

The parrot mapped out a trail for the two to follow. Then he said, "On your mark. Get set. Go!" And the parrot flew to the finish line to meet the winner.

The agouti took off down the road in a hurry. After a little while, he began to get tired. "Why am I in such a hurry? There is no way the beetle could run faster than me and win the race," bragged the agouti. He began to walk rather than run, but as he was walking, he began to think it would probably be best if he were to finish the race quickly-then he could truly rest. So off he ran again, as fast as he could go.

As agouti came upon the finish line, he saw something that made his eyes become as big as mangoes. Sitting right beside the beautiful parrot with the green and gold feathers was the little brown beetle. The agouti's mouth dropped open with surprise.

"I don't believe what I am seeing. How did you ever beat me?" asked the agouti in amazement as he came to the finish line. "I never saw you run past me."

The little brown beetle spread his wings out to the side and replied, "The parrot didn't say we had to run the race." *(spread the beetle's wings)*

The agouti was shocked by what he saw. "I didn't know you had wings!" he exclaimed. "Proud agouti, you should never judge someone by what's on the outside," said the parrot. Then the parrot gave the little brown beetle his prize—a beautiful coat of gold and green.

"Congratulations, little beetle, on winning the race," said the parrot. "No longer will you be the color brown."

To this day, however, the agouti still remains the same brown color he always was.

Source for Puppet Presentation

Cherry, Lynne. *The Great Kapok Tree: A Tale of the Amazon Rain Forest*. San Diego, CA: Harcourt Brace Jovanovich, 2000. (32 pages)

Following the picture book *The Great Kapok Tree*, develop a puppet presentation version of the story. Use posterboard to create likenesses of each character in the story: a man, a boa constrictor, a bee, a monkey, a toucan, a tree frog, a jaguar, a tree porcupine, an anteater, a three-toed sloth, and a child. Attach each character to a craft stick (paint sticks, available at paint supply stores, are sturdier than craft sticks). The storyteller may hold the puppets or have children from the group hold them.

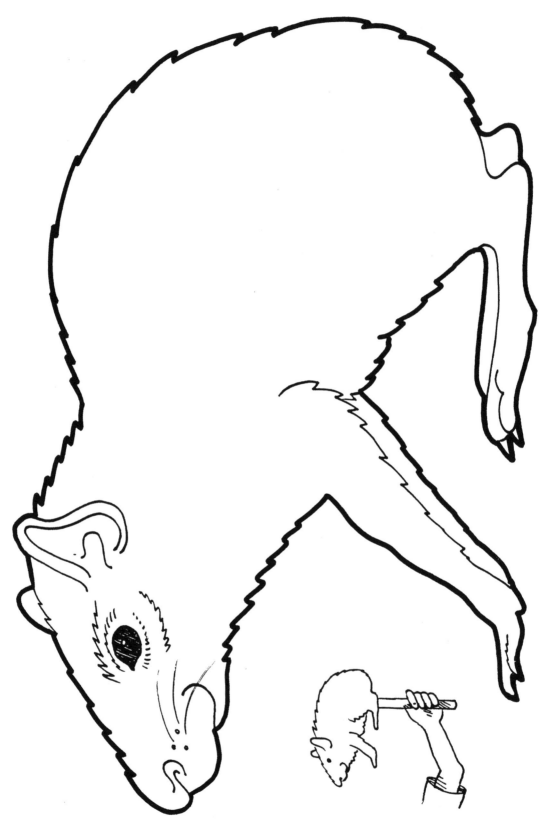

Figure 2.1 **Agouti**

Figure 2.2 **Beetle**

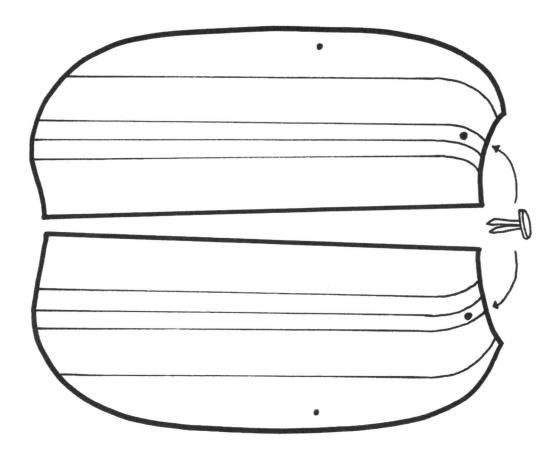

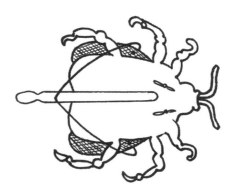

Figure 2.3 **Beetle Wings**   Figure 2.4 **Beetle Puppet Example**

Sources for Oral Stories

MacDonald, Margaret Read. "Monkeys in the Rain: A Folktale from Brazil." In *Five-Minute Tales: More Stories to Read and Tell When Time Is Short*. Atlanta, GA: August House Publishers, 2007. (pages 15–17)
   This quick audience-participation story includes echoing and body motions that children can add to the tale.

Taylor, Sean. *The Great Snake: Stories from the Amazon*. Illustrated by Fernando Vilela. London: Frances Lincoln Children's Books, 2008. (60 pages)
   A collection of nine stories including "The Legend of Jurutaí," a story of a bird who falls in love with the moon.

Thornhill, Jan. "Mouse and Tapir." In *Folktails: Animal Legends from around the World*. Toronto, ONT: Maple Tree Press, 2006. (pages 28–31)
   The short story is about a time when all the animals were hungry, yet Tapir seemed to be getting fatter. With the help of Mouse, the animals find out what the sneaky Tapir is doing.

Fingerplays, Songs, Action Rhymes, and Games

Kapok Tree Guessing Game

Play this game to introduce the book *The Great Kapok Tree* by Lynne Cherry (see "Books to Read Aloud"). Use Figures 2.5 through 2.12 to make flannel board figures for the game. Trace the tree patterns (half-patterns) on folded felt and cut along the solid, curved lines in the treetop to make flaps. Because of the detail, you may want to photocopy the patterns of the animals and color them. Glue small pieces of felt to the backs of the paper figures so they will hold to the flannel board.

Figure 2.5 **Kapok Tree Trunk** Figure 2.6 **Butterfly** Figure 2.7 **Monkey** Figure 2.8 **Toucan**
Figure 2.9 **Jaguar** Figure 2.10 **Tree Frog** Figure 2.11 **Boa Constrictor**

align with fold

Figure 2.12 **Kapok Treetop**

Kapok Tree Guessing Game by Dee Ann Corn and Sandy Shropshire

To play this guessing game, the storyteller hides the animals behind the flaps. The animals in the game include a butterfly, a monkey, a toucan, a jaguar, a tree frog, and a boa constrictor. The object of the game is for the children to guess where the monkey is hiding. During the game, have children say this verse:

> Little monkey we want to see,
> Are you in the Kapok tree?

Repeat this verse as the storyteller lifts each flap, one after each repetition, until the monkey is found.

"Five Little Monkeys"

In this action rhyme, substitute the Portuguese numbers 1 through 5:

1. *um* [OONG]
2. *dois* [DOH-eez]
3. *três* [TRAY-ees]
4. *quatro* [KWAH-troo]
5. *cinco* [SEEN-koo]

Five Little Monkeys (author unknown)

Five (*cinco*) little monkeys, sitting in the tree. (*show five fingers*)
[chorus]
Teasing Mr. Crocodile,
"You can't catch me, you can't catch me!" (*shake index finger*)
Along comes Mr. Crocodile, quiet as can be. (*with palms together,
slowly stretch out arms to represent the crocodile*)
SNAP! (*clap hands*)
Four (*quarto*) little monkeys, sitting in the tree. (*show four fingers*
[chorus]
Three (*três*) little monkeys, sitting in the tree. (*show three fingers*)
[chorus]
Two (*dois*) little monkeys, sitting in the tree. (*show two fingers*)
[chorus]
One (*um*) little monkeys, sitting in the tree. (*show one finger*)
[chorus]
No more monkeys, sitting in the tree. (*shake head back and forth*)

Sources for Fingerplays, Songs, Action Rhymes, and Games

Beall, Pamela Conn and Susan Hagen Nipp, with Nancy Spence Klein. "Ciranda" (Circle Game). In *Wee Sing around the World*. New York: Price Stern Sloan, 2006. Book with compact disc. "Ciranda" is a circle game sung in both Portuguese and English.

Putumayo Kids. "Vila Sésamo" (One Small Voice). In *Sesame Street Playground*. New York: Putumayo World Music, 2008. Compact disc.
> Vila Sésamo is the Portuguese version of the song "One Small Voice" that was featured in the *Sesame Street* television show.

Putumayo World Music. "Bonjour Pra Você" (Good Morning to You). In *World Playground*. New York: Putumayo World Music, 1999, Compact disc.
> Sung in Portuguese, the national language of Brazil, this song is a *carimbó*, a style of dance from the Amazon River Basin.

Putumayo World Music. *Brazilian Playground*. New York: Putumayo World Music, 2007. Compact disc.
> *Brazilian Playground* features some of Brazil's most popular styles of music like the samba, bossa nova, and forró. Putumayo offers free learning guides to use in conjunction with the compact disc at http://www.putumayo.com/sites/default/files/uploads/userfiles/file/Brazilian _Playground_Teaching_Guide.pdf.

Stewart, Georgiana. "Samba Parade." In *Multicultural Bean Bag Fun*. Long Branch, NJ: Kimbo Educational, 2009. Compact disc.
> Children can celebrate Carnival by forming a parade line using a bean bag to circle over their heads.

Media Choices

Show a DVD or a downloadable movie as a transition between storytelling activities and crafts.

Countries of the World: Brazil. Wynnewood, PA: Distributed by Schlessinger Media, 2004. DVD, 13 min.
> Follow Laura through her home city of Rio de Janeiro. From an outdoor market to restaurants, museums, and the beach, Laura visits many of the city's features. Laura and her family end the evening going to the annual Carnival festivities. Her culture, traditions, and history are highlighted through her daily journey.

Go Diego Go! Rainforest Fiesta! Hollywood, CA: Paramount Pictures, 2009. DVD, 99 min.
> This DVD includes four episodes from the television program *Go, Diego Go!* In the episode *Linda the Llama Saves Carnival*, Diego needs to find Linda the Llama so she can bring the basket of goodies and musical instruments to the top of for the Carnival parade.

Rainforest (Jungle). Wynnewood, PA: Distributed by Schlessinger Media, 2004. DVD, 27 min.
> This beautiful and fascinating Eyewitness DVD highlights aspects of the multiple layers of the rainforest. Animals, fruits, and products we use are all discussed in this DVD. Although all of the rainforests of the world are discussed, the Amazon jungle is highlighted.

Totally Tropical Rain Forest. Washington, DC: National Geographic, 2005. DVD, 40 min.
> Spin, the animated globe, takes us on a tour of the many layers of the Amazon rainforest. From the ground floor level, including the river, to the canopy, we are shown the many unique animals that live in the Amazon. This light-hearted, entertaining DVD is geared towards the kid audience.

Crafts and Other Activities

Choose a craft suited for the age level of the group and the time allotted for the story time.

Amazon Mobile

The Amazon region is home to many unique, beautiful plants and animals. Have children create a mobile representing Amazon flora and fauna.

Supplies

Crayons or colored markers
Wire hanger
Paper
Glue stick

Yarn
Scissors
Hole Punch

Figure 2.13 **Mobile Example**

See Figure 2.13 for a sample illustration of the mobile. Photocopy Figures 2.14 through 2.18. Make two copies of each figure for each child, if desired, to make two-sided mobile ornaments. Color the figures before cutting (cut along the thick, outside lines only). Color suggestions: poison dart frog—red and black, or yellow and black, on a green leaf; bromeliad—red flower with green leaves; blue morpho butterfly—blue wings with black edges; howler monkey—reddish brown; macaw—a mixture of yellow, red, green, and blue. If making two-sided figures, use a glue stick to attach matching pieces back to back (white liquid glue can cause wrinkling on lightweight paper unless used sparingly). Punch holes where indicated. Tie pieces of yarn with loose knots to the paper figures and tight knots to the hanger (use various lengths of yarn so the figures will hang at various lengths). Trim the ends of the yarn pieces at the knots.

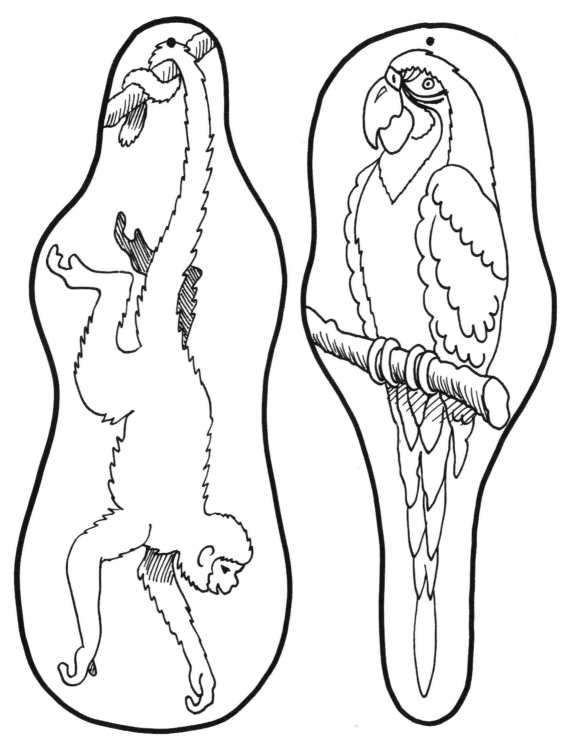

Figure 2.14 **Howler Monkey**   Figure 2.15 **Macaw**

Figure 2.16 **Poison Dart Frog**   Figure 2.17 **Bromeliad**   Figure 2.18 **Blue Morpho Butterfly**

From *Travel the Globe: Story Times, Activities, and Crafts for Children, Second Edition* by Desiree Webber,
Dee Ann Corn, Elaine Harrod, Sandy Shropshire, Shereen Rasor, and Donna Norvell (in memoriam).
Santa Barbara, CA: Libraries Unlimited. Copyright © 2013.

Carnival Mask

Brazilian people enjoy celebrating holidays. One of the most famous holidays they celebrate is Carnival, which is observed during the four days before Lent. People dress in colorful costumes and masks and dance to samba music in the streets. Brazil has what are known as samba schools. These schools parade down the streets, dancing to the music. Members in each school have the same costumes and do the same dance. The schools are judged and awarded prizes.

In this craft project, children create masks similar to those worn for Carnival. After they have completed their masks, play Carnival-style music and have a Brazilian Carnival parade! Play songs from *Brazilian Playground* by Putumayo Kids (see "Sources for Finger-plays, Songs, Action Rhymes, and Games").

Supplies

Thick posterboard (any color)
Scissors
White glue
Glitter

Sequins
Feathers
Craft sticks

See Figure 2.19 for a sample illustration of the carnival mask. Trace and cut the sample mask in Figure 2.20 on thick posterboard for each child. Where indicated on the mask pattern, have each child securely attach a craft stick to the back of the mask. Children glue feathers around the back edge of the mask so that the ends of the quills are not visible from the front. Decorate with sequins and glitter.

Figure 2.19 **Carnival Mask Example**

attach craft stick to back

Figure 2.20 **Carnival Mask**

Sources for Craft Ideas and Activities

Evans, Linda, Karen Backus, and Mary Thompson. *Art Projects from around the World: Grades 1–3*. New York: Scholastic, 2006. (pages 50–55)

Create a rainforest puppet or a pop-up rainforest tree frog. Step by step instructions are included for the puppet and frog pattern for the tree frog.

Castaldo, Nancy F. *Rainforests: An Activity Guide for Ages 6–9*. Chicago: Chicago Review Press, 2003. (144 pages)

Information, activities, and crafts relating to rainforests around the world including the Amazon rainforest are presented.

Ross, Kathy. *Crafts for Kids Who Are Wild about Rainforests*. Illustrated by Sharon Lane Holm. Brookfield, CT: Millbrook Press, 1997. (48 pages)

Twenty simple crafts you can make including a "Window Toucan" and a "Foot and Hands Macaw" are part of this creative book.

Chapter 3

Let's Visit the Caribbean Islands

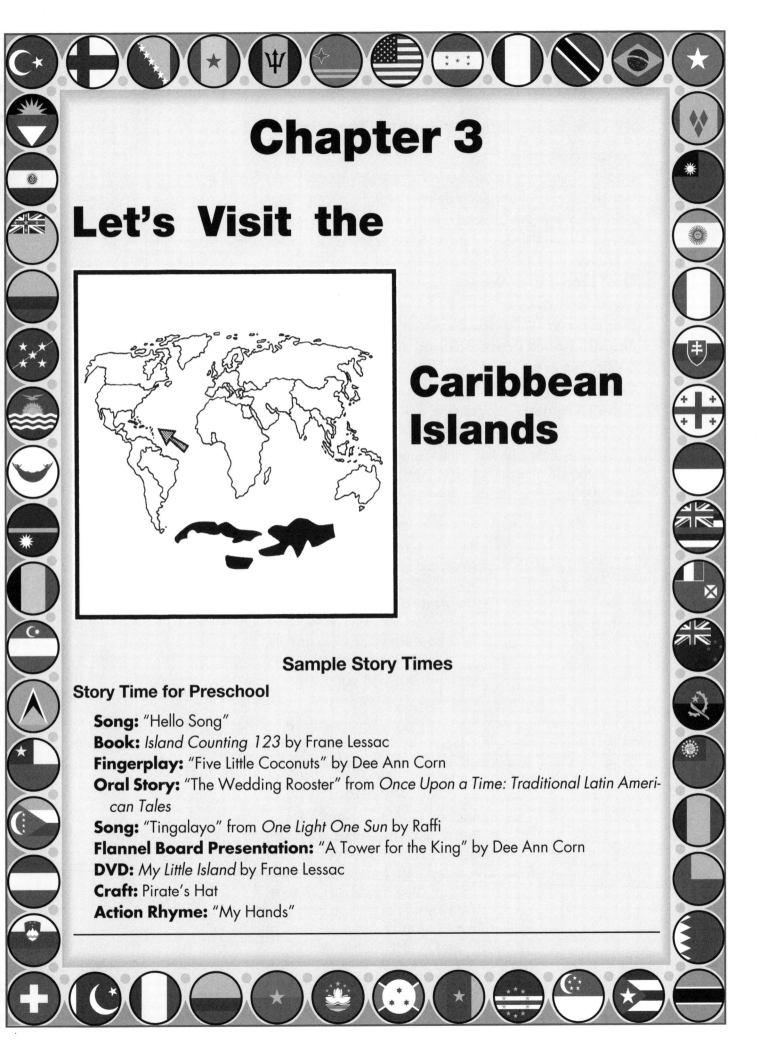

Sample Story Times

Story Time for Preschool

Song: "Hello Song"

Book: *Island Counting 123* by Frane Lessac

Fingerplay: "Five Little Coconuts" by Dee Ann Corn

Oral Story: "The Wedding Rooster" from *Once Upon a Time: Traditional Latin American Tales*

Song: "Tingalayo" from *One Light One Sun* by Raffi

Flannel Board Presentation: "A Tower for the King" by Dee Ann Corn

DVD: *My Little Island* by Frane Lessac

Craft: Pirate's Hat

Action Rhyme: "My Hands"

Story Time for Kindergarten through Third Grade

Song: "Hello Song"
Book: *Kallaloo!: A Caribbean Tale* by David and Phillis Gershator
Song: "Day O" from *Baby Beluga* by Raffi
Book: *Over in the Ocean* by Marianne Berkes
Song: "Three Little Birds" from *World Travels: World Music for Kids* by Cedella Marley Booker
Oral Story: "The Wedding Rooster" from *Once Upon a Time: Traditional Latin American Tales*
Fingerplay: "I'm a Little Palm Tree" by Dee Ann Corn
Flannel Board Presentation: "A Tower for the King" by Dee Ann Corn
DVD: *Dive to the Coral Reefs*
Craft: Sandy Beach Collage
Action Rhyme: "My Hands"

Begin the story time with the "Hello Song." Then sing the song again, substituting the word *hello* with the Dominican Republic (Spanish) greeting *hola* [OH-lah]. (See p xxix for "Hello Song" music.)

Hello Song

Hello ev'rybody,
And how are you? How are you?
Hello ev'rybody,
And how are you today?
OH-lah ev'rybody,
And how are you? How are you?
OH-lah ev'rybody,
And how are you today?

End the story time with the "My Hands" action rhyme, substituting the words *thank you* with the Dominican Republic (Spanish) word *gracias* [GRAH-see-ahs], and *goodbye* with *adios* [ah-DYOHS]. Have children stand up and follow the actions in the rhyme.

My Hands

My hands say GRAH-see-ahs. *(hold up hands)*
With a clap, clap, clap. *(clap hands)*
My feet say GRAH-see-ahs. *(point to feet)*
With a tap, tap, tap. *(stamp or tap feet)*
Clap! Clap! Clap! *(clap hands)*
Tap! Tap! Tap! *(stamp or tap feet)*
Turn myself around and bow. *(turn and bow)*
ah-DYOHS. *(wave goodbye)*

Books to Read Aloud

Berkes, Marianne. *Over in the Ocean: In a Coral Reef*. Illustrated by Jeanette Canyon. Nevada City, CA: Dawn Publications, 2004. (26 pages)
> Based on the traditional song "Over in the Meadow," this book introduces different types of animals that can be found in the ocean. Extending activities can be found at http://dawnpub.com/activities/OverInTheOcean_Activities.pdf.

Cherry, Lynne. *The Sea, the Storm, and the Mangrove Tangle*. New York: Farrar Straus Giroux, 2004. (40 pages)
> A seed from a mangrove tree floats in the Caribbean Sea, then takes root and grows on an island shore, providing a home to many animals and benefiting various other plants and animals.

Deedy, Carmen Agra. *Martina the Beautiful Cockroach: A Cuban Folktale*. Illustrated by Michael Austin. Atlanta, GA: Peachtree Publishers, 2007. (32 pages)
> In this Cuban folktale, the sweet Martina the cockroach is trying to select a husband with the help of her family.

Gershator, David and Phillis Gershator. *Kallaloo!: A Caribbean Tale*. Illustrated by Diane Greenseid. New York: Marshall Cavendish, 2005. (32 pages)
> Based on the classic tale "Stone Soup," an old woman finds a magic shell to make kallaloo, a Caribbean gumbo.

Gershator, Phillis. *Rata-Pata-Scata-Fata: A Caribbean Story*. Illustrated by Holly Meade. Long Island City, NY: Star Bright Books, 2005. (32 pages)
> Jun Jun tries saying the magic phrase "rata-pata-scata-fata" to make his chores do themselves.

Gershator, Phillis. *Sambalena Show-Off*. Illustrated by Leonard Jenkins. New York: Simon & Schuster, 2011. (25 pages)
> Sambalena is a big show-off. One day, he begins to show off by dancing around with a pot on his head, when it becomes stuck.

Isadora, Rachel. *Caribbean Dream*. New York: Puffin, 2002. (32 pages)
> This poetic picture book captures the way of life on the islands of the Caribbean.

Lessac, Frane. *Island Counting 123*. Cambridge, MA: Candlewick Press, 2005. (25 pages)
> A simple counting book highlighting the people, places, animals, and objects found in the Caribbean Islands.

MacDonald, Amy. *Please, Malese!: A Trickster Tale from Haiti*. Illustrated by Emily Lisker. New York: Farrar Straus Giroux, 2002. (32 pages)
> Malese, a trickster man, thinks of clever ways to trick his neighbors into getting things for free. It is fun to act out the "half a bottle of water" trick to show how this sleight of hand works.

Picayo, Mario. *A Caribbean Journey from A to Y (Read and Discover What Happened to the Z)*. Illustrated by Earleen Griswold. New York: Campanita Books, 2007. (60 pages)
> An enlightening ABC book that leads the reader from Aruba to Yams, leaving them to wonder what words will begin with the letter Z.

Silva Lee, Alfonso. *My Island and I: The Nature of the Caribbean*. Illustrated by Alexis Lago. Saint Paul: PANGAEA, 2002. (32 pages)
> A colorful picture book about the natural ecology of an island.

Storace, Patricia. *Sugar Cane: A Caribbean Rapunzel*. Illustrated by Raul Colon. New York: Hyperion Books for Children, 2007. (48 pages)
> A retelling of Rapunzel with the Caribbean islands as the backdrop. This book is appropriate for school-age children with its wonderfully poetic text.

Zephaniah, Benjamin. *J Is for Jamaica*. Illustrated by Prodeepta Das. London: Frances Lincoln Limited, 2006. (32 pages)
    An ABC book highlighting the beautiful island of Jamaica using photographs for each letter of the alphabet.

Storytelling

"A Tower for the King" Flannel Board Presentation

"A Tower for the King" is a retelling of a folktale from the Dominican Republic about a king who wanted to touch the moon. See Figures 3.1 through 3.5 for patterns. Trace the patterns on felt, or photocopy and color them. If photocopying, glue small pieces of felt to the backs of the paper figures so they will hold to the flannel board. Make seven boxes for the king to stand on (using Figures 3.4 and 3.5, or by simply cutting seven felt squares of various sizes). Place the figures on the flannel board as they are introduced in the story.

"A Tower for the King," retold by Dee Ann Corn

Many years ago, there lived a king who was known throughout his kingdom as being very commanding. He always thought he was right, and no one was to question his authority. *(place the king on the flannel board)*

One evening, the king stepped out onto his balcony to enjoy the evening breeze. He looked up at the sky and saw the moon. *(place the moon on the flannel board)* He watched it and admired how large and wonderful it was. Oh how he wanted to reach up and touch it! For days, the king could not stop thinking about the moon. He wouldn't eat because he thought about the moon. He finally decided he had to find a way to touch the moon. So he sent for his royal carpenter. *(place the royal carpenter on the flannel board)*

"Find a way for me to touch the moon!" the king commanded of the carpenter.

The carpenter could not understand why the king had commanded his help. Of all the wise people in the kingdom, surely there were others with better ideas. The carpenter only knew about building things out of wood. He certainly didn't know anything about the moon! In fact, the only thing he knew was that the moon was very far away. It seemed impossible that the king would be able to reach it.

Still, the king had given him a command, so the carpenter went home and tried to think of a way for the king to touch the moon. He was not able to come up with any ideas that he believed would work. *(remove the royal carpenter from the flannel board)* A couple of days had passed when the king sent for the carpenter. *(place the royal carpenter on the flannel board)*

The king asked the carpenter if he had found a way for him to reach the moon. And the carpenter said, "Your Royal Highness, I don't believe it is possible for you to touch the moon."

"Nonsense!" shouted the king. "Find a way or you will die!"

So the carpenter left the palace fearing for his life. He didn't sleep at all that night, trying to think of a way to please the king. *(remove the royal carpenter from the flannel board)*

After a few days, the king again sent for the carpenter. *(place the royal carpenter on the flannel board)* The carpenter came before the king once again, but this time he had an idea. He told the king that he was a carpenter and knew only about building things out of wood. Would the king want a tower to the moon built out of wooden boxes?

The king liked the idea, and summoned everyone in the kingdom to bring him their boxes. As all the boxes were collected, the carpenter stacked them, one on top of another, until all the boxes were stacked. However, there were not enough. *(place three boxes on the flannel board and stack them)*

The carpenter returned to the king and told him that they were out of boxes and the tower was not yet tall enough. The king commanded that all the wood in the kingdom be delivered to him to make more boxes.

The carpenter built more boxes and then began to stack them on top of the others, making the tower taller and taller. Sadly, the tower was still too short. *(place two more boxes on the flannel board and stack them on the other boxes)*

The royal carpenter went back to the king and told him that he had now used all the wood in the kingdom, yet the tower was still not tall enough to touch the moon. The king then ordered that all the trees in the kingdom were to be cut down and made into more boxes.

The carpenter became concerned. "My King, should we really cut down all the trees in the kingdom?" asked the carpenter.

"Cut down every last one, from the beautiful, flamboyant tree to the stately palm tree!" demanded the king.

The carpenter, remembering that the king did not like to be questioned, left the palace to have every tree cut down and made into boxes. When the work was done, the new boxes were stacked on the tower. *(place the two remaining boxes on the flannel board and stack them on the other boxes)*

The carpenter returned to the king and told him that his tower was complete. Excited, the king rushed to the tower and began to climb. He climbed and climbed and climbed, until he was above the clouds and could no longer be seen. The king reached the top of the tower, stood up, and reached out. His fingers were almost touching the moon, but not quite. *(place the king on top of the boxes)*

"I need one more box!" called down the king from above the clouds.

"But Your Highness, we have no more boxes, no more wood, and no more trees. There is nothing to give you!" shouted the carpenter up to the king.

The king did not care to hear this. He was determined to touch the moon. "Then take one from the bottom!" commanded the king.

The carpenter wondered if he was hearing the king correctly. Surely the king did not want him to take one of the boxes from the bottom of the tower.

The king called down again, "I order you to take a box from the bottom, immediately! With one more box on my tower, I will be able to touch the moon!"

The carpenter shook his head and took a box from the bottom of the tower, just as he was ordered. *(remove the bottom box from the flannel board)* You can guess what happened next: The tower came tumbling down, along with the king. And the king never bothered the carpenter again.

Figure 3.1 **King**   Figure 3.2 **Royal Carpenter**   Figure 3.3 **Moon**

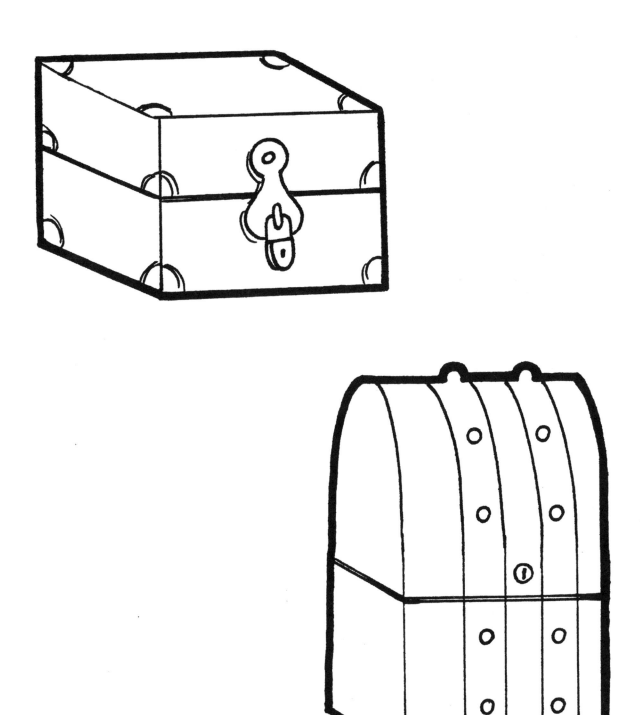

Figure 3.4 **Box**   Figure 3.5 **Box**

Sources for Oral Stories

Hayes, Joe. *Dance, Nana, Dance / Baila, Nana, baila: Cuban Folktales in English and Spanish.*
Illustrated by Mauricio Trenard Sayago. El Paso, TX: Cinco Puntos Press, 2008. (128 pages)
A collection of 13 stories and folklore from the island of Cuba. Some of the stories in this bilingual book have musical verses that encourage children to participate.

Holt, David and Bill Mooney. *More Ready-To-Tell Tales from around the World.* Little Rock, AR:
August House Publishers, 2000. (256 pages)
This collection includes five tales that are retellings of stories from the Caribbean region. It also includes tips on ways to tell the tales.

Martinez, Rueben. "The Wedding Rooster." In *Once Upon a Time: Traditional Latin American
Tales.* Illustrated by Raul Colon. New York: Rayo, 2010. (pages 11–19)
In this bilingual story, Rooster is on his way to his uncle's wedding when he gets a dirty beak pecking at a kernel of corn. This leads to a cumulative tale of his quest to clean his beak.

Fingerplays, Songs, Action Rhymes, and Games

"I'm a Little Palm Tree"

(sung to "I'm a Little Teapot") by Dee Ann Corn

I'm a little palm tree, standing tall, *(stand with arms above head)*
Here on an island, round and small. *(make a circle with arms)*
When I start to see the wind begin, *(wave hands above head)*
They just blow me around, see me bend. *(bend back and forth at the waist)*

"Five Little Coconuts"

by Dee Ann Corn

(put up five fingers and count down one finger at a time as you tell the rhyme)
Five little coconuts on de seashore;
One washed away, an' den der was four.
Four little coconuts hanging in de tree;
One fell down, an' den der was three.
Three little coconuts admiring the view;
One rolled away, an' den der was two.
Two little coconuts playing in de sun;
One got lost, an' den der was one.
One little coconut sitting by de sea;
He put down his roots, an' den became a tree.

Sources for Fingerplays, Songs, Action Rhymes, and Games

Bernier-Grand, Carmen T. *Shake It, Morena! and Other Folklore from Puerto Rico.* Illustrated by Lulu
Delacre. Brookfield, CT: Millbrook Press, 2002.
Follow a young girl in the course of her day through different songs, games and stories.

Buffett, Jimmy and Kermit the Frog and the All-Amphibian Band. "Caribbean Amphibian." In *Elmo-palooza!* New York: Koch Records, 2008. Compact disc.
> This is a fun song for preschoolers about a frog in a coconut tree.

Holmes, Brent. *Island Tunes for Kids.* [s.l.]: Fun Tunes for Kids, 2011. Compact disc.
> This wonderful compact disc contains original songs about the islands. Great for all ages. Compact disc may be ordered at http://www.funtunesforkidswholesale.com.

Raffi. "Day O." In *Baby Beluga*. Cambridge, MA: Shoreline Records, 1980. Compact disc.
> "Day O" is a traditional work song from the island of Trinidad.

Raffi. "Tingalayo." In *One Light One Sun*. Cambridge, MA: Shoreline Records, 1996. Compact disc.
> Raffi sings this traditional Caribbean song about a little donkey.

Raffi, Aaron Nigel Smith, Maria Medina-Serafin, Buckwheat Dural, Taj Mahal, Karan Casey, Bill Miller, et al. "Three Little Birds." In *World Travels: World Music for Kids*. Redway, CA: Music for Little People, 2010. Compact disc.
> In this compact disc, Bob Marley's mother, Cedella Marley Booker, sings this happy song about not worrying.

Stewart, Georgiana. "Bahama Beach Game." In *Multicultural Bean Bag Fun*. Long Branch, NJ: Kimbo Educational, 2009. Compact disc.
> Using a bean bag, have the children sit in a circle and listen to the directions in the music.

Media Choices

Show a DVD or a downloadable movie as a transition between storytelling activities and crafts.

Dive to the Coral Reefs. Lincoln, NE: GPN Educational Media, 2003. DVD, 30 min.
> This feature book by Paul Erickson, Les Kaufman, and Elizabeth Tayntor from Reading Rainbow describes the many plants and animals that make the coral reef their home.

Gibbons, Gail. *Ocean Creatures Collection*. Pine Plains, NY: Live Oak Media, 2006. DVD, 26 min.
> This collection of stories includes the books *Sharks* and *Whales* by Gail Gibbons with simple narration and authentic sounds of the ocean.

My Little Island. Lincoln, NE: GPN Educational Media, 2006. DVD, 29 min.
> In this Reading Rainbow selection, LeVar Burton spends a day on the island of Montserrat. The featured book, *My Little Island* by Frane Lessac, is about a boy who brings a friend along when he visits his birthplace of Montserrat in the Caribbean Islands.

Crafts and Other Activities

Choose a craft suited for the age level of the group and the time allotted for the story time session.

Sandy Beach Collage

The Caribbean beaches are among the most beautiful in the world. Tourists, as well as the residents, enjoy these beaches. Popular activities at the beach include sunning, swimming, snorkeling, and searching for shells.

Supplies

8½- by 11-inch posterboard	Blue construction paper
White glue	Scissors
White glue	Seashells (small sizes)
Water	Crayons
Bowl	
Paintbrush	
Sand	

Figure 3.6 **Sandy Beach Collage Example**

See Figure 3.6 for a sample illustration of the sandy beach collage. In a bowl, mix white glue with enough water that the glue can be spread on the posterboard using a paintbrush. Paint a thin coat of the glue-and-water mixture onto the posterboard. While the glue is wet, sprinkle sand over the posterboard; shake or tap off the excess. Using Figure 3.7 as a pattern, cut three blue strips and glue them to the lower border of the posterboard to make the waves. Photocopy Figures 3.8 through 3.12 for children to color and cut out (to save time, photocopy the patterns on colored paper.) Have children glue the pictures into place to create a beach scene. If desired, photocopy Figures 3.4 and 3.5 (the boxes from the flannel board story "A Tower for the King"), which resemble treasure chests, for children to add to the collage. Finally, glue seashells to the collage to add depth.

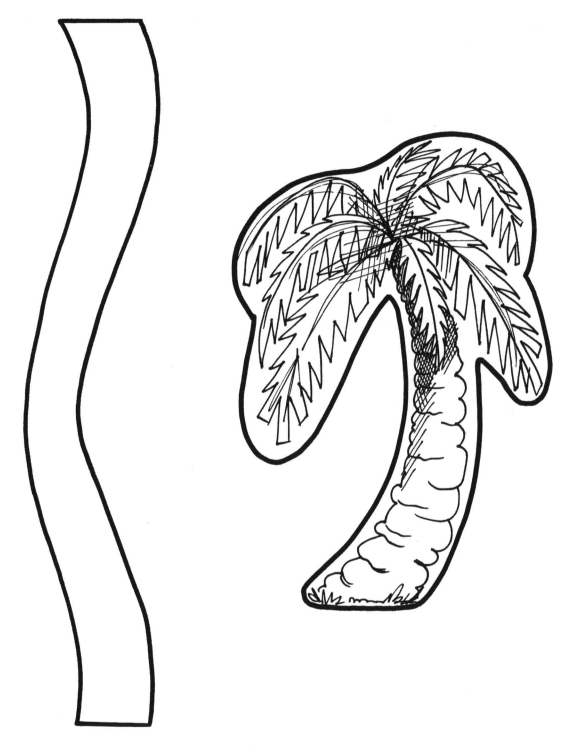

Figure 3.7 **Ocean wave**   Figure 3.8 **Palm Tree**

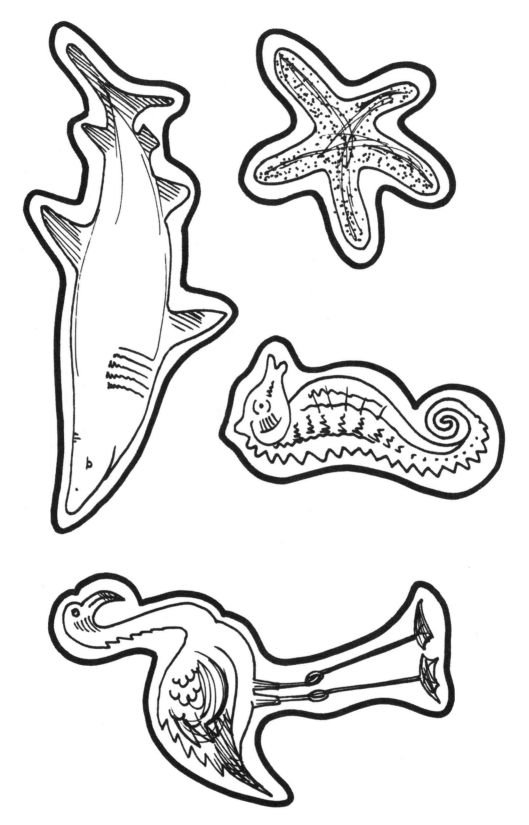

Figure 3.9 **Shark**   Figure 3.10 **Starfish**   Figure 3.11 **Sea Horse**   Figure 3.12 **Flamingo**

Pirate's Hat

From the sixteenth century to the eighteenth century, pirates made their homes in the Caribbean islands. During this period, Spain controlled the islands, and French, Dutch, and English pirates attacked and robbed the Spanish ships. Many of these ships were bringing supplies and treasures from Spain to the new land. Later, during the seventeenth century, pirates began to attack ships from all nations. Many of the pirate ships raised a black flag that featured a white skull and crossbones. This is a quick and easy craft project, ideal for preschoolers.

Figure 3.13   **Pirate Hat Example**

Supplies

Scissors
Stapler
Black construction paper

White construction paper
Pencil
Glue sticks

See Figure 3.13 for a sample illustration of the pirate hat. Trace and cut Figures 3.14 through 3.16 to make the hat, skull, and crossbones. Trace the hat pattern on black construction paper, and the skull and crossbones on white construction paper. Glue the skull and crossbones to the front of the hat. Staple a 2- by 18-inch strip of paper to the ends of the hat to make a headband.

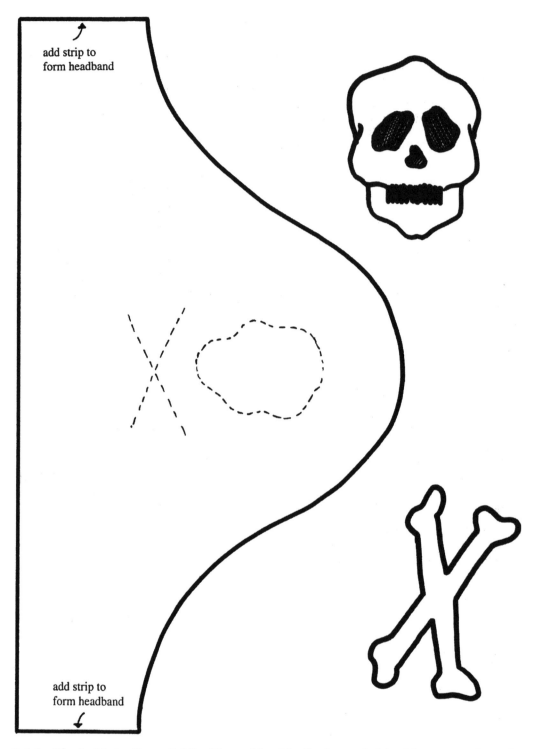

Figure 3.14 **Pirate Hat**   Figure 3.15 **Pirate Hat Skull**   Figure 3.16 **Pirate Hat Crossbones**

Sources for Craft Ideas and Activities

Braman, Arlette N. *Kids around the World Create!: The Best Crafts and Activities from Many Lands.* Illustrated by Jo-Ellen Bosson. New York: John Wiley& Sons, 1999. (pages 98–100)
Make maracas similar to those used to make music in the Caribbean islands using water bottles.

Evans, Linda, Karen Backus, and Mary Thompson. *Art Projects from around the World: Grades 1–3.* New York: Scholastic, 2006. (pages 45–47)
Design a colorful Caribbean-style house like those found in the islands.

Mofford, Juliet Haines. *Recipe and Craft Guide to the Caribbean.* Hockessin, DE: Mitchell Lane Publishers, 2011. (64 pages)
This book contains simple, easy recipes and crafts from the Caribbean region. Each craft or recipe gives information and history on why it is important to the area.

Temko, Florence. *Traditional Crafts from the Caribbean.* Illustrated by Randall Gooch. Minneapolis, MN: Learner Publications Company, 2001. (64 pages)
Includes traditional crafts from different regions of the islands such as a Grenadian spice hanger, Jamaican woven fish, and Barbadian shell craft.

Chapter 4

Let's Visit

China (Peoples' Republic of China)

Sample Story Time

Story Time for Preschool

Song: "Hello Song"

Book: *Panda-monium* by Cynthia Platt

Action Rhyme: "Mayling's Hammer" by Desiree Webber

Book: *Empty Pot* by Demi

Action Rhyme: "Chinese New Year" in *Multicultural Bean Bag Fun* by Georgiana Stewart.

Flannel Board/Audience Participation: "The Dragon Who Ate the Sun" by Desiree Webber

Action Rhyme: "Five Red Dragons" by Desiree Webber

DVD: *Stone Soup* by Jon J. Muth

Craft: Dragon Puppet

Action Rhyme: "My Hands"

Story Time for Kindergarten through Third Grade

Song: "Hello Song"
Book: *Stone Soup* by Jon J. Muth
Book: *The Magic Pillow* by Demi
Action Rhyme: "Mayling's Hammer" by Desiree Webber
Flannel Board/Audience Participation: "The Dragon Who Ate the Sun" by Desiree Webber
Book: *Lin Yi's Lantern: A Moon Festival Tale* by Brenda Williams
DVD: *Lon Po Po* by Ed Young
Game: Pin the Tail on the Dragon
Action Rhyme: "My Hands"

Begin the story time with the "Hello Song." Then sing the song again, substituting the word *hello* with the Mandarin Chinese greeting, pronounced "KNEE-how". (See p. xxix for "Hello Song" music.)

Hello Song

Hello ev'rybody,
And how are you? How are you?
Hello ev'rybody,
And how are you today?
KNEE-how ev'rybody,
And how are you? How are you?
KNEE-how ev'rybody,
And how are you today?

End the story time with the "My Hands" action rhyme, substituting the words *thank you* with the Mandarin Chinese word pronounced "SHAY shay," and *goodbye* with the Mandarin Chinese word, pronounced "shy JEN." Have children stand up and follow the actions in the rhyme.

My Hands

My hands say SHAY shay. *(hold up hands)*
With a clap, clap, clap. *(clap hands)*
My feet say SHAY shay. *(point to feet)*
With a tap, tap, tap. *(stamp or tap feet)*
Clap! Clap! Clap! *(clap hands)*
Tap! Tap! Tap! *(stamp or tap feet)*
Turn myself around and bow *(turn and bow)*
shay JEN *(way goodbye)*

Books to Read Aloud

Cleveland, Rob. *The Archer and the Sun: A Tale from China.* Illustrated by Baird Hoffmire. Atlanta, GA: August House Publishers, 2008. (24 pages)
> Once there were too many suns in the sky. An archer shot down all but one sun to keep the earth from being scorched. The single sun hid behind a mountain and then the earth became too cold. The lion, the rabbit, and finally the rooster attempt to call the sun into the sky.

Compestine, Ying Chang. *The Runaway Wok: A Chinese New Year Tale.* Illustrated by Sebastiá Serra. New York: Dutton Children's Books, 2011. (32 pages)
> A magical wok helps a poor family celebrate the Chinese New Year with food, gifts, and gold coins to share with others.

Demi. *The Empty Pot.* New York: Henry Holt and Company, 1990, 2011. (32 pages)
> An emperor wants to choose a successor. He gives all the children seeds and asks them to return in one year with their results. Only one boy remains truthful and arrives a year later with an empty pot.

Demi. *The Magic Pillow.* New York: Margaret K. McElderry Books, 2008. (36 pages)
> A young boy stays at an inn during a terrible snow storm. A magician lets the boy sleep on a magic pillow that shows him what life would be like if he were rich and famous. The boy decides that his current life is something to be enjoyed and treasured.

Grandis, John. *The Travel Game.* Illustrated by R. W. Alley. New York: Clarion Books, 2009. (32 pages)
> Tad lives above his family's tailor shop in Buffalo, New York. After the family eats lunch, Tad and his aunt Hattie always play the travel game. On this particular afternoon they travel to Hong Kong, China.

Haskins, Jim. *Count Your Way through China.* Illustrated by Dennis Hockerman. Minneapolis, MN: Lerner Publishing Group, 1988. (24 pages)
> The Mandarin Chinese characters for numbers one through ten are introduced alongside information about the culture, government, and history of China. A pronunciation guide is provided.

Lin, Grace. *Thanking the Moon: Celebrating the Mid-Autumn Moon Festival.* New York: Alfred A. Knopf, 2010. (28 pages)
> A simple tale that shows a family celebrating the Mid-Autumn Moon Festival, which is celebrated at night with colorful lanterns, moon cakes, moon-shaped fruits such as grapes, and round cups of tea.

Muth, Jon J. *Stone Soup.* New York: Scholastic Press, 2003. (32 pages)
> The author takes this traditional folktale and sets it in China. Three monks visit a town in which no one trusts his or her neighbor and no one shares.

Platt, Cynthia. *Panda-monium!* Illustrated by Veronica Vasylenko. Wilton, CT: Tiger Tales, 2011. (32 pages)
> Panda bear Beckett is hungry for bamboo to eat. In his journey to find bamboo, other pandas join him. The rhyming text makes this a fun read-aloud.

Santore, Charles. *The Silk Princess.* New York: Random House, 2007. (36 pages)
> Princess Hsi-Ling Chi sees a cocoon fall into her mother's tea. She pulls at the thread, which grows in length. Soon the princess is running out of the garden, beyond the palace walls, and into the mountains with her long silk string. A kindly gentleman shows her how the silk thread can be woven into beautiful, expensive fabric. (K–3) Educator's Guide available on

publisher's website, http://www.randomhouse.com/catalog/teachers_guides/97803758 36640.pdf.

Tucker, Kathy. *The Seven Chinese Sisters*. Illustrated by Grace Lin. Park Ridge, IL: Albert Whitman & Company, 2003. (32 pages)
    A starred review in *Booklist* states that *The Seven Chinese Sisters* is a great read-aloud. Six sisters outsmart a dragon to save the seventh sister from being eaten.

Williams, Brenda. *Lin Yi's Lantern: A Moon Festival Tale*. Illustrated by Benjamin Lacombe. Cambridge, MA: Barefoot Books, 2009. (32 pages)
    A young boy is sent to the market to buy items for the Moon Festival, such as moon cakes, star fruits, rice, yams, and peanuts, for Uncle Hui. If there is enough money left over, he may purchase a red rabbit lantern for the festival.

Yolen, Jane. *The Seeing Stick*. Illustrated by Daniela Jaglenka Terrazzini. Philadelphia, PA: Running Press Book Publishers, 1977, 2009. (32 pages)
    Princess Hwei Ming is blind, and her father has offered a fortune in jewels to anyone who can help her see. An old man travels to the palace in Peking to help Hwei Ming see through his carved seeing stick. Illustrations evolve from black and white to full color.

Storytelling

"The Dragon Who Ate the Sun" Audience-Participation Flannel Board Presentation

"The Dragon Who Ate the Sun," an audience-participation story, is based on an ancient belief that a solar eclipse was caused by a giant dragon eating the sun. People would come out into the streets pounding on their cooking pots to scare away the dragon. Of course, they were successful in their efforts because the sun always returned.

Refer to Figures 4.1 through 4.3 for flannel board pattern pieces. Some pieces will be cut from felt and placed on the flannel board. Other pieces will be cut from card stock and manipulated using florist wire.

Use yellow felt for the sun, blue felt for the ocean, white card stock for the moon, and green card stock for the dragon. To create water, representing the Yellow Sea, cut a 14-by 10-inch rectangle of blue felt. Scallop the top edge of the rectangle to represent ocean waves. Place the ocean on the flannel board before beginning the narration.

Attach a 12-inch piece of florist wire to both the dragon and moon using a small piece of tape. This allows easy manipulation of the figures as the story is told. When the white moon is placed in front of the sun, there will be a halo of yellow around the moon—just as the moon has a halo of sunlight during a total eclipse.

"The Dragon Who Ate the Sun" calls for audience participation. At the appropriate time, have children clap their hands or drum on coffee cans or oatmeal containers (whatever is available) to scare away the dragon. Before the presentation, explain that an eclipse is caused by the moon moving between the sun and the earth, blocking our vision of the sun. Place the sun on the flannel board and slowly move the moon across it. Pause when the moon completely covers the sun and discuss how dark it would be on earth without the sun's light.

Note: Flannel board figures may also be photocopied on paper as a substitute to felt. Photocopy and color the patterns. Glue small pieces of felt on the backs of the paper figures so they hold to the flannel board.

"The Dragon Who Ate the Sun" by Desiree Webber

A long time ago, in the depths of the Yellow Sea near China, there lived a young dragon. (*place the dragon in the water [blue felt], and make him swim about*) Although the dragon was young, he was the size of ten skyscrapers. He had four legs, a pair of strong wings, and large paws with claws like a tiger. His body was covered with fish scales, and he had two long whiskers which grew from each side of his wide, wide mouth. His parents named him Zhenshu [*zen-chew*], which means "pearl."

Zhenshu loved to swim in the sea among the other creatures. But often, Zhenshu would swim close to the surface of the water, watching the sunlight glitter and dance upon the waves. Zhenshu would look up into the sky (*place the sun on flannel board*) at the warm, round sun.

"I wish the sun lived in the Yellow Sea," Zhenshu told his parents.

"But the sun belongs in the sky," they answered. "Without the sun, the plants and trees would wither and die, and the people would starve."

Still, everyday, Zhenshu would watch the sun, until one day when he decided that the sun must come to live with him. Zhenshu flew out of the water and into the sky. (*move the dragon up to the sun*) Up into the atmosphere he flew, until he was next to the sun.

Afraid that he would not be able to hold the sun safely in his paws, Zhenshu decided to swallow it. (*move the dragon close to the sun*) He opened his mouth wider and wider and began to swallow the sun. (*slowly slide the dragon's mouth and throat over the sun as you continue the story*)

Down on earth, in cities such as Peking and Qingdao, people pointed to the sky: A dragon was eating the sun! Everyone ran into their houses and grabbed their cooking pots and brass kettles. They began to bang loudly on their cookery. (*have children clap their hands or bang their drums*)

Bang! Bong! Bang!

Bang! Bong! Bang! went all the pots and kettles.

Then, suddenly, everyone stopped: The sun was gone! (*slide the dragon completely over the sun, blocking it from view*) Bright stars twinkled in the purple-black sky, and flowers closed their petals.

Up in the sky, Zhenshu was uncertain what to do. He wanted the sun, but the loud clamoring of cooking pots frightened him.

Bang! Bong! Bang! went the pots and kettles again. (*have children clap their hands or bang their drums*)

Bang! Bong! Bang!

Reluctantly, Zhenshu opened his mouth and released the sun. (*move the dragon back so that the sun appears to go up his throat and mouth*) He returned to the sea and was no longer afraid. (*move the dragon down to the water*) Deep in the water, Zhenshu could no longer hear the bang, bong, bang of the pots and kettles.

Figure 4.1 **Dragon**

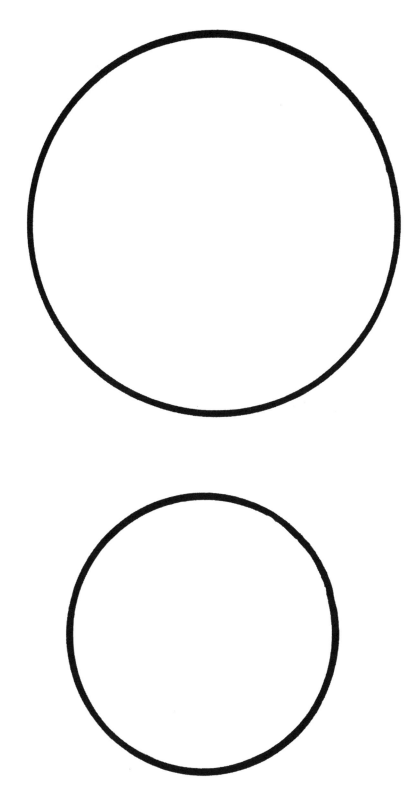

Figure 4.2 **Sun** Figure 4.3 **Moon**

Chinese Calligraphy Story

Louis, Catherine. *Liu and the Bird: A Journey in Chinese Calligraphy*. Translated by Sibylle Kazeroid. Calligraphy by Feng Xiao Min. New York: North-South Books, 2003, 2006. (36 pages)

Young Liu decides to visit his grandfather who lives on the other side of the mountain from his home. As the reader turns the pages of the book, there are elements from the story displayed on each page, such as a moon, star, rice, and trees. There are three squares, one for each element. The top square shows a drawing of the item, the second square shows an early pictograph of the item, and the third box shows the modern Chinese character for the item. Duplicate the Chinese characters on 8½- by 11-inch sheets of paper and laminate, or create a PowerPoint slide for each character. Read the story aloud, displaying the Chinese characters as they appear in the story.

After the story presentation, give each child a sheet of paper, a calligraphy-style paint brush (small, soft, with pointed tip), and nonpermanent, washable paints. Let them create their own pictographs for elements in the story such as mountain, bird, tree, or house. The author also includes several activities at the end of the book, such as "Flashlight Picture Magic."

Tangram Story

Tompert, Ann. *Grandfather Tang's Story*. Illustrated by Robert Andrew Parker. New York: Random House, 1990, 1997. (32 pages)

Grandfather Tang and his granddaughter Soo use tangrams to tell a story about two fox fairies who play a dangerous game that almost cost them their friendship.

Tangrams are an ancient Chinese puzzle game. School-age children enjoy creating figures using tangram puzzle pieces. Give each child a tangram set made from posterboard or card stock. Refer to Figure 4.4 for a tangram pattern. Use 11- by 14-inch sheets of paper, or larger, to make a flip chart of tangram figures from the book *Grandfather Tang's Story*.

Read the story aloud, showing the book's illustrations. Read the story aloud a second time, stopping to show each tangram character on the flip chart. Ask children to duplicate each character using their tangram puzzle pieces. Explain that all seven pieces must be used and that each piece must touch at least one other puzzle piece.

Note: This activity may be more appropriate as the basis for an entire story time or as an extending activity for the media center or classroom. It may require 30 to 40 minutes, depending upon the age of the group and their familiarity with tangrams.

Fingerplays, Songs, Action Rhymes, and Games

"Mayling's Hammer" Fingerplay

Share the book *Count Your Way through China* with children. Teach them the Chinese words for the numbers one through ten (see below) and then present this action rhyme, which is based on a children's verse known as either "Johnny's Hammer" or "Peter's Hammer" (author unknown).

Figure 4.4 **Tangram**

This action rhyme may be performed two ways. One method is to have children show the number of hammers with their fingers. Then they pound their fists on the palms of their other hands as they hammer.

Another method is to have the children stand and use their arms, legs, and heads as hammers. For example, first you hammer with your right arm, moving your arm up and down in a hammering motion (one hammer); then you hammer with your right and left arms (two hammers); then you hammer with both arms and your right leg by stamping your foot (three hammers); then you hammer with both arms and both legs (four hammers); and finally, you hammer with both arms, both legs, and your head, by nodding the head up and down (five hammers).

Counting Pronunciation Guide

1. pronounced "ee"
2. pronounced "rr"
3. pronounced "sahn"
4. pronounced "zuh"
5. pronounced "wuu"

Mayling's Hammer by Desiree Webber

Mayling pounds with one (ee) hammer,
One (ee) hammer, one (ee) hammer,
Mayling pounds with one (ee) hammer,
Then she pounds with two (rr).
Mayling pounds with two (rr) hammers,
Two (rr) hammers, two (rr) hammers,
Mayling pounds with two (rr) hammers,
Then she pounds with three (sahn).
Mayling pounds with three (sahn) hammers,
Three (sahn) hammers, three (sahn) hammers,
Mayling pounds with three (sahn) hammers,
Then she pounds with four (zuh).
Mayling pounds with four (zuh) hammers,
Four (zuh) hammers, four (zuh) hammers,
Mayling pounds with four (zuh) hammers,
Then she pounds with five (wuu).
Mayling pounds with five (wuu) hammers,
Five (wuu) hammers, five (wu) hammers,
Mayling pounds with five (wu) hammers,
Then she goes to sleep.

"Five Red Dragons" Fingerplay

Five Red Dragons by Desiree Webber

Five red dragons flying in the sky, *(stretch arms out)*
The first one said, "I can soar high!" *(reach arms above head and stand on tip toes)*
The second one said, "Watch me dive low." *(bend at waist with arms outstretched)*

The third one said, "Into the clouds I blow." *(puff cheeks and blow hard)*
The fourth one said, "I can swallow the moon." *(make arms like a jaw—open and shut)*
The fifth one said, "Hear the drums? Let's zoom, zoom zoom!"
(stretch arms out and soar)

"Pin the Tail on the Dragon" Game

Supplies

Draw an enlarged outline of dragon on poster board or paper, minus the tail. Use the dragon puppet figure (Figure 4.5) as a pattern.

Cut a paper tail for each child using the dragon puppet figure (Figure 4.5) as a pattern.
Blindfold
Transparent tape
Optional: Treats for prizes

Directions

Fasten the dragon drawing on the wall at about shoulder height for the children. Give each child a paper tail with transparent tape placed at the large end of the tail. (The tape should be placed so that it sticks on both the tail and the dragon drawing.) Start 10 feet away from the wall. Blindfold each child, one at a time, and have him or her walk forward to the drawing and attempt to tape the tail to the drawing. The child who tapes his or her tail the closest to where the tail belongs is the winner.

Sources for Fingerplays, Songs, Action Rhymes, and Games

"Chinese New Year/Dancing Dragon." In *Hanukkah & Chinese New Year*. Long Branch, NJ: Kimbo Educational, 1999, 2002. CD-ROM.
   Use a story time parachute or large piece of cloth for this activity. The leader takes one end and the children grab on one at a time to create a parade dragon during the song.

MacMillan, Kathy and Christine Kirker. "Kids around the World Wake Up." In *Storytime Magic: 400 Fingerplays, Flannelboards, and Other Activities*. Chicago, IL: American Library Association, 2009. (page 28)
   This rhyme can easily be converted into an action rhyme with children stretching, yawning, and speaking greetings from various countries, including China.

"Red Dragonflies." In *Storytime Magic: 400 Fingerplays, Flannelboards, and Other Activities* by Kathy MacMillan and Christine Kirker. Chicago, IL: American Library Association, 2009. (page 29)
   This rhyme can be developed into a fingerplay for story time.

Stewart, Georgiana. "Chinese New Year." In *Multicultural Bean Bag Fun*. Long Branch, NJ: Kimbo Educational, 2009. Compact disc.
   Children toss and catch their bean bags while making faces and roaring like dragons in a parade.

Media Choices

Show a DVD or downloadable movie as a transition between storytelling activities and crafts.

Lon Po Po: A Red-Riding Hood Story from China by Ed Young. Norwalk, CT: Weston Woods, 2006. DVD, 14 min.

While the mother is gone, a wolf comes to the door posing as the children's grandmother, called "Po Po." The three children cleverly escape the wolf.

More Stories from Near and Far. Norwalk, CT: Weston Woods, 2006. DVD.
   This collection includes *Who's in Rabbit's House?* by Verna Aardema, *The Beast of Monsieur Racine* by Tomi Ungerer, *The Story about Ping* by Marjorie Flack, and *The Great White Man-Eating Shark* by Margaret Mahy. *The Story about Ping* is 10 minutes in length. Ping, a duck, becomes separated from his family as they sail down the Yangtze River in China.

Muth, Jon J. *Stone Soup.* Norwalk, CT: Weston Woods, 2011. DVD, 13 min.
   The author takes this traditional folktale and sets it in China with three monks visiting a small town in which no one trusts his or her neighbor and no one shares.

Winter Holiday Stories, Vol. II. Norwalk, CT: Weston Woods, 2007. DVD.
   This collection includes *The Drummer Boy, One Zillion Valentines* by Frank Modell, and *Sam and the Lucky Money* by Karen Chinn. *Sam and the Lucky Money* is 11 minutes in length. Sam receives $4.00 in red envelopes called "leisees" as "lucky money" to celebrate the Chinese New Year. He and his mother go shopping in Chinatown, and Sam cannot decide what to buy until he meets a homeless man with no shoes.

Crafts and Other Activities

Choose a craft suited for the age level of the group and the time allotted for the story time session.

Chinese New Year

Suggested Reading

Otto, Carolyn. *Celebrate Chinese New Year.* Washington, DC: National Geographic Society, 2009. (32 pages)
   Otto presents the preparations, celebrations, food, decorations, and gifts that take place during the Chinese New Year holiday.

Suggested Websites

If there is Internet access along with an LCD projector, screen, or interactive whiteboard, show video clips of dragon parades or dragon dances that are accessible through YouTube.com, such as:

- February 21, 2007, http://www.youtube.com/watch?v=iRVhf9Yrdjw
- March 20, 2008, http://www.youtube.com/watch?v=n3bwreD_w3s
- January 29, 2006, http://www.youtube.com/watch?v=4WUnWPpRsIM
- February 23, 2011, http://www.youtube.com/watch?v=VsAzR4Am4I0 (Chinatown, San Francisco)

Chinese New Year is one of the most popular celebrations in China. It is held sometime in January or February, depending upon the phase of the moon, to usher in the spring season. People buy new clothes and gifts for family and friends, cook special foods, and receive red envelopes with money inside. One of the highlights of the Chinese New Year celebration is the dragon parade or dragon dance. The dragon has a large, beautifully decorated head. Underneath the dragon's head is a dancer who leads the dragon along the parade route jumping and twisting. Attached to the dragon's head is a large piece

attach straws or craft sticks to back at arrows

Figure 4.5   **Dragon Puppet**

of colorful cloth representing its body. Several people hold the dragon's body as they dance through the parade.

The "Dragon Puppet" craft is an individual project. The "Chinese New Year Dragon" craft is a group project—children make a dragon for their own New Years' parade.

Dragon Puppet

Supplies

Green posterboard or construction paper	Scissors
Tissue paper—various colors (cut into 1-inch squares)	Drinking straws or large craft sticks (two per child)
Glue sticks	Clear tape
Pencils	

Enlarge Figure 4.5 to 200 percent to create the pattern for this craft. Make a copy for each child. Have children trace their pattern on green posterboard or construction paper and cut out the dragon (for young children, supply precut dragons). Tape two straws or two large craft sticks to the back of the dragon where indicated in Figure 4.5, leaving enough room between the straw or sticks for manipulation of the puppet with both hands. Glue various colors of tissue-paper squares to the front of the puppet, creating the appearance of dragon scales.

Children can manipulate their dragon puppets like miniature Chinese New Year dragons on parade by moving the straws or sticks backward and forward to create a rippling effect.

Chinese New Year Dragon

Supplies

Cardboard box	Decorative materials (construction paper, washable tempera paints, washable markers, streamers, feathers, buttons, tissue paper, ribbon, etc.)
Brown or white wrapping paper on a roll	
Clear tape	
White glue	

See Figure 4.6 for a sample illustration of the Chinese New Year dragon. Create the dragon's head using a cardboard box large enough to fit over a child's head but not too heavy to carry. An adult should precut the eyes and cut slots in the side of the box to be used as handles. Have two or three children either paint the box or cover it with construction paper. Then use streamers, feathers, buttons, tissue paper, and ribbons to decorate the head. (If desired, an adult may paint and decorate the box beforehand to save time.)

Give each child a 36-inch section of brown or white wrapping paper to decorate with paints or markers. They are creating a colorful body for the dragon. After all the sections

Figure 4.6 **Chinese New Year Dragon Example**

are decorated, tape them together to form the body of the dragon. Tape should be applied on the inside for a cleaner appearance. Then tape the body to the top of the dragon's head.

One child holds the dragon's head by the handles while the other children support the dragon's body above their heads. Have children move around the room (or any other large space) to perform their own dragon parade. Refer to the "Chinese New Year/Dancing Dragon" song under "Sources for Fingerplays, Songs, Action Rhymes, and Games" for music to play.

Sources for Craft Ideas and Activities

Gould, Roberta. *The Kids' Multicultural Craft Book: 35 Crafts from around the World.* Charlotte, VT: Williamson Publishing, 2004. (pages 66–68)
Includes directions for making a "Chinese Children's Hat." Hats are designed using craft materials to look like one of the "good luck" animals, such as a dragon, pig, dog, or tiger.

Mattern, Joanne. *Recipe and Craft Guide to China.* Hockessin, DE: Mitchell Lane, 2011.
Mattern's book provides instructions, along with color photographs, for making several crafts such as paper cutouts, kites, dragon boats, dough-clay panda bears, red lanterns, and paper firecrackers.

Michaels, Alexandra. *The Kids' Multicultural Art Book: Art & Craft Experiences from around the World.* Nashville, TN: Williamson Books, 2007. (pages 142–147)
There are two crafts for China, "Good-Luck Dragon" and "Traditional Papercuts," that can be used by children in second grade and higher. The "Good-Luck Dragon" may be used by younger children with assistance by an adult.

Press, Judy. *Around-the-World Art & Activities: Visiting the 7 Continents through Craft Fun*. Nashville, TN: Williamson Books, 2000. (pages 49–51)
> The "Chinese Paper Fan" is a simple craft utilizing paper, markers, and transparent tape to make a unique and useful item.

Speechley, Greta. *World Crafts*. New York: Gareth Stevens Publishing, 2010. (pages 22–23)
> Children cut out a dragon head and attach a folded accordion tail to create an attractive New Year dragon. Book includes pattern for dragon head. Appropriate for school-age children with adult assistance.

Chapter 5

Let's Visit

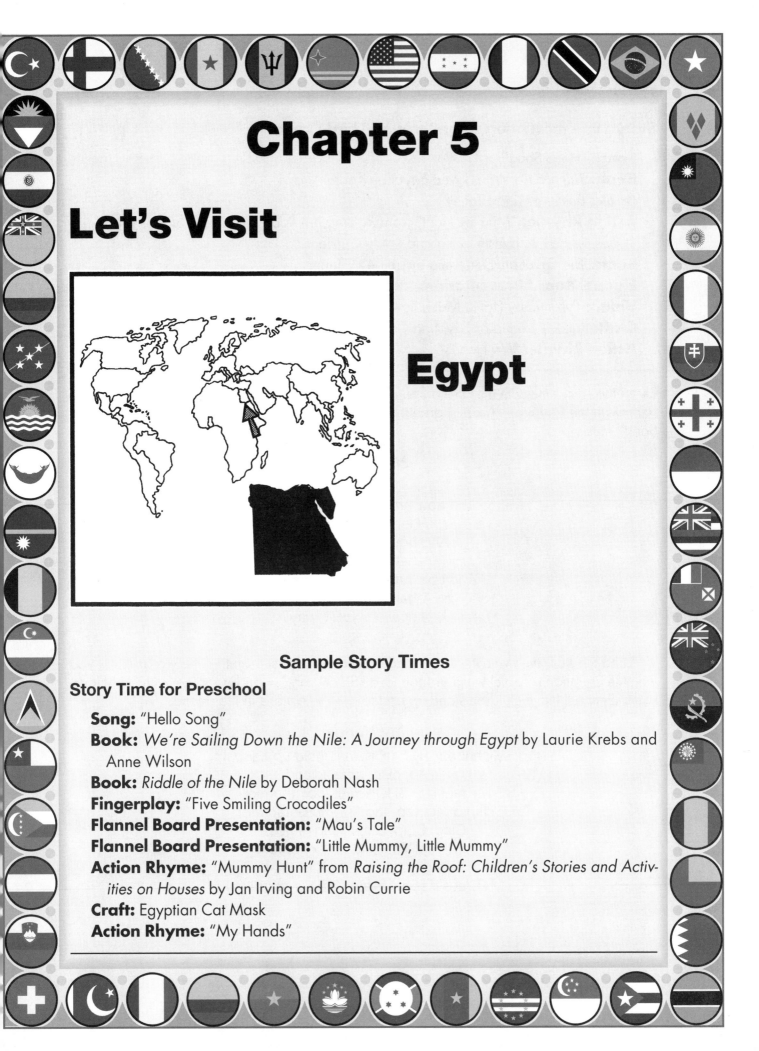

Egypt

Sample Story Times

Story Time for Preschool

Song: "Hello Song"

Book: *We're Sailing Down the Nile: A Journey through Egypt* by Laurie Krebs and Anne Wilson

Book: *Riddle of the Nile* by Deborah Nash

Fingerplay: "Five Smiling Crocodiles"

Flannel Board Presentation: "Mau's Tale"

Flannel Board Presentation: "Little Mummy, Little Mummy"

Action Rhyme: "Mummy Hunt" from *Raising the Roof: Children's Stories and Activities on Houses* by Jan Irving and Robin Currie

Craft: Egyptian Cat Mask

Action Rhyme: "My Hands"

Story Time for Kindergarten through Third Grade

Song: "Hello Song"
Book: *The Mouse Who Saved Egypt* by Karim Alrawi
Book: *Bastet* by Linda Talley
Action Rhyme: "Mummy Hunt" from *Raising the Roof: Children's Stories and Activities on Houses* by Jan Irving and Robin Currie
Book: *The Egyptian Cinderella* by Shirley Climo
Flannel Board Presentation: "Mau's Tale"
Video: *Pyramid* by David Macaulay
Craft: Paper Pyramid or Egyptian Cat Mask
Action Rhyme: "My Hands"

Begin the story time with the "Hello Song." Then sing the song again, substituting the word *hello* with the Egyptian (Arabic) greeting pronounced "A-hal-an." (See p. xxix for "Hello Song" music.)

Hello Song

Hello ev'rybody,
And how are you? How are you?
Hello ev'rybody,
And how are you today?
A-hal-an ev'rybody,
And how are you? How are you?
A-hal-an ev'rybody,
And how are you today?

End the story time with the "My Hands" action rhyme, substituting the words *thank you* with the Egyptian (Arabic) word pronounced "SHOK-ran,",= and *goodbye* with "MAE-aes-sae-LAE-mae." Have children stand up and follow the actions in the rhyme.

My Hands

My hands say SHOK-ran. *(hold up hands)*
With a clap, clap, clap. *(clap hands)*
My feet say SHOK-ran. *(point to feet)*
With a tap, tap, tap. *(stamp or tap feet)*
Clap! Clap! Clap! *(clap hands)*
Tap! Tap! Tap! *(stamp or tap feet)*
Turn myself around and bow. *(turn and bow)*
MAE-aes-sae-LAE-mae. *(wave goodbye)*

Books to Read Aloud

Alrawi, Karim. *The Mouse Who Saved Egypt*. Illustrated by Bee Willey. Northampton, MA: Crocodile Books, 2011. (24 pages)
A mouse repays the kindness to the young prince who had rescued her in the desert. A retelling of an ancient Middle Eastern folktale.

Bower, Tamara. *The Shipwrecked Sailor: An Egyptian Tale with Hieroglyphs*. New York: Antheneum, 2000. (32 pages)
A shipwrecked sailor on a magic island befriends the Prince of Punt and is then given many gifts by the prince when he is finally rescued and returns home to Egypt. Includes phrases in hieroglyphs with their translations. Recommended for school-age children.

Climo, Shirley. *The Egyptian Cinderella*. Illustrated by Ruth Heller. Lodi, NJ: Marco Book Co., 2009. (32 pages)
In this Egyptian version of Cinderella, Rhodopis, a slave girl, is chosen to be queen by the pharaoh. Recommended for school-age children.

Farmer, Nancy. *Clever Ali*. Illustrated by Gail De Marcken. New York: Orchard Books, 2006. (36 pages)
Young Ali's father is the keeper of the pigeons for the wicked sultan of Cairo. When Ali disobeys, he must cross the snowy mountains of Syria in order to save his father from the sultan. Recommended for school-age children.

Hamilton, Martha and Mitch Weiss. *The Well of Truth: A Folktale from Egypt*. Illustrated by Tom Wrenn. Atlanta, GA: August House Story Cove, 2009. (32 pages)
When Goat, Rooster, and Donkey decide to try their hand at farming, all goes well until Donkey's appetite gets the best of him. In this tale from Egypt, Donkey learns the price of being greedy and discovers that the truth will always come out, even if it comes from the bottom of a well.

Hartland, Jessie. *How the Sphinx Got to the Museum*. Maplewood, NJ: Blue Apple Books, 2010. (40 pages)
The repetitive cadence describes the history of Hatshepsut's sphinx and how it came to be in the Metropolitan Museum of Art in New York City. Recommended for school-age children.

Krebs, Laurie. *We're Sailing Down the Nile: A Journey through Egypt*. Illustrated by Anne Wilson. Cambridge, MA: Barefoot Books, 2007. (40 pages)
A group of children travel the Nile River and see some of the best-known sites in Egypt.

Maldonado, Cristina Falcón. *1, 2, 3 Suddenly in Egypt: The Eye of Horus*. Illustrated by Marta Fàbrega. Hauppauge, NY: Barron's Educational Series, 2011. (33 pages)
Martin uses the key his grandfather gave him to open a secret storeroom, where a magic necklace and special travel album take him on a trip through Egypt.

Nash, Deborah. *Riddle of the Nile*. London, England: Frances Lincoln Children's Books, 2006. (24 pages)
Baby Crocodile is on an adventure down the Nile River to try to solve the riddle that will prove him worthy of becoming king of the Nile. Facts are interspersed on each page and directions for the Pyramid Fortune Game are included at the end of the book.

Schachner, Judy. *Skippyjon Jones in Mummy Trouble*. New York: Scholastic, 2006. (32 pages)
Skippy goes into his closet and on an adventure to ancient Egypt, where he must answer the riddle of the "Finx" in order to enter the mummy's tomb.

Schuh, Mari. *Look Inside a Pyramid*. Mankato, MN: Capstone Press, 2009. (24 pages)
Includes informative facts about the pyramids of Egypt, including labeled photographs and diagrams.

Sollinger, Emily. *Diego's Egyptian Expedition.* Illustrated by Warner McGee. New York: Simon Spotlight/Nickelodeon, 2009. (24 pages)
   Diego goes on an adventure through Egypt with his friend Medina. There they learn about desert animals, including camels, and see the Great Pyramids.

Talley, Linda. *Bastet.* Illustrated by Itoko Maeno. Kansas City, MO: MarshMedia, 2001. (32 pages)
   Bastet lives on the streets of Cairo with her best friend Sabah. The two cats dream of seeing Tutankhamen's golden mask in the Egyptian Museum, but Bastet comes to find out that friendship is more important and valuable.

Walsh, Jill Paton. *Pepi and the Secret Names: Help Pepi Crack the Hieroglyphic Code.* Illustrated by Fiona French. London: Frances Lincoln Children's Books, 2009. (32 pages)
   Pepi helps his father by gathering the animals for the artwork of the royal tomb. The hieroglyphic key is provided at the end of the book for fun decoding of the animals' secret names. Recommended for school-age children.

Would, Nick. *The Scarab's Secret.* Illustrated by Christina Balit. London: Frances Lincoln Children's Books, 2011. (32 pages)
   The small scarab beetle Khepri saves the pharaoh's life. Includes a historical end note on tomb building and the pharaohs.

Storytelling

"Mau's Tale" Flannel Board Presentation

Cats were first domesticated in Egypt, held a special place in Egyptian worship, and were sacred because they were associated with the cat goddess, Bastet. Bastet was the goddess of joy who loved music and dance. She had a pretty Egyptian cat's head with a narrow snout and large pointed ears. Many families, rich or poor, owned a cat in ancient Egypt. Even the pharaohs had pet cats.

Share this story and discover many interesting facts about Egyptian cats. See "Cat Mummy," "Bastet, Cat Goddess," "Egyptian Woman," "Mau," "Mother Cat with Kittens," and "Bubastis Temple" (Figures 5.1 through 5.6) for patterns. Trace the patterns on felt, or photocopy and color them. If photocopying, glue small squares of felt to the backs of the paper figures so they will hold to the flannel board. Place the figures on the flannel board as they are introduced in the story.

"Mau's Tale" by Donna Norvell

Mau was a yellow-striped tabby kitten who lived with her mother, a brother, and a sister. *(place the mother cat with kittens on the flannel board)* One day, when Mau and her family were asleep in their warm cozy basket, Mau began to dream. She was a sleek Egyptian cat. She dreamed of the exciting and strange story their mother had just told them. There were pyramids, palm trees, and pharaohs. *(take basket off and place Mau on the flannel board)*

Suddenly, Mau opened her eyes; there was sand all around, and so many strange smells. What were those large stone buildings she could see in the distance? Then she knew: She was in that far-away place called Egypt that her mother had described to them. It was the home of her ancestor cats many, many years ago—in fact, about 3,500 years ago. It was in Egypt that people first made pets of cats. Cats were greatly admired by the Egyptians because they were great hunters and protected the grain storages from rats and mice.

Mau remembered her mother saying that many of her ancestors once lived in a city called Bubastis along a large river called the Nile. These cats lived with families in palaces, homes, and huts. *(place the temple on the flannel board)* At the center of the city was a grand temple where the statue of Bastet was kept. *(place the statue of Bastet on the flannel board)* Bastet was the Cat Goddess.

Then Mau heard music. She could see boats floating down the Nile, and there were people dancing, clapping their hands, and beating on drums and singing. It was the Spring Festival in honor of Bastet. *(place the Egyptian woman on the flannel board)* The Egyptian women wore glittering jewelry and lined their eyes with black makeup, like cats' eyes.

Mau's mother also told her that all cats were sacred in ancient Egypt. If a house was on fire, the cats were the first to be saved. Killing a cat was punishable by death. And it was forbidden to take cats out of Egypt. The Romans and the Greeks smuggled them out, though, and that is why cats are found all over the world today.

As Mau was prowling through the streets, she saw another strange sight: A small boy and his mother and father were crying. Their family cat had died, and they had shaved off their eyebrows out of respect and grief. They proceeded to prepare their cat for a special burial, so he would be ready for his life in the next world. They wrapped him tightly in pieces of cloth, mummifying him. *(place the cat mummy on the flannel board)* They also caught mice and mummified them so the mummy cat would have food. Mau thought this was all rather strange, but interesting. However, thinking of mice was making Mau hungry.

What was this new smell? Could it be? Kitty Chow, here in Egypt? Then Mau yawned and stretched. She woke up and realized she was in the basket with her family at home. *(remove all pieces from flannel board and place the mother cat with her kittens on the flannel board)* There was her mother, her brother, and her sister, but where did Egypt go? Across the ocean—far, far away.

Figure 5.1 **Cat Mummy**   Figure 5.2   **Bastet, Cat Goddess**   Figure 5.3   **Egyptian Woman**

Figure 5.4 **Mau** Figure 5.5 **Mother Cat with Kittens**

Figure 5.6 **Bubastis Temple**

Fingerplays, Songs, Action Rhymes, and Games

Feldman, Jean. "Alligator Sock Puppet." *Puppets & Storytime*. New York: Teaching Resources, 2005. (page 11)
> The rhyme "See you later, alligator! After awhile, crocodile!" is accompanied by directions to make a sock puppet and a chant to focus children's attention.

Low, Elizabeth Cothen. "If You Should Meet a Crocodile" and "She Sailed Away on One Fine Day." In *Big Book of Animal Rhymes, Fingerplays, and Songs*. Westport, CT: Libraries Unlimited, 2009. (page 1)
> This action rhyme includes the line, "The crocodile sleeps upon the Nile."

Pirotta, Saviour. "Counting Chickens: A Story from Egypt" *Around the World in 80 Tales*. Illustrated by Richard Johnson. Boston, MA: Kingfisher, 2007. (page 114)
> This story could be retold as an action rhyme acting out the steps in Farouk's story that lead him to learn a lesson about paying attention to the present time and not "counting his chickens" before they hatch.

Scott, Barbara A. *1,000 Fingerplays & Action Rhymes: A Sourcebook & DVD*. New York: Neal Schuman Publishers, 2010. (pages 243–244)
> Fun action rhymes include "One Little Crocodile" sung to the tune of "Six Little Ducks," "I'm a Little Crocodile" sung to the tune of "I'm a Little Teapot," and "Baby Crocodile" sung to the tune of "I'm Bringing Home a Baby Bumblebee." There are also motions included in the margin.

"Little Mummy, Little Mummy" Flannel Board Game

Preschool children will enjoy this flannel board guessing game with a repeating rhyme. Use the "Pyramid" and "Cat Mummy" figures (Figures 5.7 and 5.8) to make the figures for this game. Trace the patterns on felt, or photocopy and color them. If photocopying, glue small squares of felt to the backs of the paper figures so they will hold to the flannel board. Make five pyramids, each a different color: red, yellow, orange, blue, and green.

"Little Mummy, Little Mummy" by Desiree Webber and Sandy Shropshire

To play this game, the storyteller places all the pyramids on the flannel board, hiding the cat mummy behind one of them. Do not let the children see where the mummy is placed. Have the children say the following rhyme, and the storyteller removes each colored pyramid from the flannel board. Repeat the process until the Little Mummy is found. This is clearer worded this way.

Little Mummy, Little Mummy are you hid
Underneath the (red, yellow, orange, blue, green) pyramid?

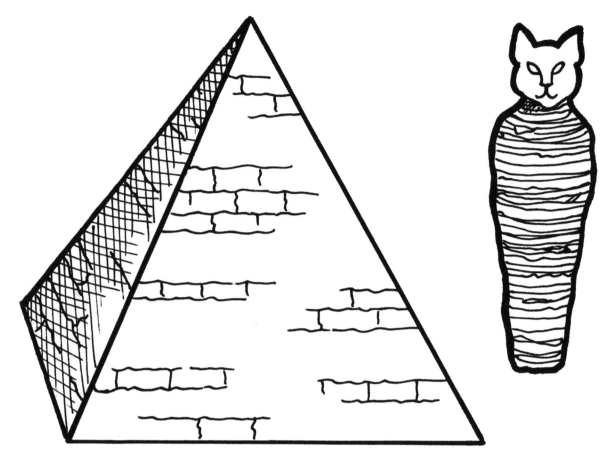

Figure 5.7 **Pyramid**   Figure 5.8 **Cat Mummy**

"Five Smiling Crocodiles" Fingerplay

The landscape of ancient Egypt was created by the Nile River, the longest river in the world. Once a year, after torrential rainstorms, the river overflowed its banks. This was a blessing for the people of Egypt because they could plant their crops in the rich soil left by the fertile river mud. Of all the wildlife found along the Nile, the crocodile was the most feared.

The crocodile was the symbol for the ancient Egyptian god Sebek. In the city Crocodopolis, one of the duties of the priests was to keep a live crocodile fat and healthy. After it died, it was mummified and placed into a special tomb. (See books about crocodiles at the end of this fingerplay, which might be used to supplement the fingerplay that follows.)

Photocopy one set of five crocodile finger puppets (Figure 5.9) and four sets of 10 fish finger puppets (Figure 5.10) on white tagboard or construction paper. Use markers to color the crocodiles green; color the sets of fish red, blue, orange, and green. Cut out the crocodiles and fish and tape or glue each to a finger attachment (make six copies of Figure 5.11). Tape together the three flaps of each finger puppet attachment. It will fit over the tip of each finger like a thimble.

Choose four children to help perform this fingerplay. Give each child a set of fish. As each color is introduced in the fingerplay, have the child with that color of fish approach the storyteller and make the fish swim around the crocodiles (the child will have a fish puppet on each finger of one hand). As each crocodile swims away, remove a finger puppet. Have all children participate when the crocodiles grunt, hiss, growl, and roar.

Five Smiling Crocodiles by Donna Norvell

Five little crocodiles,
Floating down the Nile.
Each of them had a great big smile.
GRUNT! HISSSS! GROWL! ROAR!
They were enjoying their play that sunshiny day,
When a large school of red fish swam their way.
One little crocodile forgot about play . . .
Something yummy in his tummy was his wish,
As he swam away after the red fish.
Four little crocodiles,
Floating down the Nile.
Each of them had a great big smile.
GRUNT! HISSSS! GROWL! ROAR!
They were enjoying their play that sunshiny day,
When a large school of blue fish swam their way.
One little crocodile forgot about play . . .
Something yummy in his tummy was his wish,
As he swam away after the blue fish.
Three little crocodiles,
Floating down the Nile.
Each of them had a great big smile.
GRUNT! HISSSS! GROWL! ROAR!
They were enjoying their play that sunshiny day,

When a large school of orange fish swam their way.
One little crocodile forgot about play . . .
Something yummy in his tummy was his wish,
As he swam away after the orange fish.
Two little crocodiles,
Floating down the Nile.
Each of them had a great big smile.
GRUNT! HISSSS! GROWL! ROAR!
They were enjoying their play that sunshiny day,
When a large school of green fish swam their way.
One little crocodile forgot about play . . .
Something yummy in his tummy was his wish,
As he swam away after the green fish.
One little crocodile,
Floating down the Nile.
He no longer had a great big smile.
His friends were gone and so were the fish,
So he swam back home with a swish, swish, swish.

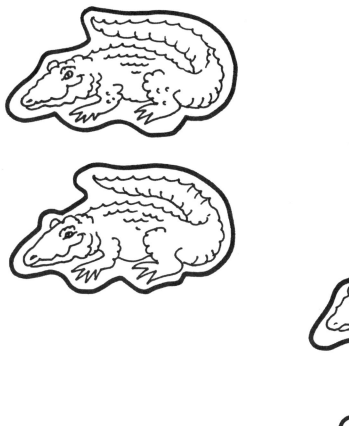

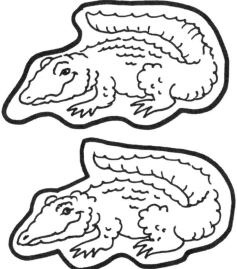

Figure 5.9 **Crocodile Finger Puppets**

Figure 5.10　**Fish Finger Puppets**

Figure 5.11 **Finger Puppet Attachments**

Books about Crocodiles

Llewellyn, Claire. *Starting Life: Crocodile.* Illustrated by Simon Mendez. Chanhassen, MN: NorthWord Press, 2004. (24 pages)
This book contains realistic illustrations of a crocodile's life cycle on interesting layered pages.

Sirota, Lyn. *Crocodiles.* Mankato, MN: Capstone Press, 2010. (24 pages)
The full-color photographs and simple text provide interesting and informative facts about crocodiles.

Welsbacher, Anne. *Crocodiles.* Mankato, MN: Capstone High-Interest Books, 2003. (32 pages)
Engaging facts about crocodiles, including a section on page 28 about Egypt titled "Ancient Beliefs."

"Mummy Wrap" Game

Have children pair off and then give each pair several rolls of toilet paper. One child stands straight with arms by his or her sides and acts as the mummy. The other child does the wrapping. Time the pairs: Who can wrap their mummy the quickest?

Irving, Jan and Robin Currie. "Mummy Hunt." In *Raising the Roof: Children's Stories and Activities on Houses.* Englewood, CO: Teacher Ideas Press, 1991. (65 pages) Reprinted with permission.

"Mummy Hunt" Action Rhyme

"Mummy Hunt" by Jan Irving and Robin Currie

We're going on a mummy hunt,
We're going to swish through the sand. *(rub hands together)*
Here we are at the pyramid.
Open the creaking door. *(move arm as if opening the door)*
Eeeeeeek.
Look, there's writing on the walls. *(point)*
It's hieroglyphics—it says, "Walk this way."
Let's tiptoe. *(tiptoe in place)*
Shhhhh, shhhhh. *(put index finger to lips)*
Here is the inner chamber and . . .
King Tut!
He's having a party.
Let's dance! *(dance Egyptian style)*
Time to go.
Better tiptoe out so they don't miss us. *(tiptoe)*
Read the hieroglyphics. *(point)*
It says "This way out."
Open the door.
Eeeek. *(move arm as if opening the door)*
And slam it shut.
Bang. *(clap)*
Back through the swishing sand. *(rub hands together)*
And back to our home.

Brush the sand out of your clothes. *(brush self)*
Do you remember how to dance like King Tut?
(dance as before)

King Tut Dance

Martin, Steve. "King Tut." In *Kids Wanna Rock*. Oklahoma City: Melody House, 1996. Compact disc. Streaming digital version available on SongFacts.com. October 12, 2011. http://www.songfacts.com/detail.php?id=3813.
A humorous song with a catchy tune for dancing.

Play this song after the action rhyme "Mummy Hunt" (above) and have the children dance like King Tut. Or play the song after the craft "Egyptian Cat Masks" (see "Crafts and Other Activities") and have children dance while holding their cat masks to their faces.

Media Choices

Show a DVD or downloadable movie as a transition between storytelling activities and crafts.

Disney's Little Einsteins- The Legend of the Golden Pyramid. Burbank, CA: Walt Disney Studios, 2007. DVD, 30 min.
The Little Einstein Kids travel through the desert of Egypt, down the Nile River, to visit the Sphinx and explore inside a pyramid.

NeoK12. *Educational Videos, Lessons, and Games for K-12 School Kids: Ancient Egypt*. October 12, 2011. http://www.neok12.com/Ancient-Egypt.htm.
A collection of short streaming video segments include headings such as "Secret of the Pyramids," "Sphinx and Great Pyramids," and "Tut's Treasures." Includes the statement: "All videos & lessons on NeoK12 have been reviewed by K–12 teachers."

Crafts and Other Activities

Choose a craft suited for the age level of the group and the time allotted for the story time.

Egyptian Cat Mask

Children enjoy making masks that look like Bastet, the Egyptian cat goddess of joy who loved music and dancing. After making the masks, have them dance to Egyptian music, such as "King Tut." (See "Fingerplays, Songs, Action Rhymes, and Games.")

Supplies

Yellow posterboard	Craft sticks
Orange construction paper	Clear tape
Black construction paper	Scissors
Hot-glue gun and glue sticks	Pencils
Black and orange markers	Hole punch

See Figure 5.12 through 5.14 for patterns. Enlarge the cat mask pattern and accompanying pieces by 20 percent if desired.

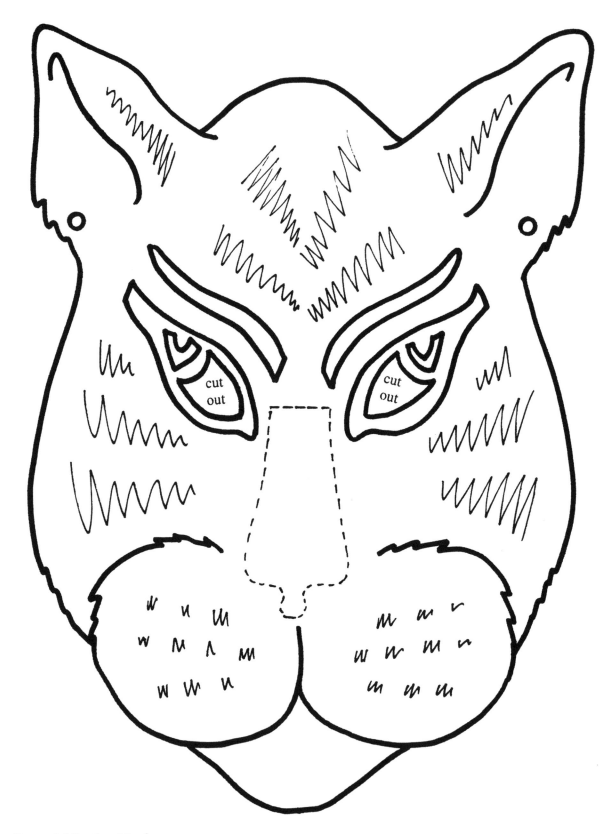

Figure 5.12 **Cat Mask**

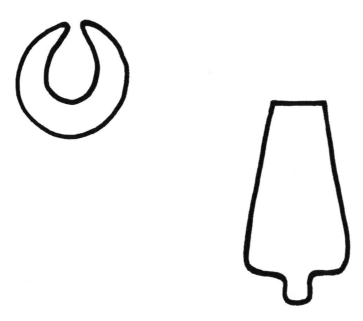

Figure 5.13 **Cat Mask Earring**   Figure 5.14   **Cat Mask Nose**

Using yellow posterboard, trace and cut out the cat mask (for younger children, precut the mask and eye holes). An adult should hot glue (or tape) a craft stick to the back of the mask. Using orange construction paper, trace and cut out the nose and earrings (precut for younger children). Glue the nose into place. To make whiskers, glue 4-inch by ¼-inch strips of black construction paper to the face beside the nose. Curl the ends if desired. Using a black marker, color the eyebrows and bold lines around the eyes. Using an orange marker, color the wavy "tabby cat" stripes. Punch a hole in each ear where indicated using a hole punch. Insert the earrings into the holes and attach them behind the ears with tape.

Paper Pyramid

Some of the oldest stone buildings in the world are the Great Pyramids of Egypt. The pharaohs had the pyramids built to serve as their tombs after they died. The pyramids are so colossal because they had to hold all the pharaoh's treasures that were to be with him in his next life. It took up to 20 years to build one pyramid. The largest pyramid, the Great Pyramid of Giza, the tomb of Pharaoh Cheops, is 40 stories high.

In this craft project, children make a pyramid using a piece of posterboard.

Supplies

Light-brown or tan posterboard or tagboard   Scissors

Clear tape   Fine-tipped colored markers

Use the "Paper Pyramid" pattern (Figure 5.15) for the pyramid. On light-brown or tan tagboard, photocopy and cut out a pyramid for each child. Have children refer to the "Hieroglyphic Examples" (Figure 5.15) and draw brightly colored designs on the sides of their pyramids. Fold the triangular sides upward to form a pyramid and tape them into place.

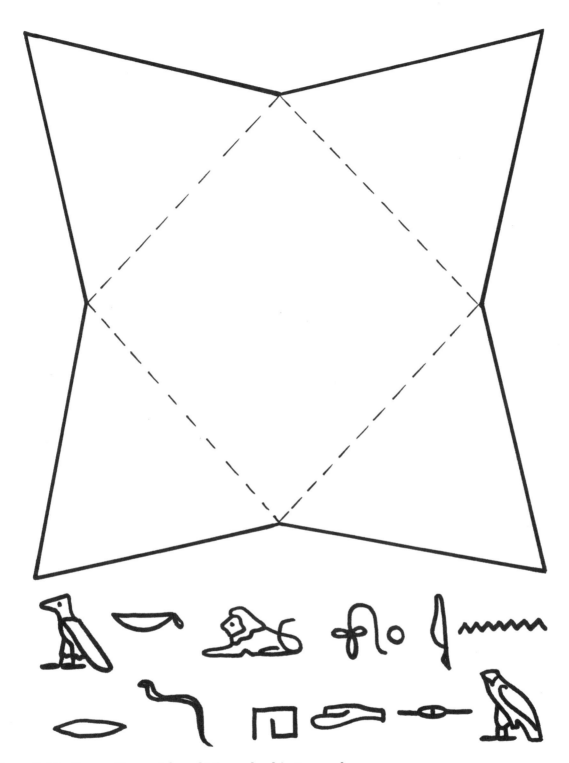

Figure 5.15 **Paper Pyramid and Hieroglyphic Examples**

Sources for Craft Ideas and Activities

Cressy, Judith. *What Can You Do with a Paper Bag?* San Francisco, CA: Chronicle Books, 2001.
Children will enjoy making the "Easy Egyptian Queen's Headdress" found on page 27. School-age children can construct the "Advanced Pharaoh's Headdress" found on pages 31 through 33.

Michaels, Alexandria. *The Kids' Multicultural Art Book: Ages 3–9.* Nashville, TN: Williamson Books, 2007. (157 pages)
Includes a craft for Egyptian worry beads made from paper with easy-to-find-and-use materials.

Press, Judy. *The Little Hands Big Fun Craft Book.* Illustrated by Loretta Trezzo Braren. Nashville, TN: Williamson Books, 2008.
Children will enjoy making the beautiful "Egypt: Crackled Egg Art" from pages 80 and 81.

Speechley, Greta. *Crafts for Kids: Myths and Tales Book.* Danbury, CT: The Brown Reference Group, 2003.
The myths and stories are brought to life with the "Ancient Egyptian Phoenix Clip" found on page 20 and 21.

Stilton, Geronimo. *The Mummy With No Name.* New York: Scholastic, 2005. (128 pages)
This book, intended for children from second through fourth grade, is an adventure mystery. It has many facts about ancient Egypt throughout the story, as well as a section in the back full of activities including "Mummy Chain," "Egyptian Spiders," and "The Mummy Dance."

Chapter 6

Let's Visit

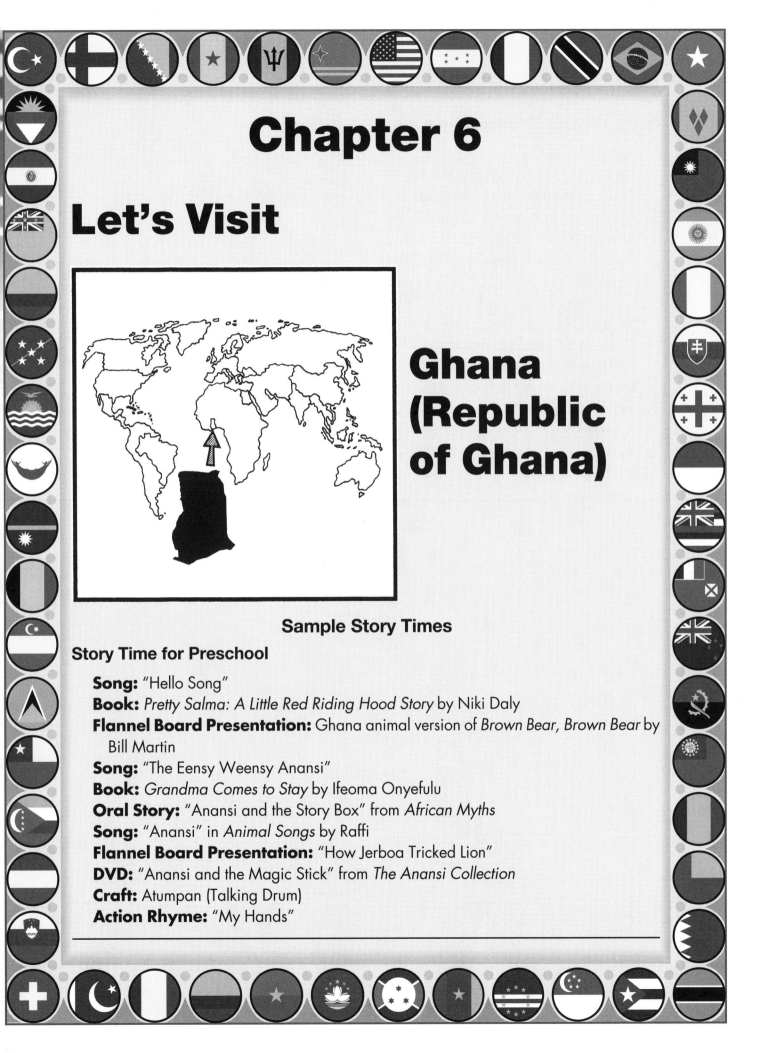

Ghana (Republic of Ghana)

Sample Story Times

Story Time for Preschool

Song: "Hello Song"

Book: *Pretty Salma: A Little Red Riding Hood Story* by Niki Daly

Flannel Board Presentation: Ghana animal version of *Brown Bear, Brown Bear* by Bill Martin

Song: "The Eensy Weensy Anansi"

Book: *Grandma Comes to Stay* by Ifeoma Onyefulu

Oral Story: "Anansi and the Story Box" from *African Myths*

Song: "Anansi" in *Animal Songs* by Raffi

Flannel Board Presentation: "How Jerboa Tricked Lion"

DVD: "Anansi and the Magic Stick" from *The Anansi Collection*

Craft: Atumpan (Talking Drum)

Action Rhyme: "My Hands"

Story Time for Kindergarten through Third Grade

Song: "Hello Song"

Book: *Kofi and His Magic* by Maya Angelou

Flannel Board Presentation: "Anansi and the Rock" from *Multicultural Folktales: Stories to Tell Young Children*

Song: "Anansi" in *Animal Songs* by Raffi.

Book: *One Hen: How One Small Loan Made a Big Difference* by Katie Smith Milway

Oral Story: "The Man Who Didn't Know What Minu Meant" from *Noodlehead Stories: World Tales Kids Can Read and Tell*

Song: "Che Che Kule" from *World Travels: World Music for Kids* by Aaron Nigel Smith

Flannel Board Presentation: "How Jerboa Tricked Lion"

DVD: *American Cultures for Children: African-American Heritage*

Craft: Royal Ashanti Crown and Ring

Action Rhyme: "My Hands"

Begin the story time with the "Hello Song." Then sing the song again, substituting the word *hello* with the Twi greeting *Akwaaba* [ah-KWAH-bah]. (See p. xxix for "Hello Song" music.)

Hello Song

Hello ev'rybody,
And how are you? How are you?
Hello ev'rybody,
And how are you today?
ah-KWAH-bah ev'rybody,
And how are you? How are you?
ah-KWAH-bah ev'rybody,
And how are you today?

End the story time with the "My Hands" action rhyme, substituting the words *thank you* with the Twi word *meda ase* [may-DAH-say], and *goodbye* with *nantew yiye* [nan-ti yeah]. Have children stand up and follow the actions in the rhyme.

My Hands

My hands say may-DAH-say. *(hold up hands)*
With a clap, clap, clap. *(clap hands)*
My feet say may-DAY-say. *(point to feet)*
With a tap, tap, tap. *(stamp or tap feet)*
Clap! Clap! Clap! *(clap hands)*
Tap! Tap! Tap! *(stamp or tap feet)*
Turn myself around and bow. *(turn and bow)*
Nan-ti yeah. *(wave goodbye)*

Books to Read Aloud

Angelou, Maya. *Kofi and His Magic.* Illustrated by Margaret Courtney-Clarke. New York: Crown Books for Young Readers, 2003. (48 pages)
Meet Kofi, a young Ashanti boy who lives in the town of Bonwire, as he uses his "magic" (imagination) to travel to other places. The beautiful photographs in this book introduce readers to the West African culture. A wonderful book to read along with the "Royal Ashanti Crown and Ring" craft on page 99.

Cummings, Pat. *Ananse and the Lizard: A West African Tale.* New York: Henry Holt and Company, 2002. (39 pages)
Ananse has a plan to marry the chief's daughter and someday become the chief himself until Lizard outsmarts him.

Daly, Niki. *Pretty Salma: A Little Red Riding Hood Story from Africa.* New York: Clarion Books, 2006. (24 pages)
The retelling of "Little Red Riding Hood" set in Ghana introduces readers to two Ghanaian words: *ntama* (a wrap-around skirt) and *atumpan* (a talking drum). This is a wonderful book to go along with using the atumpan (talking drum) craft on page 98. Have the children use rattles, clapping sticks, and drums to frighten Mr. Dog away at the end of the story.

Jarman, Julia. *The Magic Backpack.* Illustrated by Adriano Gon. New York: Crabtree Publishing, 2004. (48 pages)
Josh travels to Ghana using his magic backpack to visit his Uncle William's cocoa plantation to pick up the chocolate ingredient for his class project. This is a wonderful read-aloud for younger elementary children.

Kurtz, Jane. *In the Small, Small Night.* Illustrated by Rachel Isadora. New York: Greenwillow Books, 2005. (32 pages)
On Abena and her brother Kofi's first night in America, they remember their home back in Ghana by telling two Ashanti stories.

McDermott, Gerald. *Anansi the Spider: A Tale from the Ashanti.* New York: Henry Holt and Company, 1987. (48 pages)
Anansi has six sons with special gifts, which they each use when Anansi gets into trouble.

Milway, Katie Smith. *One Hen: How One Small Loan Made a Big Difference.* Illustrated by Eugenie Fernandes. Toronto, ON: Kids Can Press, 2008. (32 pages)
In a Ghanaian village, a young boy turns a small loan for one hen into a flourishing farm.

Mitchell, Rhonda. *The Talking Cloth.* New York: Orchard Books, 2001. (32 pages)
Amber visits her Aunt Phoebe, who shows her a beautiful *adinkra* cloth from Ghana. Aunt Phoebe tells her the significance of the patterns and colors used in the cloth.

Musgrove, Margaret. *The Spider Weaver: A Legend of Kente Cloth.* Illustrated by Julia Cairns. New York: The Blue Sky Press, 2001. (32 pages)
Two expert weavers go into the forest to trap some animals for food and come upon a magically unique web created by a beautiful spider. This is the story of how the spider shared her secret with the two weavers to create the design for what is known as *kente* cloth.

Onyefulu, Ifeoma. *Deron Goes to Nursery School.* London: Frances Lincoln Children's Books, 2009. (24 pages)
The simple text in this book lends itself to the preschooler showing the similarities of children beginning school in Ghana with children in any country.

Onyefulu, Ifeoma. *Grandma Comes to Stay*. London: Frances Lincoln Children's Books, 2009. (24 pages)
> Stephanie is excited because her grandma is coming to visit. This simple story is a great read-aloud for preschoolers, showing the everyday life of a little girl who lives in Ghana. Photographs of Stephanie's drum and drums used at the Osu Homowo Festival would be a great introduction to the atumpan (talking drum) craft in this chapter.

Provencal, Francis and Catherine McNamara. *Nii Kwei's Day: From Dawn to Dusk in a Ghanaian City*. New York: Frances Lincoln Children's Books, 2010. (32 pages)
> Meet seven-year-old Nii Kwei as he takes us on a journey through his day. He introduces us to his home, school, pastimes, and food.

Storytelling

"How Jerboa Tricked Lion" Flannel Board Presentation

"How Jerboa Tricked Lion" is a folktale of the Hausa people in northern Ghana. See Figures 6.1 through 6.5 for patterns. Trace the patterns on felt, or photocopy and color them. If photocopying, glue small pieces of felt to the backs of the paper figures so they will hold to the flannel board. If performing the story for a large group of children, enlarge the patterns 100 percent to make the figures easier to see. Place the figures on the flannel board as they are introduced in the story.

"How Jerboa Tricked Lion" retold by Dee Ann Corn

Lion was the most powerful animal in all the land. *(place the lion on the right side of the flannel board)* He was eating all the other animals. So the animals got together to talk about this terrible problem. After much discussion, the animals came up with the best solution they could: They decided to choose one animal at random every day to give to Lion to eat. They hoped this would satisfy him and make him happy. They went to Lion and asked him if he would leave them alone if they brought him one animal every morning for breakfast. Lion agreed.

The first morning, they chose Gazelle and took her to Lion. *(place the gazelle on the flannel board)* Lion did not bother the other animals that day. The next morning, Roan Antelope was chosen and sent to Lion. *(place the roan antelope on the flannel board)* This continued every morning, until it was Jerboa's turn. *(remove the gazelle and the roan antelope from the flannel board)*

Jerboa had an idea. *(place the jerboa on the left side of the flannel board)* He told all the animals he would go to Lion alone. The next day, as the sun came up, Lion waited for Jerboa. But Jerboa stayed in his hole until noon. Lion was getting very impatient and decided to go look for Jerboa because he had missed his breakfast and was getting hungry. He began to walk through the forest, roaring as loud as he could, searching for Jerboa. He was extremely angry.

Jerboa heard Lion roaring a little way down the road. Jerboa smiled and climbed a tree so he could see Lion. Lion came closer, then closer, and closer still, until he was right beneath Jerboa. *(place the lion beneath the jerboa)*

Jerboa asked, "Why are you roaring so loudly?"

Lion looked up and said, "I waited for you all morning and you never came."

"Well," Jerboa began, "I was on my way to your house with some honey for you to enjoy with your meal when the lion in the well took it."

Lion replied, "Take me to this lion."

Jerboa said, "He was in the well over there when I saw him, and he told me he was much more powerful than you." *(place the well on the flannel board)*

Lion became furious. He walked over to the well and looked in—and there was the lion, staring back at him. *(place the lion next to the well on the flannel board)* Lion didn't know it was his own reflection in the well.

"You are right, Jerboa," said Lion. "There is a lion down in the well. Lion asked the other lion in the well for the honey. But the lion in the well only mimicked him. Lion roared as loud as he could and jumped into the well to attack the lion. *(remove the lion from the flannel board)* That was the last time Lion was ever seen.

Jerboa returned to the animals and told them what had happened, and that they could live in peace once again.

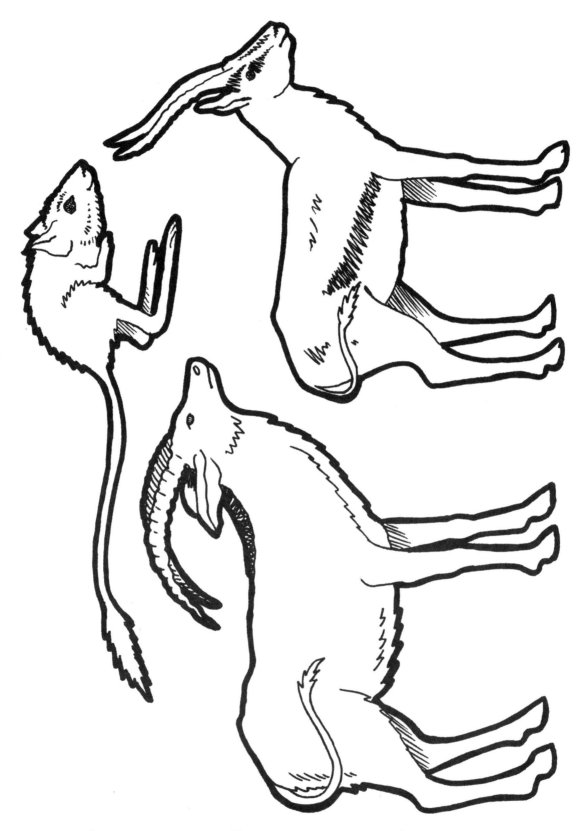

Figure 6.1 **Jerboa**   Figure 6.2 **Gazelle**   Figure 6.3 **Roan Antelope**

Figure 6.4 **Lion**   Figure 6.5 **Well**

Sources for Flannel Board Presentations

Create a West African animal version of *Brown Bear, Brown Bear, What Do You See?* by Bill Martin. Using nine animals from the country of Ghana, substitute the Ghanaian wildlife for the animals in the original book. Examples of animals native to Ghana are baboon, bush pig, buffalo, antelope, lion, leopard, hippo, gazelle, and python.

Sierra, Judy and Robert Kaminski. "Anansi and the Rock." In *Multicultural Folktales: Stories to Tell Young Children*. Phoenix, AZ: Oryx Press, 1991. (page 46)
Anansi becomes greedy after not having anything to eat. He finds a magical stone that makes millet into flour and decides to take it home for himself. This simple-to-tell story includes flannel board patterns to make.

Sources for Oral Stories

Hamilton, Martha and Mitch Weiss. "The Man Who Didn't Know What Minu Meant." In *Noodlehead Stories: World Tales Kids Can Read & Tell*. Little Rock, AR: August House Publishers, 2006. (page 66)
This easy-to-tell story is about a foolish man who thinks he knows everything and makes an assumption about understanding a different language.

Hull, Robert. *Stories from West Africa*. Illustrated by Tim Clarey. Austin, TX: Raintree Steck-Vaughn Publishers, 2000.
This collection of stories includes four tales from the Ghana region of West Africa: "Anansi and Hate-to-be-Contradicted," "The Monster Sasabonsam versus the Wonder Child," "The First City of Wagudu," and "The Man Who Learned the Language of Animals."

Morris, Neil. "Anansi and the Story Box." In *African Myths*. New York: Windmill Books, 2009. (pages 18–21)
Anansi must capture four different creatures to trade the sky god for his collection of stories.

Washington, Donna L. "Anansi's Fishing Expedition." In *A Pride of African Tales*. Illustrated by James Ransome. New York: Harper Collins Publishers, 2004. (pages 1–11)
This fun tale is about how Anansi tries to trick Onini into being his fishing partner and doing all of the work. Yet Onini ends up tricking Anansi into doing everything and Onini getting the fish.

Fingerplays, Songs, Action Rhymes, and Games

"Beat the Drum"

(sung to "Row, Row, Row Your Boat") by Dee Ann Corn

Beat, beat, beat the drum,
Rum, Pum, Pum, Pum, Pum.
Listen to the sounds it makes,
Watch us have some fun.
Play, play, play the drum,
Rum, Pum, Pum, Pum, Pum.
Hear it talk and tell a tale,
Listen everyone.

"The Eensy Weensy Anansi" Action Rhyme

Sung to "The Eensy Weensy Spider"; substitute the word *spider* with the word *Anansi* (a-NAHN-see).

(Traditional Rhyme) Eensy Weensy Anansi

The eensy weensy Anansi went up the waterspout *(move one hand up
opposite arm like a spider)*
Down came the rain *(raise hands and drop them while wiggling fingers)*
And washed Anansi out *(move hands from center outwards)*
Out came the sun *(make a circle with hands above head)*
And dried up all the rain,
And Eensy Weensy Anansi *(move hand up arm again)*
Went up the spout again.

Che Che Koolay Singing Game

Che Che Koolay is a traditional singing game that children play in Ghana. The players stand in a circle with one person in the middle who is the leader (or "It"). The leader places his or her hands on his or her head and sings "Che Che Koolay" (a nonsense phrase). The players in the circle follow the leader and repeat the line. The leader sings the next line with hands on shoulders, and the players in the circle follow and repeat the phrase. The game continues with hands on hips, hands on knees, and hands on ankles for the last phrase. When the song ends, the leader falls down and the players follow. Then, suddenly, the leader stands up and tags one of the other players before they can stand up (the players cannot stand up before the leader). The person who is tagged becomes the leader. Note: It might be more appropriate for a story time to have children stand in place and follow the leader without forming a circle and playing tag.

Sources for Fingerplays, Songs, Action Rhymes, and Games

Beall, Pamela Conn, and Susan Nipp, with Nancy Spence Klein. "Tue, Tue." In *Wee Sing around the World*. Los Angeles, CA: Price Stern Sloan, 2006. Book with compact disc.
"Tue Tue" is a circle game. Compact disc includes music and directions for playing the game.

"Little One Mine." In *Babies Presents International Lullabies*. [s.l.]: Lakeshore Records, 2010. Compact disc.
A beautiful instrumental of *"Little One Mine,"* a traditional song from Ghana.

Raffi. "Anansi." In *Animal Songs*. Burlington, MA: Rounder Music, 2008. Compact disc.
A fun song about Anansi, who is half spider and half human.

Raffi, Aaron Nigel Smith, Maria Medina-Serafin, Buckwheat Dural, Taj Mahal, Karan Casey, Bill Miller, et al. "Che Che Kule." In *World Travels: World Music for Kids*. Redway, CA: Musical Kidz, 2010. Compact disc.
A fun traditional call-and-response song from Ghana.

Media Choices

Show a DVD or a downloadable movie as a transition between storytelling activities and crafts.

Families of Ghana. Cincinnati, OH: Master Communications, Inc., Library Video Company, 2009. DVD, 30 min.
    Introduces viewers to two children from both an urban and a rural setting in Ghana. This DVD brings out the similarities of children all around the world.

Kimmel, Eric A., Janet Stevens, and Jerry Terheyden. *The Anansi Collection.* New York: Live Oak Media, 2003. DVD, 47 min.
    "Anansi and the Magic Stick," "Anansi and the Talking Melon," "Anansi Goes Fishing," and "Anansi and the Moss-Covered Rock" are the four tales that are included on this delightful DVD. Each tale is read by Jerry Terheyden word for word from the original book text.

Mitchell, Trish, Sissy Yates, Andrew Schlessinger, and Phylicia Rashad. *American Cultures for Children: African-American Heritage.* Wynnewood, PA: Schlessinger Media, 2006. DVD, 25 min.
    An entertaining DVD that introduces the many sights and sounds of Africa, including Ghana. Kente cloth, an Adinkra cloth craft, and an Anansi the Spider story are presented.

Crafts and Other Activities

Choose a craft suited for the age level of the group and the time allotted for the story time.

Atumpan (Talking Drum)

Atumpan drumming is one of the oldest traditions in Ghana. Atumpan drums are used in celebrations, ceremonies, and storytelling as well as for sending messages. It is said that a good drummer can make the drums "talk" by imitating the pitch patterns of the language.

In this craft project, children create their own talking drums. Children can enjoy playing their drums while reading *Grandma Comes to Stay* by Ifeoma Onyefulu. An example of a talking drum can be found in *Ghana* by Lyn Larson (Minneapolis: Lerner Publications, 2011), page 41.

Supplies

Coffee cans, oatmeal containers, or baby formula cans with plastic lids

Construction paper

Scissors

Crayons or colored markers

Pencils

Clear tape

Cotton balls

Precut the construction paper to fit around the cans or containers that children will be using. Have children decorate the construction paper with crayons or markers. Tape the construction paper around the cans or containers. (If the cans or containers do not have plastic lids, use masking tape to make the membrane across the top of the can or container.) Have children tape a cotton ball to a pencil to make the drumstick.

Royal Ashanti Crown and Ring

The Asante, or Ashanti, people value gold above all other metals. Gold has been mined in the Ghana area since the 1300s. Gold jewelry is still worn widely throughout Ghana. At one time, however, gold jewelry was only worn by royalty.

Have children make an Ashanti crown and ring like those worn by Ashanti royalty. An example of gold worn in Ghana by an Asante woman can be found in *Ghana* by Lyn Larson (Minneapolis: Lerner Publications, 2011), page 12.

Supplies

Posterboard	White glue
Pasta—various	Scissors
shapes and sizes	Stapler or clear tape
Gold spray paint	

Figure 6.6   **Crown and Ring Example**

See Figure 6.6 for a sample illustration of the crown and ring. Prepaint the pasta with gold spray paint. Using "Crown, Ring Band and Ring Top" patterns (Figures 6.7 through 6.9), create an Ashanti gold crown and a gold ring. Using posterboard, trace and cut out the patterns. Have children decorate the crown and the ring top by gluing the gold-colored pasta to the posterboard. Staple or tape the ring band around the child's finger, and glue the ring top, decorated with pasta, to the ring band. Staple or tape together the back of the crown so it will fit tightly around the child's head.

Note: For older children, it may be necessary to add a 2-inch-wide band to the crown to accommodate a larger head.

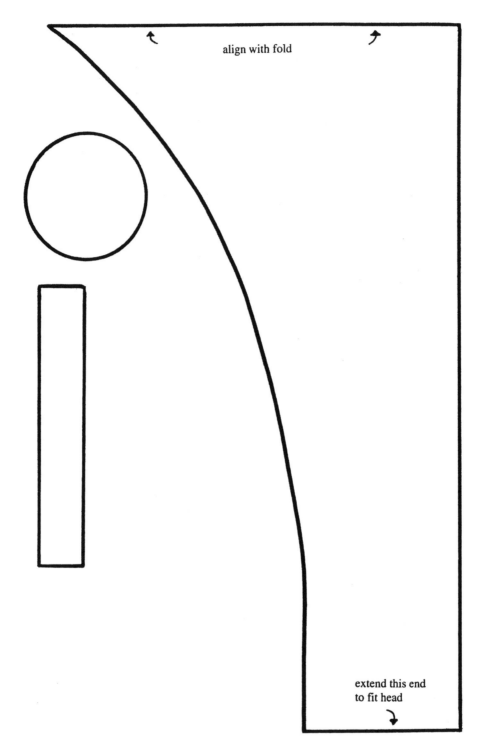

align with fold

extend this end
to fit head

Figure 6.7 **Crown**   Figure 6.8 **Ring Band**   Figure 6.9 **Ring Top**

Sources for Craft Ideas and Activities

Evans, Linda, Karen Backus, and Mary Thompson. *Art Projects from around the World, Grades 1–3: Step-by-Step Directions for 20 Beautiful Art Projects That Support Learning about Geography, Culture, and Other Social Studies Topics*. New York: Teaching Resources, 2006. (pages 7–9)
Weave a paper pattern similar to the colorful kente cloth made by the Ashanti people of Ghana.

Garner, Lynne. *African Crafts: Fun Things to Make and Do from West Africa*. Chicago: Chicago Review Press, 2008. (48 pages)
This book mainly focuses on Ghana with step-by-step instructions for different crafts. It includes a brief history and background of the culture of both West Africa and Ghana.

Gould, Roberta. *Kids' Multicultural Craft Book: 35 Crafts from around the World*. Illustrated by Sarah Rakitin. Charlotte, VT: Williamson Publishing, 2004. (pages 34–37)
Create a talking drum from Ghana using latex gloves and clay flowerpots.

Michaels, Alexandra. *The Kids' Multicultural Art Book: Art & Craft Experiences from around the World*. Nashville, TN: Williamsonbooks, 2007. (157 pages)
Several crafts from Africa are shown, including "Akua-ba Doll," "Paper Kufi," and "Kente Paper Weaving."

Mooney, Carla. *Amazing Africa Projects You Can Build Yourself*. Illustrated by Megan Stearns. White River Junction, VT: Nomad Press, 2010. (pages 37–38, 78–79)
Create an adinkra stamping similar to those by the Asante artists using potatoes and stamp pads, and make a mancala game known as Oware out of egg cartons and dried beans.

Chapter 7

Let's Visit

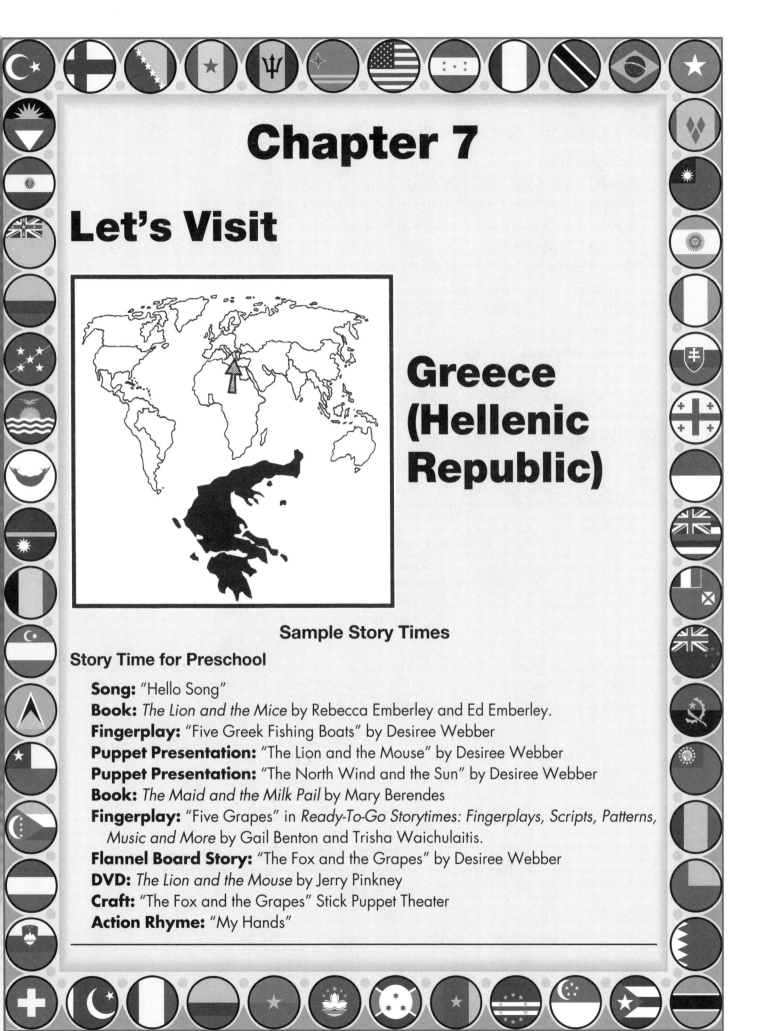

Greece (Hellenic Republic)

Sample Story Times

Story Time for Preschool

Song: "Hello Song"
Book: *The Lion and the Mice* by Rebecca Emberley and Ed Emberley.
Fingerplay: "Five Greek Fishing Boats" by Desiree Webber
Puppet Presentation: "The Lion and the Mouse" by Desiree Webber
Puppet Presentation: "The North Wind and the Sun" by Desiree Webber
Book: *The Maid and the Milk Pail* by Mary Berendes
Fingerplay: "Five Grapes" in *Ready-To-Go Storytimes: Fingerplays, Scripts, Patterns, Music and More* by Gail Benton and Trisha Waichulaitis.
Flannel Board Story: "The Fox and the Grapes" by Desiree Webber
DVD: *The Lion and the Mouse* by Jerry Pinkney
Craft: "The Fox and the Grapes" Stick Puppet Theater
Action Rhyme: "My Hands"

Story Time for Kindergarten Through Third Grade

Song: "Hello Song"
Book: *Lousy Rotten Stinkin' Grapes* by Margie Palintini
Fingerplay: "Five Greek Fishing Boats" by Desiree Webber
Book: *The Orphan: A Cinderella Story from Greece* by Anthony Manna
Puppet Presentation: "The North Wind and the Sun" by Desiree Webber
Oral Story: "The Crow and the Pitcher"
Dance: "Greek Zorba Dance" in *Folk Dance Fun* by Georgiana Stewart
DVD: *The Lion and the Mouse* by Jerry Pinkney
Craft: Fish Mosaic
Action Rhyme: "My Hands"

Begin the story time with the "Hello Song." Then sing the song again, substituting the word *hello* with the Greek greeting pronounced "yassas," which means both "hello" and "good-bye." (See p. xxix for "Hello Song" music.)

Hello Song

Hello ev'rybody,
And how are you? How are you?
Hello ev'rybody,
And how are you today?
Yassas ev'rybody,
And how are you? How are you?
Yassas ev'rybody,
And how are you today?

End the story time with the "My Hands" action rhyme, substituting the words *thank you* with the Greek word pronounced "ef-har-eesto," and *goodbye* with "yassas". Have children stand up and follow the actions in the rhyme.

My Hands

My hands say ef-har-eesto. *(hold up hands)*
With a clap, clay, clap. *(clap hands)*
My feet say ef-har-eesto. *(point to feet)*
With a tap, tap, tap. *(stamp or tap feet)*
Clap! Clap! Clap! *(clap hands)*
Tap! Tap! Tap! *(stamp or tap feet)*
Turn myself around and bow. *(turn and bow)*
Yassas. *(wave goodbye)*

Books to Read Aloud

Some of the books selected for reading aloud, such as *Ant and Grasshopper* by Luli Gray, are based on fables attributed to a freed Greek slave named Aesop. Aesop is said to have lived about 620 to 560 B.C. Not a lot of information is known about him, but references about him appear in ancient writings. Some believe he may have come originally from Ethiopia. Aesop is considered the author of many popular fables that were passed along orally for several hundred years before being written down. A fable is a story that has a stated moral or lesson at the end. Children are delighted by the animal characters and simple storylines found in Aesop's tales.

Aesop's Fables: A Pop-up Book of Classic Tales. Illustrated by Chris Beatrice and Bruce Whatley. Paper engineering by Kees Moerbeek. New York: Little Simon, 2011. (14 pages)
  The pop-up features of the stories will delight young readers. Some of the smaller, side-panel pop-ups may be difficult to manage during story time, so the reader should be familiar with the text in order to effectively show the pop-ups without having to read each word.

Berendes, Mary. *The Maid and the Milk Pail.* Illustrated by Nancy Harrison. Mankato, MN: Peterson Publishing Company, 2011. (24 pages)
  While carrying a pail of milk on her head, a milkmaid daydreams of all the money she is going to make. When she dreams that she will toss her head at jealous onlookers, her pail of milk falls to the ground.

Emberley, Rebecca and Ed Emberley. *The Lion and the Mice.* New York: Holiday House, 2011. (28 pages)
  This is a brightly illustrated version of Aesop's fable featuring mice who come to the aid of a captured lion.

Forest, Heather. *The Contest between the Sun and the Wind.* Illustrated by Susan Gaber. Atlanta, GA: August House Publishers, 2008. (32 pages)
  The sun challenges the wind to a contest of strength. Whoever can force a man to remove his coat is the strongest. Based on a fable attributed to Aesop, the lesson is that gentleness wins over force.

Gray, Luli. *Ant and Grasshopper.* Illustrated by Giuliano Ferri. New York: Margaret K. McElderry Books, 2011. (32 pages)
  Ant works hard collecting food and counting his stored supplies every day. Meanwhile Grasshopper sings and plays his fiddle, not worrying about tomorrow. When winter arrives, Grasshopper knocks on the door of Ant's home.

Lowry, Amy. *Fox Tales: Four Fables from Aesop.* New York: Holiday House, 2012. (32 pages)
  This collection presents four separate stories, including the well-known "Fox and the Grapes" fable. The other stories may not be as familiar, but readers will enjoy their message such as "never trust a flatterer" in "The Crow and the Fox." A great read-aloud and beautifully illustrated.

Manna, Anthony and Christodoula Mitakidou. *The Orphan: A Cinderella Story from Greece.* Illustrated by Giselle Potter. New York: Schwartz & Wade, 2011. (40 pages)
  An orphan is left with her stepmother, who treats her cruelly. With gifts from the sun, moon, and sea, the young woman attracts the prince with her beauty.

Naidoo, Beverly. *Aesop's Fables.* Illustrated by Piet Grobler. London: Francis Lincoln Children's Books, 2011. (49 pages)
  A collection of Aesop-inspired tales written by Beverly Naidoo, who grew up in South Africa. In the introduction, Naidoo proposes that Aesop may have been captured somewhere in

North Africa and taken to Greece to become a slave. She says that many of the animals in Aesop's fables were African animals and that Aesop's name is similar to the "old Greek word for black African: 'Ethiop.' " Storyteller can read one or two selections from this unique collection during story time.

Oppenheim, Shulamith Levey. *Yanni Rubbish*. Illustrated by Doug Chayka. Honesdale, PA: Boyds Mills Press, 1999. (32 pages)
Yanni helps with the family business of collecting rubbish in his Greek village. His friends tease him, which hurts his feelings. He comes up with an idea to end the teasing after seeing a photo of his parents on their wedding day.

Palintini, Margie. *Lousy Rotten Stinkin' Grapes*. Illustrated by Barry Moser. New York: Simon & Schuster Books for Young Readers, 2009. (32 pages)
Fox thinks of an elaborate plan to pick some grapes, but his efforts fail. Unable to listen to the suggestions of others, he leaves in a huff, stating that the grapes are lousy, rotten. and stinky anyway.

Pinkney, Jerry. *The Lion and the Mouse*. Boston: Little, Brown and Company, 2009. (40 pages)
This is a wordless version of the well-known Aesop's fable. The only text is a few animal sounds, which add to the atmosphere of the story. The setting for the book is the African Serengeti of Tanzania and Kenya. This wordless book is great for librarians and teachers to share using either audience participation or quietly with music in the background.

Storytelling

"The Lion and the Mouse" and "The North Wind and the Sun" Puppet Presentations

"The Lion and the Mouse" and "The North Wind and the Sun" are retellings of Aesop's fables using stick puppets. Copy the puppet patterns on posterboard, cut them out, and hot glue paint sticks or craft sticks to the backs of the puppets (paint sticks, available at paint supply stores, are sturdier than craft sticks). To make the puppets colorful and attractive, use colored posterboard or use crayons to color the puppets. Storyteller may hold the puppets or have children from the group hold them.

Note: If performing the story for a large group of children, enlarge the patterns 100 percent to make the figures easier to see. Lamination (after coloring the puppets) can add brightness, and it makes the puppets more durable.

"The Lion and the Mouse"

Two puppets and one prop are needed for this puppet play: the mouse, the lion, and a 12- by 12-inch net made by weaving and hot gluing macramé string. Use Figures 7.1 and 7.2 to make the lion and mouse puppets. Ask three children to help tell the story. Have one child hold the lion puppet, another child the mouse puppet, and a third child the net. At the appropriate time during the narration, have the child with the net throw it over the lion. Have the child with the mouse make the puppet nibble at the net, freeing the lion.

Figure 7.1 **Lion**   Figure 7.2 **Mouse**

"The Lion and the Mouse" retold by Desiree Webber

Now, as you know, the lion is the king of beasts—mighty and fearsome. One day, the lion was resting in the shade of a tree after walking through his domain. Suddenly, a little mouse scurried across the lion's paw. The lion trapped the mouse, picked him up by his tail, and brought the mouse close to his face.

"Please," begged the mouse. "I did not see you. Let me go and someday I will do a favor for you."

The lion did not think the little mouse could ever do anything for him, but he was in a generous mood. So he let the mouse go.

Several days later, the lion was walking through the jungle when a net from a hunter's trap fell upon him without warning. The lion roared out in anger and fear. Deep in the jungle, the little mouse heard the lion's roar and ran quickly to help. When he saw the ropes that entangled the lion, the little mouse began to chew through the net, and soon the king of beasts was free.

"See," said the mouse. "Even a little one can help a great one."

"The North Wind and the Sun"

Use Figures 7.3 and 7.4 to make wind and sun puppets for this puppet play. Ask three children to help tell the story. Have one child hold the North Wind puppet, another child the Sun puppet, and have a third child, wearing a piece of cloth as a cloak, play the role of the traveler.

"The North Wind and the Sun" retold by Desiree Webber

One day, the North Wind and the Sun were arguing as to which one was stronger. Looking down from the sky, the North Wind and the Sun saw a traveler on horseback who was wearing a cloak upon his shoulders. The Sun said, "Whoever can make the traveler remove his cloak first will be named the strongest."

The North Wind tried first. Gathering up his forces, he blew down with all his strength upon the man. Cold air swirled around the man, tugging furiously at his cloak, but the man just gathered his cloak closer around his body. The harder the North Wind blew, the tighter the man clutched his cloak.

"My turn," said the Sun, coming out from behind the clouds. He began to shine warm, gentle rays upon the earth. The man opened his cloak and continued riding. The Sun shone warmer and warmer until, finally, the man tossed off his cloak, glad to be free of it.

Moral: Persuasion is better than force.

"The Fox and the Grapes" Flannel Board Story

Tell the Aesop's fable "The Fox and the Grapes" using a flannel board. This fable may be found in *Fox Tales: Four Fables from Aesop* by Amy Lowry (see "Books to Read Aloud") or in *Aesop's Fables* retold by Alice Shirley (see "Sources for Oral Stories"). Use Figures 7.8 and 7.9 from "The Fox and the Grapes" stick puppet theater craft to tell this story. Use brown felt to make the grape arbor. (Refer to "Stick Puppet Theater Example," Figure 7.7, for a sample illustration.) Use violet and green felt to make the grapes and leaves. Draw details of the grapes and leaves with a black felt-tip marker. Using red construction paper, draw and cut out a two-sided fox and attach a piece of florist wire in between. (Refer to Figure 7.8.) While telling the story, manipulate the wire to make the fox jump at the grapes.

Figure 7.3 **North Wind**

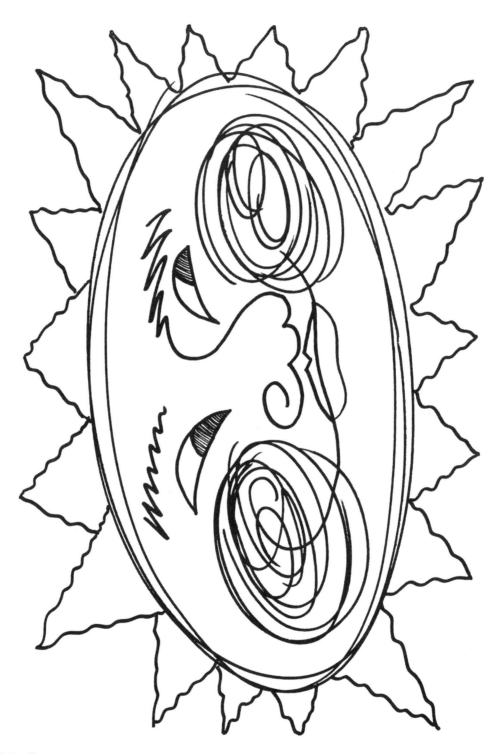

Figure 7.4 **Sun**

Sources for Flannel Board Presentation

Sierra, Judy. "The Miller, the Boy and the Donkey." In *The Flannel Board Storytelling Book*, 2nd ed. New York: H.W. Wilson, 1997. (pages 229–233)
> This humorous tale is about a miller and his son who lose their donkey after following the advice of others. Patterns and instructions are included.

"The Crow and the Pitcher" Oral Story

Use a small, clear pitcher (or jar) and marbles as props to tell this classic fable from Aesop. Fill the pitcher halfway full with water. While telling the story, drop the marbles into the pitcher one by one, letting children watch as the water rises to the top.

"The Crow and the Pitcher" retold by Desiree Webber

A thirsty crow found a pitcher halfway full with water. It tried and tried to drink but was unable to reach the water with its beak. The crow stopped to think of a plan to save itself. At last, an idea struck: Taking pebbles lying nearby, the crow dropped one pebble *(begin dropping marbles into the pitcher)* after another into the pitcher until, finally, the water reached the top, where the crow was able to drink.
> Moral: Little by little a goal is reached.

Sources for Oral Stories

Cech, John. *Aesop's Fables*. Illustrated by Jarrie Martin. New York: Sterling Publishing Company, 2009. (40 pages)
> Cech's collection includes favorite and no-so-familiar Aesop's fables. Most tales are only a paragraph or two in length and can be easily memorized to tell aloud.

Shirley, Alice. *Aesop's Fables*. London: Pavilion Children's Books, 2009. (157 pages)
> This large collection of Aesop's tales is beautifully illustrated. Most of the stories are very short and can be memorized to tell orally during the story time session.

Young, Cy. *Aesop's Fables*. Phoenix, AZ: Tradebit, n.d. Audio download at http://www.tradebit .com/filedetail.php/100330025-aesop-s-fables.
> Narrator Cy Young tells and sings a selection of Aesop's fables. The fables are intermixed among the story of Aesop, a table maker who interacts with different animals that come into his shop.

Fingerplays, Songs, Action Rhymes, and Games

"Five Greek Fishing Boats" Fingerplay

For this fingerplay, the storyteller begins with five fishing boat puppets, one on each finger. Bend down a finger each time a boat exits the poem. Children hold up five fingers and follow along. To make finger puppets, photocopy Figures 7.5 and 7.6 on white construction paper. Use markers to color the boats. Laminate and cut out the boats and finger attachments. Tape together the three flaps of each finger attachment. This fits over the tip of each finger like a thimble. Tape a boat to each finger attachment.

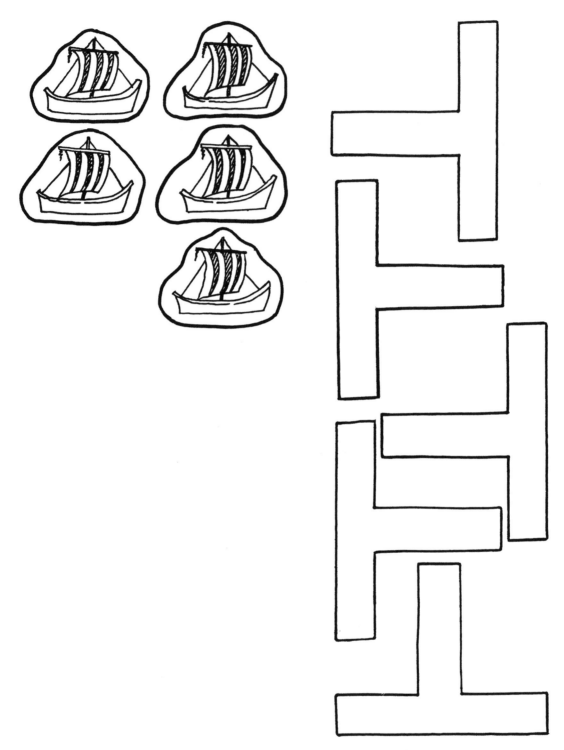

Figure 7.5 **Boat Finger Puppets**   Figure 7.6 **Finger Puppet Attachments**

Five Greek Fishing Boats by Desiree Webber

Five Greek fishing boats looking to moor;
One found a harbor, and then there were four.
Four Greek fishing boats trolling the sea;
One caught its limit, and then there were three.
Three Greek fishing boats sailing the blue;
One saw Poseidon, and then there were two.
Two Greek fishing boats up before dawn;
One sailed for Crete, and then there was one.
One Greek fishing boat under the sun;
It charted for home, and then there were none.

Sources for Fingerplays, Songs, Action Rhymes, and Games

Benton, Gail and Trisha Waichulaitis. " 'Cause They're Grapes!" In *Ready-To-Go Storytimes: Fingerplays, Scripts, Patterns, Music and More*. New York: Neal-Schuman Publishers, 2003. (page 3)
This action rhyme is about crushing, squeezing, tasting, and eating grapes. A great extending activity for the "The Fox and the Grapes" flannel board story. *Ready-To-Go Storytimes* comes with accompanying music for the action rhyme on the enclosed compact disc.

Benton, Gail and Trisha Waichulaitis. "Five Grapes." In *Ready-To-Go Storytimes: Fingerplays, Scripts, Patterns, Music and More*. New York: Neal-Schuman Publishers, 2003. (page 4)
Children will enjoy this simple five-count fingerplay about grapes.

Glykeria. "Tik Tik Tak" by Glykeria. In *Putumayo Kids Presents World Playground*. New York: Putumayo World Music, 1998. Compact disc.
"Tik Tik Tak" is sung in Greek. One of the instruments in the song is a bouzouki, which is a popular stringed instrument like a guitar. This song is a good choice to play in the background while children work on crafts or before story time begins. The website has teacher resources at http://www.putumayokids.com.

Stewart, Georgiana. "Children's Song." In *Multicultural Rhythm Stick Fun*. Long Branch, NJ: Kimbo Educational, 1992. Compact disc.
Children use rhythm sticks (or clap their hands) to this song about Greece.

Stewart, Georgiana. "Greek Zorba Dance." In *Folk Dance Fun*. Long Branch, NJ: Kimbo Educational, 1984. Compact disc.
The dance is 2 minutes in length and is a great activity for children to stand up and move their bodies. The dance can be done in a line or a circle. Children follow the directions and make dance movements such as snapping their fingers and tapping their feet.

Stewart, Georgiana. "A Visit to My Friend." In *Children of the World: Multicultural Rhythmic Activities*. Long Branch, NJ: Kimbo Educational, 1991. Compact disc.
Children move in a circle as they clap, wave, hop, and more to music from Mexico, Russia, and Greece.

Media Choices

Show a DVD or downloadable movie as a transition between storytelling activities and crafts.

Countries of the World: Greece. Wynnewood, PA: Schlessinger Media, 2007. DVD, 13 min. Available digitally on Safari Montage.
    Nine-year-old Viviane shares her life in the capitol city of Athens. The audience meets her family and enjoys their outings to the National Gardens, an outdoor market, and the changing of the Presidential Guard in front of the Parliament building, plus the family's preparation for the Easter celebration. Information about ancient and modern Greece is shared in an enjoyable video presentation. Teacher guides are also available at http://www.libraryvideo.com.

Pinkney, Jerry. *The Lion and the Mouse.* Norwalk, CT: Weston Woods, 2010. DVD, 12 min.
    Illustrator Jerry Pinkney places the setting for this well-known tale in the African Serengeti. This is a wordless picture book, so the film's production team uses animal sounds, music, and singing, in conjunction with the illustrations, to tell the story. The publisher has an online study guide for educators.

Crafts and Other Activities

Choose a craft suited for the age level of the group and the time allotted for the story time.

"The Fox and the Grapes" Stick Puppet Theater

The Greeks are well known for their theater. During the fourth century B.C., the actors were always male and wore character masks that showed the emotions they were expressing.

In this craft project, children create a puppet theater for the Aesop's fable "The Fox and the Grapes."

Supplies

Light-yellow or light-blue posterboard   White glue
Brown construction paper   Scissors
Purple or dark-blue construction paper   Pencils
Colored markers or crayons

Introduce the fable "The Fox and the Grapes" before beginning this craft project. (See *Fox Tales: Four Fables from Aesop* by Amy Lowry [in the section "Books to Read Aloud"] or *Aesop's Fables* retold by Alice Shirley [in the section "Sources for Oral Stories"]). Each child needs an 8½- by 11-inch piece of light-yellow or light-blue posterboard, with a slit cut 1 inch from the bottom and 2 inches from each side (see "Stick Puppet Theater Example," Figure 7.7).

Use Figures 7.8 and 7.9 to make the fox puppet and the grapes for the arbor. The fox puppet is two-sided and should be precut or predrawn for younger children. Have older children trace and cut out their puppets using red construction paper. Glue a ½- by 6-inch strip of posterboard between the two fox pattern pieces, or a craft stick or straw can be substituted for the posterboard strip.

Make the grape arbor by gluing strips of brown construction paper onto the poster-board (see "Stick Puppet Theater Example," Figure 7.7). Cut an outline of hanging grapes from purple and the leaves from green construction paper (or photocopy the grape pattern on white paper and have children color them). Glue the grapes in the middle and upper corners of the arbor.

To perform the fable, insert the fox puppet through the slit from the back of the poster-board. Children make the fox jump up at the grapes as they tell the story.

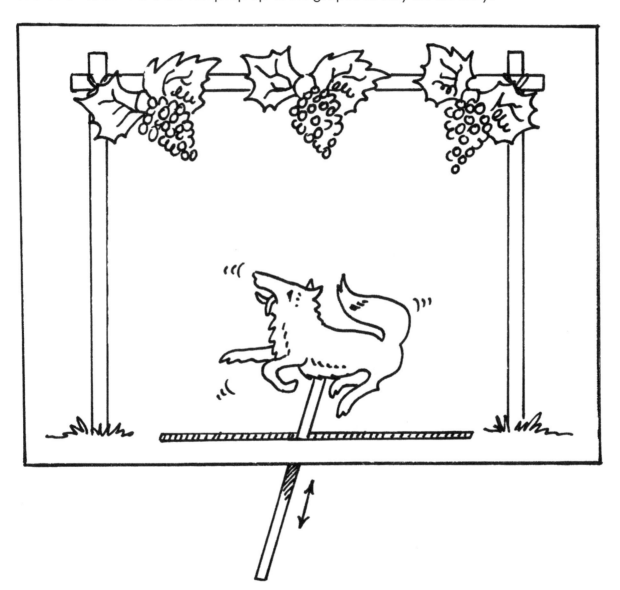

Figure 7.7   **Stick Puppet Theater Example**

Figure 7.8 **Foxes**   Figure 7.9 **Grapes**

Fish Mosaic

Archeologists have found mosaics in Greece that date back to the fourth century B.C. These early mosaics often had only two colors and were created using pebbles. For example, a typical background was created using black or blue pebbles, while the figure was created using white or light-brown pebbles. Later mosaics were created from cut glass, stones, or clay tiles. Some Greeks decorated the floors of their homes with mosaics.

In this craft project, children create mosaics using posterboard and construction paper. The fish design was chosen because of the importance of fishing as an industry in Greece. It is also a simple design for most children. However, depending upon the age and abilities of the group, other designs for mosaics might include mythological creatures, such as the Cyclops or Medusa, or a simple graphic arrangement using two or more colors.

Supplies

Brown posterboard
White or light-yellow construction paper
Blue construction paper

White glue
Paper cutter

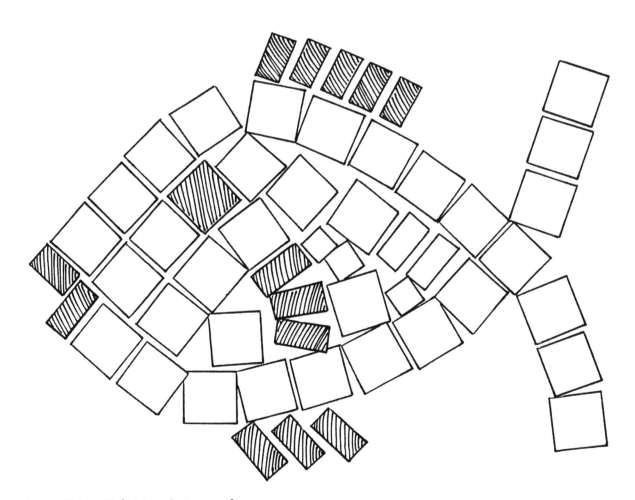

Figure 7.10   **Fish Mosaic Example**

See Figure 7.10 for an example of a fish mosaic. An adult should precut an 8½- by 11-inch piece of white or light-yellow posterboard for each child. This will serve as the background for the mosaic. Precut the white construction paper into 1-inch squares. Then cut some of the blue construction paper into 1-inch squares and some into ½- by 1-inch rectangles.

The children create the fish mosaic by gluing squares of paper to the posterboard in the shape of a fish. Use white squares for the body and blue squares for the eyes and fins.

Sources for Craft Ideas and Activities

Hawes, Alison. *Go Greek!* New York: Crabtree Publishing Company, 2011. (32 pages)
> Several crafts are featured along with information about ancient Greek life. Some of the simple crafts are a soldier's shield from card stock, a "protective eye" from a paper plate and poster paints, or knucklebone-game pieces from self-hardening clay.

Speechley, Greta. *Arts & Crafts for Myths and Tales*. New York: Gareth Stevens, 2010. (pages 10–11, 22–23, and 26–27)
> There are three crafts that are appropriate for extending activities for children in second to third grade: (1) a lyre from paper plates and yarn; (2) a Cyclops eye from egg crate and glue; and (3) a Trojan horse using small boxes, toilet tissue tubes, and felt or construction paper.

Van Vleet, Carmella. *Explore Ancient Greece!* Illustrated by Alex Kim. Chicago, IL: Nomad Press, 2008. (90 pages)
> Contains a variety of games, activities, recipes, and crafts. For example there is a game of tag plus a simple craft entitled "papyrus poetry roll."

Chapter 8

Let's Visit

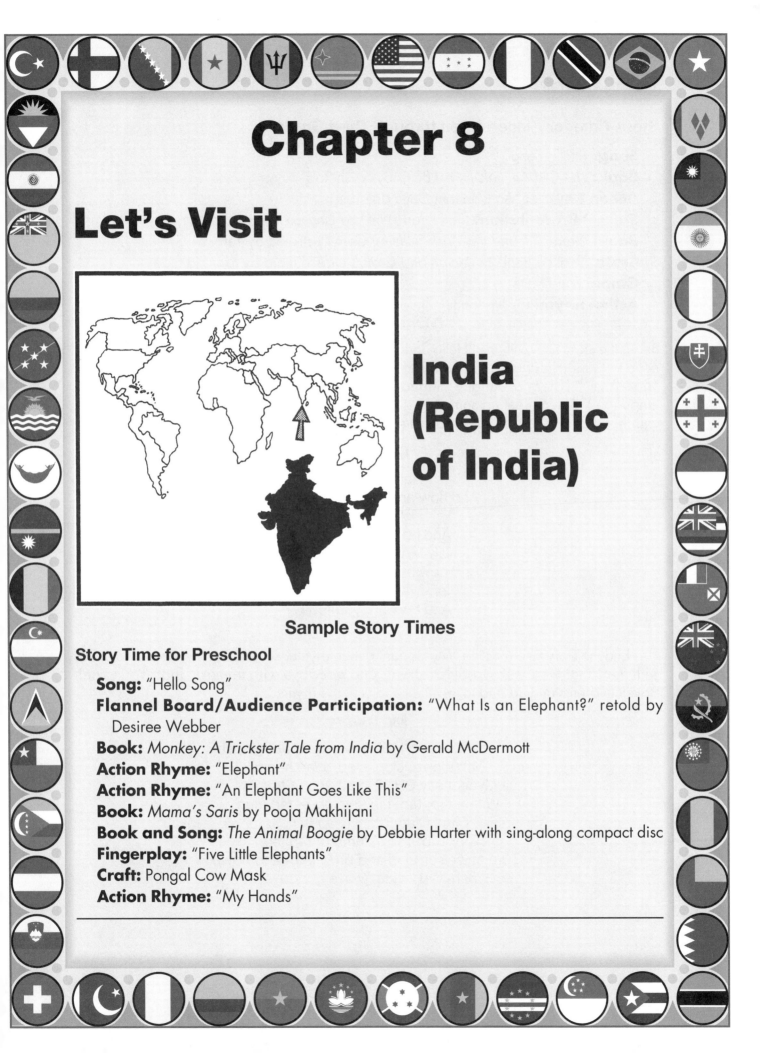

India (Republic of India)

Sample Story Times

Story Time for Preschool

Song: "Hello Song"

Flannel Board/Audience Participation: "What Is an Elephant?" retold by Desiree Webber

Book: *Monkey: A Trickster Tale from India* by Gerald McDermott

Action Rhyme: "Elephant"

Action Rhyme: "An Elephant Goes Like This"

Book: *Mama's Saris* by Pooja Makhijani

Book and Song: *The Animal Boogie* by Debbie Harter with sing-along compact disc

Fingerplay: "Five Little Elephants"

Craft: Pongal Cow Mask

Action Rhyme: "My Hands"

Story Time for Kindergarten through Third Grade

Song: "Hello Song"
Book: *The Old Animals Forest Band* by Sirish Rao
Action Rhyme: "An Elephant Goes Like This"
Puppet Presentation: "The Pearl Thief" by Desiree Webber
Book: *Great Gift and the Wish-Fulfilling Gem* illustrated by Terry McSweeney.
Craft: "Punkha (fan)" in *Recipe and Craft Guide to India* by Khadija Ejaz
Game: Pearl Race
Action Rhyme: "My Hands"

Begin the story time with the "Hello Song." Then sing the song again, substituting the word *hello* with the Hindi greeting *namaste* [nah-MAH-stee], which means both "hello" and "goodbye." (There are many languages in India, but Hindi is the country's official language.) When greeting someone, press your hands together, fingertips up, and bow your head as you say the word *namaste*. (See p. xxix for "Hello Song" music.)

Hello Song

Hello ev'rybody,
And how are you? How are you?
Hello ev'rybody,
And how are you today?
Nah-MAH-stee ev'rybody,
And how are you? How are you?
Nah-MAH-stee ev'rybody,
And how are you today?

End the story time with the "My Hands" action rhyme, substituting the words *thank you* with the Hindi word *súkriyā* [SHOE-crea], and *goodbye* with *namaste* [nah-MAH-stee]. Have children stand up and follow the actions in the rhyme.

My Hands

My hands say SHOE-crea. *(hold up hands)*
With a clap, clap, clap. *(clap hands)*
My feet say SHOE-crea. *(point to feet)*
With a tap, tap, tap. *(stamp or tap feet)*
Clap! Clap! Clap! *(clap hands)*
Tap! Tap! Tap! *(stamp or tap feet)*
Turn myself around and bow. *(turn and bow)*
nah-MAH-stee. *(wave goodbye)*

Books to Read Aloud

Brown, Marcia. *Once a Mouse . . . : A Fable Cut in Wood.* Lodi, NJ: Marco Book Company, 2009. (32 pages)
In this Caldecott Medal winner, a hermit saves the life of a mouse and magically changes the rodent into larger and larger animals until finally it becomes an arrogant tiger.

Great Gift and the Wish-Fulfilling Gem: A Story about the Power of Wishing Happiness to All Beings. Illustrated by Terry McSweeney. Cazadero, CA: Dharma Publishing, 2010. (34 pages)
A boy goes on a journey to find the "wish-fulfilling gem" in order to end poverty and hunger in his country.

Makhijani, Pooja. *Mama's Saris.* Illustrated by Elena Gomez. New York: Little, Brown and Company, 2007. (32 pages)
A young girl wants to be old enough to wear one of her mother's beautiful saris. As her mother unpacks saris, the girl asks her mother if she can wear one of them for her birthday celebration that day.

McDermott, Gerald. *Monkey: A Trickster Tale from India.* Boston: Harcourt Children's Books, 2011. (32 pages)
Crocodile tries various ways to make a meal out of Monkey, but Monkey is too smart for Crocodile.

Padma, T.V. *Growing Gold.* Illustrated by Tom Wrenn. Atlanta, GA: August House Story Cove, 2008. (32 pages)
A wise mother gets her lazy sons to help on the farm by telling them family gold is buried in the wheat field.

Rao, Sirish. *The Old Animals Forest Band.* Illustrated by Durga Bai. India: Tara Publishing, 2008. (42 pages)
This is a great read-aloud for all ages. It is a simple but well-written tale about a dog, cow, donkey, and rooster who are rejected by their masters for being too old. The foursome meet and go into the forest to live, where they find a hut inhabited by robbers. They scare off the thieves with their raucous "singing" and bring the village people running. The story is similar to the Brothers Grimm's "Bremen Town Musicians."

Sheth, Kahmira. *Monsoon Afternoon.* Illustrated by Yoshiko Jaeggi. Atlanta, GA: Peachtree Publishers, 2008. (32 pages)
A young boy finds that everyone in the household is too busy to go outside and play with him except his grandfather. Together they play and explore during the rains of the seasonal monsoon.

Sheth, Kahmira. *My Dadima Wears a Sari.* Illustrated by Yoshiko Jaeggi. Atlanta, GA: Peachtree Publishers, 2007. (32 pages)
Rupa and her sister Neha speak with Dadima (grandmother) about her favorite saris, which are passed down to the next generation. Instructions on how to wear a sari are found at the end of the book.

Wolf, Gita. *The Churki-Burki Book of Rhyme.* Illustrated by Durga Bai. India: Tara Books, 2010. (24 pages)
Two sisters, Churki and Burki, create rhymes as they go through the day collecting firewood along with a pumpkin, crab, fish, and corn for dinner.

Young, Ed. *Seven Blind Mice.* New York: Penguin Group USA, 2002. (40 pages)
   A retelling of the Indian fable "The Blind Men and the Elephant." The reader learns that it is important to seek knowledge about the "whole" and not just the "part" of something. The story also relates the days of the week and colors.

Zia, F. *Hot, Hot Roti for Dada-ji.* Illustrated by Ken Min. New York: Lee & Low Books, 2011. (32 pages)
   Aneel loves to hear his grandfather's stories about how strong he became after eating hot *roti* (flat, fried bread). Grandfather could once wrestle water buffaloes, cobras, and elephants. Aneel wants someone to cook Grandfather a stack of hot roti, but everyone is too busy. Aneel decides to cook the bread himself. A pronunciation guide is located on last page of book.

Storytelling

"What Is an Elephant?" Flannel Board Presentation

This is a retelling of a fable from India about four men (sometimes it is six men), blind from birth, who want to touch an elephant so that they can understand what type of animal it is. The ancient meaning of this story has religious significance. One age-old version ends with the moral that we are all blind in religious matters because we see the parts but not the whole.

See Figures 8.1 through 8.6 for patterns. Trace the patterns on felt, or photocopy and color them. If photocopying, glue small pieces of felt to the backs of the paper figures so they will hold to the flannel board. Place the figures on the flannel board as they are introduced in the story.

This is an audience-participation story. Encourage children to mimic actions, such as pounding one fist on the palms of their hands or moving their hands back and forth like a fan.

"What Is an Elephant?" retold by Desiree Webber

There were once four blind men who lived in a small village in India. The four were good friends and often discussed things under the shade of a large tree. *(place the four blind men on the flannel board)*

One day, an elephant driver, called a "mahout," came to the village riding an elephant. *(place the elephant on the flannel board and the elephant driver on the elephant)* Although there were many elephants in India, the four men had never seen one. They asked the elephant driver if they could examine the beast. *(remove the elephant driver from the flannel board)* The driver agreed, and the four blind men approached the elephant, exploring it with their hands.

The first man felt the foot of the elephant and said, "The elephant is like a mortar for pounding rice." *(pound fist on palm of hand)*

The second man felt the tail of the elephant and said, "No, my friend, the elephant is like a broom." *(make sweeping motions)*

"You are both wrong," said the third man, feeling the ear of the elephant. "The animal is like a broad, flat leaf." *(fan one hand back and forth)*

"I do not know what you can be thinking," said the fourth, feeling the sides of the elephant. "This magnificent beast is like a mountain—huge and endless." *(bring hands together and make a point with fingers)*

The four friends began to argue among themselves, each thinking his opinion was right, until they were interrupted by the elephant driver. *(place elephant driver on elephant)*

"You are each right, but also, each of you is wrong! When one of you says the elephant is like a mortar, you are speaking of the elephant's foot. When another of you says the elephant is like a broom, you are speaking of the elephant's tail. And when another describes the elephant as being like a broad, flat leaf, you are speaking of the elephant's ear. When the last of you describes the elephant as being like a mountain, huge and endless, you are speaking of its sides."

The four men understood the wisdom of the elephant driver's words. They had been arguing about the whole when they each knew only a portion.

Sources for Flannel Board Presentations

MacMillan, Kathy and Christine Kirker. "Lion Hide-and-Seek Flannelboard." In *Storytime Magic: 400 Fingerplays, Flannelboards, and Other Activities*. Chicago, IL: American Library Association, 2009. (page 26)
Substitute the lion with an animal indigenous to India, such as an elephant or tiger. The mother animal looks for her young behind a tree, rock, and so forth.

Sierra, Judy. "The Cat and the Parrot." In *The Flannel Board Storytelling Book*, 2nd ed. Bronx, NY: H.W. Wilson Company, 1997. (pages 198–204)
A folktale from India in which a cat goes to the parrot's house for dinner but ends up eating the parrot, the spicy cakes, a woman, a man, a donkey, an elephant, and finally two crabs. Book includes patterns. Sierra also includes instructions on how to present the tale as a humorous audience-participation story.

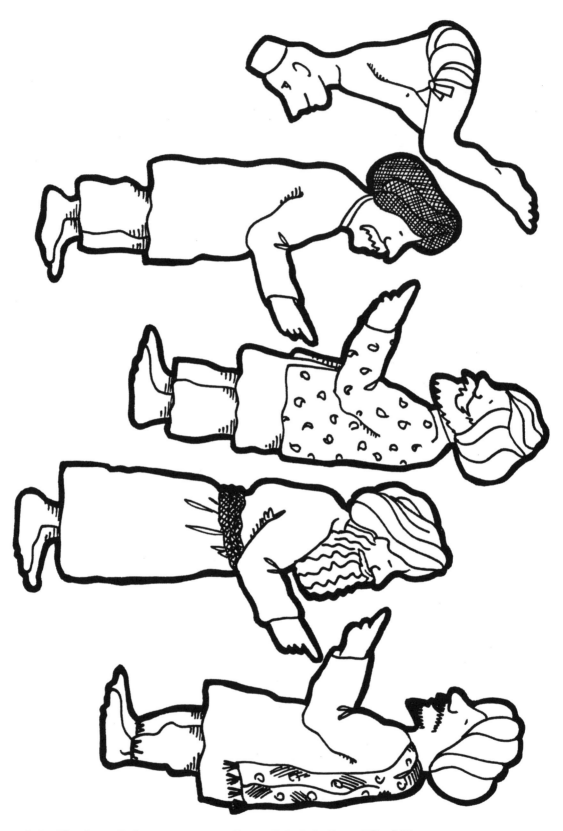

Figure 8.1 **Elephant Driver**   Figure 8.2–8.5 **Four Blind Men**

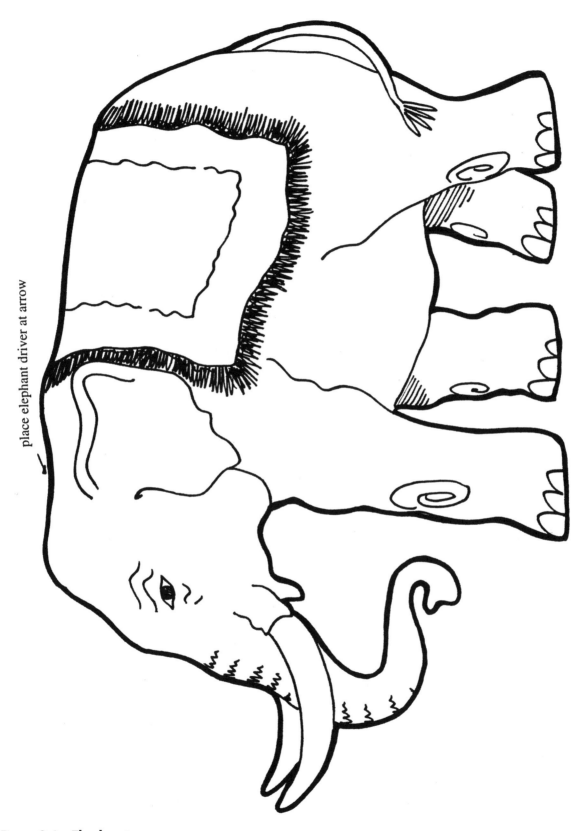

place elephant driver at arrow

Figure 8.6 **Elephant**

125

Sierra, Judy. "The Monkey and the Crocodile." In *The Flannel Board Storytelling Book*, 2nd ed. Bronx, NY: H.W. Wilson Company, 1997. (pages 234–237)
In this folktale from India, a monkey outwits the crocodile who wants to make a meal of him. Book includes patterns.

"The Pearl Thief" Puppet Presentation

Supplies

Three bags, cloth or paper, approximately 6 inches wide and 9 inches long (if cloth, sew in a drawstring) Hot glue or needle and thread Package of white pony beads (available at physical or online craft stores) (need 20 beads to tell the story)

One strand of white plastic cord, 8 inches in length (thin enough to slide pony beads on cord) One strand of pink (or some other color) plastic cord, 8 inches in length One small bowl

Figure 8.7 **Pearl Bag Example**

This puppet presentation is performed using three 6- by 9-inch cloth bags with drawstrings— see Figure 8.7. Sew or hot glue the picture of each man (Figures 8.8 through 8.10) to each of the three bags. (Lunch-size paper sacks, with the pictures of the three men glued to the front, can be substituted for the cloth bags.) Use a thin piece of cord or fold the bag closed as needed within the story.

Two of the men in this story are neighbors. One of the men is called the "kind man"; the second is called the "greedy neighbor," who later becomes known as the "pearl thief"; the third man is called the "judge."

Put two pony beads (pearls) into the kind man's bag; the pink plastic cord (strong thread), with a knot tied at one end, into the greedy neighbor's bag; and a strand of 18 pearls strung on white plastic cord (rotten thread) into the judge's bag. When the time comes, restring the judge's 18 pearls onto the greedy neighbor's thread, plus the kind man's two pearls.

Lay the three bags on your lap and have the bowl close at hand. As each character is introduced in the story, raise the appropriate bag, with the face toward the audience.

Figure 8.8 **Judge**

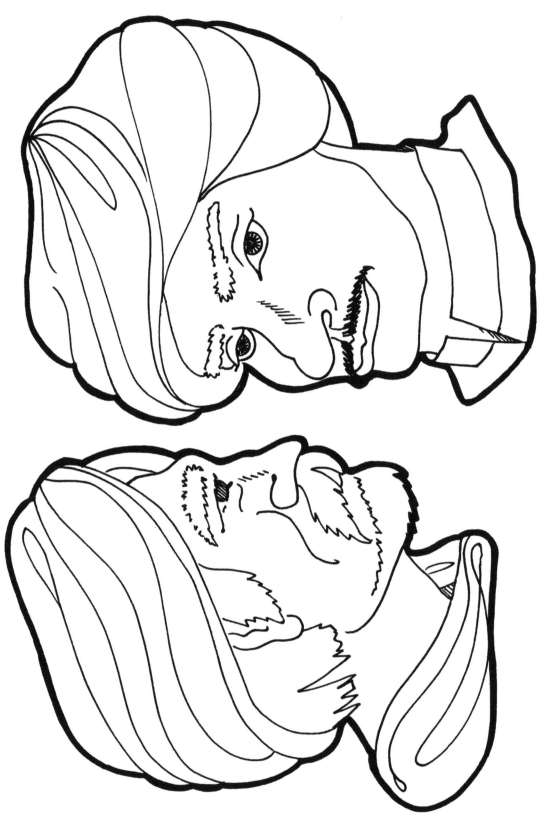

Figure 8.9 **Kind Man** Figure 8.10 **Greedy Neighbor**

"The Pearl Thief" retold by Desiree Webber

Once there was a kind and trusting man who owned two pearls. *(show the kind man)* He was about to leave on a long journey and did not want to take his treasure with him in case he should be robbed. So he asked his neighbor, *(show the greedy neighbor)* who he thought was honest, to watch over his two pearls. *(take the two pearls from the kind man's bag and drop them, one at a time, into the greedy neighbor's bag)*

The man said goodbye to his neighbor and began his long journey. During the several months he was gone, his neighbor thought and thought about the two pearls he had been trusted to protect. Slowly, greed filled his heart, and he decided to keep the pearls for himself. *(close the greedy neighbor's bag by pulling the drawstring)*

When the kind man finally returned home, he went straightaway to his neighbor. The man thanked his neighbor for caring for his pearls and asked for their return.

The neighbor looked astonished and said, "No pearls did you entrust to me. My friend, you are mistaken."

The kind man begged his neighbor for the return of the two pearls. They were the only wealth he possessed. But the greedy neighbor only said, "No pearls did you entrust to me. You are mistaken."

The kind man went immediately to the judge *(show the judge)* and told him his story. The judge summoned the greedy neighbor and asked for his version of what had happened. Again, the neighbor said, "No pearls did he entrust to me. He is mistaken."

The judge was a wise man and could read the guilt upon the greedy neighbor's face, but the judge knew he needed proof. So he sent the kind man and the greedy neighbor away and thought about the situation. *(place the kind man and greedy neighbor bags down)* Finally, he came up with a plan to catch the greedy neighbor, whom he now called "the pearl thief."

The judge went to his safe, removed 18 pearls, and strung them onto a piece of rotten thread. *(take the strand of 18 pearls out of the judge's bag and count them aloud with the children)*

The next day, the judge called for the pearl thief *(show pearl thief)* and said, "I trust an honest face such as yours. Please take these 20 pearls and restring them onto a strong piece of thread." *(place the strand of 18 pearls into the pearl thief's bag and lay the judge down)*

The pearl thief was pleased that the judge trusted him with the 20 pearls. He was sure it was a sign that the judge thought him to be innocent and that he would get away with the crime against his neighbor.

"Tonight I will restring the pearls, and tomorrow return them to the judge," the pearl thief told himself. "Then I will again be considered an honest man by all, and I will still possess my neighbor's two pearls!"

After eating his fill of dinner, the pearl thief sat down by his fire and threaded his needle with a strong piece of thread. *(take the pink cord from the pearl thief's bag)* Then he removed the pearls from the rotten thread and placed them into a bowl. *(slide the 18 pearls from the judge's strand into the bowl)*

"Now I shall restring these 20 pearls," said the thief, and he began to count each pearl as he threaded it onto the needle. *(thread the pearls onto the thief's pink thread while counting them aloud with the children)* "One, two, three, four, five . . . sixteen, seventeen, eighteen . . .

Where did the other two go?!" exclaimed the thief. Frantically, he jumped up from his seated position and began to search about the floor. He looked in the bowl again, among his clothes, around the furniture, in the entrance to his home—everywhere he had been.

"The judge will accuse me of stealing two of his pearls. What am I to do?" he moaned. Then the thief remembered the two stolen pearls he possessed. He hated to part with his treasure, but he was afraid of the judge. So he added the two stolen pearls to the strand of 18. *(add the two pearls from the pearl thief's bag)*

Again he counted the strand to make sure that he indeed had 20 pearls. *(count the pearls with the children)* "One, two three, four, five . . . sixteen, seventeen, eighteen, nineteen, and twenty." Breathing a heavy sigh of relief, the thief placed the pearls into his pocket and went to bed. *(place the strand into the pearl thief's bag)*

Early the next morning, the pearl thief hurried to the judge's house to deliver the pearls. Waiting for him was the judge and the kind man whose pearls had been stolen. *(show all three bags)*

Handing the strand of pearls to the judge, the thief loudly proclaimed, "Here are the 20 pearls you asked me to restring upon a strong piece of thread. Now you know me to be an honest man and wrongly accused by my neighbor."

"Let me count these pearls," said the judge. *(take the strand of pearls from the thief's bag and hold it up)* "I asked you to restring 20 pearls, but in *reality*, I gave you only 18 pearls. I knew that in your fear of me you would add the stolen pearls."

The pearl thief knew he had been cleverly tricked and went quietly away to prison. The kind man received his two pearls *(remove two of the pearls from the strand and place them into the kind man's bag; return the strand to the judge's bag)*, and the judge remained one of the wisest men in India.

Sources for Oral Stories

Lupton, Hugh. "Monkey See, Monkey Do." In *The Story Tree: Tales to Read Aloud*. Illustrated by Sophie Fatus. Cambridge, MA: Barefoot Books, 2001. (pages 16–23)
Monkeys steal a peddler's cart full of hats for sale. The monkeys mimic the peddler's actions of shouting, waving a stick, stamping his feet, and crying. The peddler's hats are not returned until he throws his own hat down upon the ground. Presenters may use audience participation to tell this tale.

Milford, Susan. "A Drum." In *Tales Alive! Ten Multicultural Folktales with Activities*. Illustrated by Michael A. Donato. Nashville, TN: Williamson, 2007. (pages 37–45)
A young boy helps others by giving them something he owns. In return he receives a desired gift.

Pirotta, Saviour. "The Four Magicians." In *Around the World in 80 Tales*. Illustrated by Richard Johnson. Boston, MA: Kingfisher, 2007. (pages 143–144)
Three magicians try to outdo the other by proving how smart and powerful each one is. Step by step, the three bring a tiger to life and are almost attacked before the fourth, humble magician creates a cage that captures the tiger.

Fingerplays, Songs, Action Rhymes, and Games

The following is a sampling of fingerplays and action rhymes that introduce animals from India.

"Elephant" Action Rhyme

(author unknown)

Right foot, left foot, see me go. *(step in rhythm and sway like an elephant)*
I am gray and big and slow,
I come walking down the street,
With my trunk and four big feet. *(stretch out arm by face and
swing like an elephant's trunk)*

"An Elephant Goes Like This" Action Rhyme

(author unknown)

An elephant goes like this and that. *(lift feet up and down)*
He's terribly tall, *(hold arms up high)*
And he's terribly big. *(hold arms out to the sides)*
He has no fingers, *(wiggle fingers)*
And he has no toes, *(bend over and touch toes)*
But goodness gracious, what a nose! *(stretch out arm by face and
swing like an elephant's trunk)*

Pearl Race Game

Supplies

White ping pong balls (pearls)
Palm leafs or fans

Directions

This is a game that is best played indoors. Play the game after sharing the story "Pearl Thief." The object of the game is to fan the ping pong ball (pearl) from the starting line to the finish line. Players must use their palm leaves, or fan, to move the ping pong ball from start to finish. The first player to fan his or her "pearl" across the finish line is the winner. (See instructions for "Punkha" fan in *Recipe and Craft Guide to India* by Khadija Ejaz. Hockessin, DE: Mitchell Lane, 2011. Pages 42–43)

Sources for Fingerplays, Songs, Action Rhymes, and Games

Harter, Debbie. *The Animal Boogie.* Music compact disc by Fred Penner. Cambridge, MA: Barefoot Books, 2000. (32 pages plus compact disc)

A book about animals found in the jungles of India that includes a sing-along compact disc. Share the book while singing the words.

MacMillan, Kathy and Christine Kirker. "The Elephant Hokey-Pokey." In *Storytime Magic: 400 Fingerplays, Flannelboards, and Other Activities*. Chicago, IL: American Library Association, 2009. (page 25)
Children pretend they are elephants as they put in their trunks, legs, ears, and more. Rhyme is sung to the tune of "The Hokey-Pokey."

MacMillan, Kathy and Christine Kirker. "Little Elephant." In *Storytime Magic: 400 Fingerplays, Flannelboards, and Other Activities*. Chicago, IL: American Library Association, 2009. (page 30)
This is a simple rhyme about a little elephant who loves his mother best in the whole world. Poem can be adapted to be an action rhyme.

Stewart, Georgiana. "Diwali . . . Festival of Lights." In *Multicultural Bean Bag Fun*. Long Branch, NJ: Kimbo Educational, 2009. Compact disc.
Children swing their bean bags like *diyas* (lamps) in the Festival of Lights—Diwali.

Media Choices

Show a literature-based DVD as a transition between storytelling activities and crafts. This gives children an opportunity to rest quietly for a few minutes.

Rudyard Kipling. *Rikki Tikki Tavi*. Illustrated by Jerry Pinkney. Norwalk, CT: Weston Woods, 1999. DVD, 30 min.
A mongoose named Rikki-tikki-tavi saves the family, who has befriended him, from deadly poisonous snakes, including two cobras named Nag and Nagiana. Due to the length of this DVD, it would make a good extending activity in the classroom following story time.

Young, Ed. *Seven Blind Mice*. Norwalk, CT: Weston Woods, 2007. DVD, 7 min.
Young's retelling of the Indian fable "The Blind Men and the Elephant." The reader learns that it is important to seek knowledge about the whole and not just a part of something. The story also relates the days of the week and colors.

Crafts and Other Activities

Choose a craft suited for the age level of the group and the time allotted for the story time.

Rakhi (Bracelet)

Raksha Bandhan [raksha BUND-end] is a Hindu festival honoring sisters and brothers. It is celebrated during the month of August. A sister ties a *rakhi* [raw-key] (bracelet) on her brother's arm to show her love and affection. In return, he gives her a gift and promises to protect her. See Figure 8.11.

For more information about Raksha Bandhan, see *My Hindu Year* by Cath Senker (New York: Rosen Publishing Group, 2008) or the YouTube video listed below, which shows a mother teaching her young daughter about Raksha Bandhan. In the video, the sister ties the rakhi around her brother's wrist and feeds him treats. The brother in return gives his sister a gift. Only the first minute needs to be shown, as the video repeats many of the images. http://www.youtube.com/watch?v=mtc2m0tb4t0&feature=fvsr. Posted August 5, 2009.

Supplies

Posterboard
(orange, yellow,
or pink)
Aluminum foil
Construction
paper (use
bright colors)
Buttons (metallic,
if possible)

Yarn
Glue stick
Scissors
Pencil
Hole punch
White glue or
hot-glue gun and
glue sticks

Figure 8.11   **Rakhi (Bracelet) Example**

Use Figures 8.12 through 8.16 to make a rakhi. An adult should precut all pieces for the rakhi. Each child should receive one of each piece with the exception of the leaf-shaped piece. Give each child eight leaf-shaped pieces.

Trace and cut the medium-size circle, Figure 8.12, from orange posterboard. Using a multitude of brightly colored construction paper, trace and cut the leaf-shaped pieces (Figure 8.13). The small round circle (Figure 8.14) and the flower-shaped piece (Figure 8.15) are traced from yellow and pink posterboard, respectively. The largest circle, Figure 8.16, is cut from aluminum foil. Cut a fringe around the edge of the foil using scissors. Lastly, cut a 15-inch strand of yarn for each child.

The teacher or librarian should glue the medium-size circle (Figure 8.12) to the center of the foil (Figure 8.16). The foil piece will be the bottom of the bracelet. The fringed edge of the foil will extend beyond the edge of the posterboard circle. These two pieces, when glued together, form the main part of the rakhi. When dry, punch two holes at the center, ½ inch apart, with a single-hole punch.

Children can now use the main part of the rakhi and the remaining pieces to create their bracelets. Each child should begin by threading the 15-inch length of yarn through the two holes. Thread up through the bottom and down through the other hole, looping across the top of the posterboard.

Glue the leaf-shaped pieces on top of the posterboard circle in a flower-petal design. Next, glue the flower-shaped piece (Figure 8.15) at the center of the circle, covering the yarn looped across. At the center of Figure 8.15, glue the small circle. Finish the bracelet with a decorative button glued at the center of the small circle. (If using hot glue, have an adult perform this last step.) The rakhi is now ready to be tied around the child's wrist.

Figure 8.12–8.16 **Bracelet Pieces**

Pongal Cow Mask

In the state of Tamil Nadu, in southern India, the Tamils celebrate Pongal [pon-GAL] during the middle of January. Pongal is a thanksgiving festival which lasts three days. On the first day of Pongal, bonfires are lit and a sweet rice pudding is made. On the second day, the sun is thanked, and on the third day cows and bullocks are honored as sacred animals. Their horns are brightly painted and tipped with brass ornaments. Garlands of flowers are hung around their necks. Once decorated, the cows and bullocks are paraded through the village as people play music and drum loudly.

In this craft project, children make cow masks representing the animals honored during Pongal. As a follow-up activity, have children make drums using coffee cans or oatmeal containers. Lead children in a procession around the room or library. Have some children play the drums (or other musical instruments) while the other children hold cow masks to their faces.

Supplies

Yellow posterboard   Scissors
Yellow construction paper   Pencils
White posterboard   Jumbo craft sticks
Glue sticks   Colored markers or crayons
Clear tape   Foil

Use Figures 8.17 through Figure 8.19 to make the mask. An adult should precut one cow's head, two ears, and two horns per child.

Using yellow posterboard, trace and cut out the cow's head (Figure 8.17 is a half-pattern). Cut out the openings for the eyes and nose. Trace and cut two horns (Figure 8.18) from the white posterboard and two ears (Figure 8.19) from the yellow construction paper. Fold the ears in half along the dashed lines.

Children will glue the horns and ears into place and decorate. Glue the folded ears at the top of the head, behind the mask. Color the horns using markers or crayons and glue the tips of the horns to represent the brass ornaments.

Either an adult or child can tape a craft stick to the back of the mask, at the base, to be used as a handle.

Sources for Craft Ideas and Activities

Ejaz, Khadija. *Recipe and Craft Guide to India.* Hockessin, DE: Mitchell Lane, 2011.
    Provides instructions, along with color photographs, for making several crafts such as a *chakri* (pinwheel), *punka* (fan), *doli* (palanquin), and *diya* (clay lamp).
Michaels, Alexandra. *The Kids' Multicultural Art Book: Art & Craft Experiences from around the World.* Nashville, TN: Williamson Books, 2007. (pages 124–129)
    "Twirling Palm Puppet" and "Peacock of India" are unique and fun crafts for children in second grade and higher. Both crafts may be utilized by younger children with assistance from an adult.

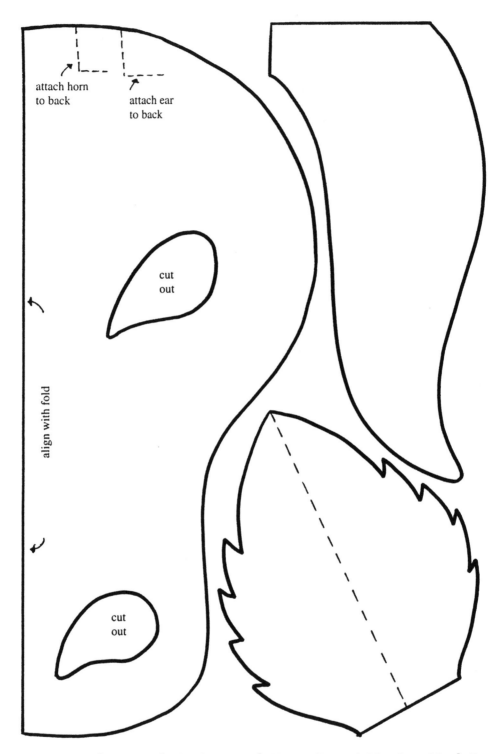

attach horn
to back

attach ear
to back

cut
out

align with fold

cut
out

Figure 8.17 **Cow Mask**   Figure 8.18 **Cow Mask Horn**   Figure 8.19 **Cow Mask Ear**

Press, Judy. *The Little Hands Big Fun Craft Book*. Nashville, TN: Williamson Books, 2008. (pages 90–91)

"Floating Diwali Candle" is an easy craft that young children can make. The basic supplies consist of a toilet-tissue tube, foil, and construction paper.

Speechley, Greta. *World Crafts*. New York: Gareth Stevens Publishing, 2010. (pages 12–13)

Indian mirror is made with a cardboard frame glued to a mirror tile. A gold-paper elephant decorates the mirror's frame, along with glitter. An adult will need to precut the cardboard frames.

Chapter 9

Let's Visit

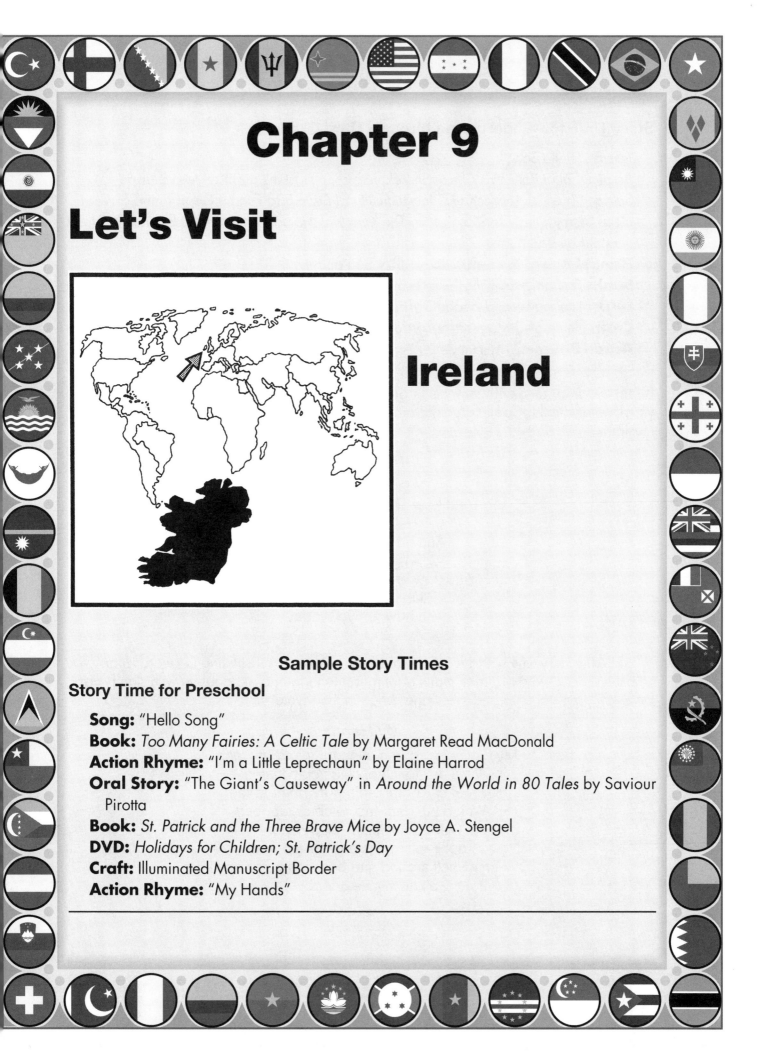

Ireland

Sample Story Times

Story Time for Preschool

Song: "Hello Song"

Book: *Too Many Fairies: A Celtic Tale* by Margaret Read MacDonald

Action Rhyme: "I'm a Little Leprechaun" by Elaine Harrod

Oral Story: "The Giant's Causeway" in *Around the World in 80 Tales* by Saviour Pirotta

Book: *St. Patrick and the Three Brave Mice* by Joyce A. Stengel

DVD: *Holidays for Children; St. Patrick's Day*

Craft: Illuminated Manuscript Border

Action Rhyme: "My Hands"

Story Time for Kindergarten through Third Grade

Song: "Hello Song"
Book: *Count Your Way Through Ireland* by Jim Haskins and Kathleen Benson
Song: "The Irish Leprechaun" in *Multicultural Bean Bag Fun* by Georgianna Stewart
Oral Story: "Just One Choice" in *The King with Horse's Ears: and Other Irish Folktales* retold by Bart Burns
Flannel Board Presentation: "Billy Beg and the Bull"
Book: *St. Patrick and the Three Brave Mice"* by Joyce A. Stengel
DVD: *Little Travelers. Episode 3: The British Isles* by Angelia Hart
Craft: Illuminated Manuscript Border
Action Rhyme: "My Hands"

Begin the story time with the "Hello Song." Then sing the song again, substituting the word *hello* with the Gaelic greeting *dia duit* [djiah gwich]. (See p. xxix for "Hello Song" music.)

Hello Song

Hello ev'rybody,
And how are you? How are you?
Hello ev'rybody,
And how are you today?
Djiah gwich ev'rybody.
And how are you? How are you?
Djiah gwich ev'rybody
And how are you today?

End the story time with the "My Hands" action rhyme, substituting the words *thank you* with the Gaelic word *go raibh maith agat* [guramahhagut] and goodbye with *slán* [slaan]. Have children stand up and follow the action in the rhyme.

My Hands

My hands say guramahhagut. *(hold up hands)*
With a clap, clap, clap. *(clap hands)*
My feet say guramahhagut. *(point to feet)*
With a tap, tap, tap. *(stap or tap feet)*
Clap! Clap! Clap! *(clap hands)*
Tap! Tap! Tap! *(stamp or tap feet)*
Turn myself around and bow. *(turn and bow)*
Slaan. *(wave goodbye)*

Books to Read Aloud

Bateman, Teresa. *Fiona's Luck.* Illustrated by Kelly Murphy. Watertown, MA: Charlesbridge, 2007. (32 pages)
> What Fiona lacks in being lucky she makes up for in being clever. She knows that getting luck back from the leprechauns will be no easy task.

Bunting, Eve. *Finn McCool and the Great Fish.* Illustrated by Zachary Pullen. United States: Sleeping Bear Press, 2010. (32 pages)
> Finn was told that catching and eating a special salmon would give him the wisdom of the world. Finn finds another way to gain the wisdom and is forever revered by others.

Burgard, Anna Marlis. *Flying Feet: A Story of Irish Dance.* Illustrated by Leighanne Dees. San Francisco: Chronicle Books, 2005. (36 pages)
> A competition between two dancers takes place for a chance to teach the people of Ballyconneely to dance.

Edwards, Pamela Duncan. *The Leprechaun's Gold.* Illustrated by Henry Cole. New York: Harper Collins Publisher, 2006. (40 pages)
> Two harpists embark on a journey to be recognized as the best harpist in Ireland, but not without a little help from a mischievous little leprechaun.

Garland, Michael. *King Puck: Inspired by an Irish Festival.* New York: Harper Collins, 2007. (32 pages)
> Finny the goat is crowned King Puck. This is based on a real tradition in Ireland in the village of Killorglin.

Haskins, Jim and Kathleen Benson. *Count Your Way through Ireland.* Illustrated by Beth Wright. Minneapolis, MN: Carolrhoda Books, 1996. (24 pages)
> Count from 1 to 10 in Gaelic while also learning about Ireland.

Krensky, Stephen. *Too Many Leprechauns or How That Pot o' Gold Got to the End of the Rainbow.* Illustrated by Dan Andreasen. New York: Simon & Schuster Books for Young Readers, 2007. (32 pages)
> Finn O' Finnegan comes home after being on an adventure to find his village over run with noisy leprechauns. Finn must devise a plan to bring peace back to his village and get rid of the leprechauns.

MacDonald, Margaret Read. *Too Many Fairies: A Celtic Tale.* Illustrated by Susan Mitchell. Tarrytown, NY: Marshall Cavendish for Children, 2010. (32 pages)
> This is a retelling of an old tale from Ireland and Scotland. When a woman complains about too much housework, fairies come to save the day—only things aren't as great as they first seem.

Stengel, Joyce A. *St. Patrick and the Three Brave Mice.* Illustrated by Herb Leonhard. Gretna, LA: Pelican Publishing Co., 2009. (32 pages)
> This traditional story of St. Patrick driving the snakes out of Ireland is given new life with the addition of three clever mice.

Storytelling

"Billy Beg and the Bull" Flannel Board Presentation

"Billy Beg and the Bull" is the story of how the loyal friendship of an animal helps a boy find happiness. See Figures 9.1 through 9.8 for patterns. Trace the patterns on felt, or photocopy and color them. If photocopying, glue small squares of felt to the backs of the paper figures so they will hold to the flannel board. Place the figures on the flannel board as they are introduces in the story.

"Billy Beg and the Bull" retold by Elaine Harrod

In the green pastures of Ireland lived Billy Beg and his bull. *(place Billy Beg and the bull on the flannel board)* They were best friends. The bull had been a gift from Billy's mother, who had died a few years before. When Billy's father remarried, the stepmother soon made it clear that she did not like Billy spending all his time with the bull. She wanted Billy to do not only his chores but also her children's chores. Billy was so unhappy that he would quickly finish his chores and run to be with his bull. They spent many hours together and were great friends.

One day, Billy overheard his stepmother say she was going to get rid of his bull. Billy knew he would never let anything happen to his bull, for it was all he had left to remind him of his mother. He told the bull of his plan for them to leave their home. The bull was a friend and agreed to follow Billy anywhere. Billy and the bull set off on their journey, not knowing where the road would take them.

As Billy and his bull traveled, they met with many challenges. The bull was wise and taught Billy many things. Billy's bull was an extraordinary animal with very special abilities. When Bill was hungry, he would reach into the bull's right ear and pull out a cloth. When Billy laid it out upon the ground, it would magically become covered with food. *(place the cloth with food on the flannel board)* After supper every evening, the bull would have the boy take a stick out of his other ear. *(place the magic stick on the flannel board)* The bull would have Billy practice with the stick as if it were a sword, and in this way Billy was learning to take care of himself.

One day as the two approached a forest, they saw another bull. The strange bull approached and told Billy and the bull they could not pass through his forest. Billy and the bull did not want to turn back, for they had come so far. Billy's bull told Billy that he would fight the other bull. He explained to Billy that if he were to lose, Billy was to make a belt from his hide. This special belt would help give Billy strength. This was, unfortunately, the outcome of the fight between the two bulls. Before the bull died, he told Billy to take the stick from his ear, and after he had made the belt from his hide, he was to wave the stick above his head.

Billy was very sad, but he did what the bull had asked him to do. He made the belt out of the hide of the bull and waved the stick above his head. Magically, the stick turned into a sword. *(place the sword on the flannel board and remove the magic stick)* After the fight, the strange bull watched in fear as Billy turned the stick into a sword. When the bull saw this, he ran away. Billy then made his way into the forest. As Billy traveled through the forest, he became a brave hunter.

One day as Billy was walking, he saw smoke. As he approached, he could see that there was an outdoor celebration. *(place the princess on the flannel board)* Many people were dancing and having a feast. Billy was invited to join the celebration. Suddenly, he noticed something coming out of the forest: It was a dragon *(place the dragon on the flannel board)* The dragon was reaching out to grab a young princess. Billy took his sword and quickly slew the dragon. He saved the princess! The people rushed in to make sure the princess was all right, and when they did, Billy slipped away into the forest. *(remove the dragon and Billy from the flannel board)*

When the princess realized that the young man who saved her was gone, she looked down and saw that, during the struggle with the dragon, the young man had lost one of his boots. *(place Billy's boot on the flannel board)* She quickly ordered the king's men to bring all the men within a 10-mile range back to the celebration to try on the boot.

Many men came to the celebration hoping that the boot would fit them, making them a hero. *(place Billy on the flannel board)* After many tries, the boot was finally slipped onto Billy's foot. The princess was so happy that she asked Billy to be her husband. At last, Billy knew his journey had come to an end. He and the princess lived a very happy life together.

"Five Little Instruments" Flannel Board Presentation

The people of Ireland have a rich musical history. Today, music continues to be an important part of Irish culture. Some of the common instruments played in Ireland are the *bodhran* [BAH-rahn] (drum), the fiddle (violin), the penny whistle (flute), the accordion, and the harp, which are featured in this flannel board presentation. See Figures 9.9 through 9.13 for patterns. Photocopy, color, and laminate the patterns. Glue small pieces of felt to the backs of the figures so they will hold to the flannel board. Place the figures on the flannel board as the instruments are introduced in the poem. (Optionally, reduce the size of the patterns and make puppets for a finger play; use Figure 5.11 to make finger attachments for the puppets.)

Five Little Instruments by Elaine Harrod and Sandy Shropshire

Here are Irish instruments to blow, to pound, to strum.
Beat the bodhran [BAH-rahn] hard and strong; it's a Celtic drum.
(Place drum on flannel board.)
Now play a penny whistle, a flute with sweetest sound.
Blow it soft; blow it loud; great music will abound!
(place the penny whistle/flute on flannel board.)
Next we'll hear the fiddle, it's a violin to some.
The notes they blend together-join in; have some fun!
(place the violin on flannel board.)
Time for the accordion with buttons, keys and folds.
Listen to the music; hear ancient tales retold.
(place the accordion on flannel board.)
Last we add the Gaelic harp-Ireland's ancient treasure.
Our Irish band is now complete; the music is such pleasure.
(place the harp on flannel board.)

Sources for Oral Stories

Burns, Batt. "Just One Choice." In *The King with Horse's Ears and Other Irish Folktales.* Illustrated by Igor Oleynikov. New York: Sterling Publishing Co., 2009. (96 pages)
    The Giant's Causeway on the northern coast of Ireland has long been the legendary home of half-human seals. In this story a half-human seal grants wishes to a family.

Figure 9.1 **Billy Beg** Figure 9.2 **Princess**

Figure 9.3 **Bull** Figure 9.4 **Cloth with Food** Figure 9.5 **Sword** Figure 9.6 **Billy's Boot**
Figure 9.7 **Magic Stick**

Figure 9.8 **Dragon**

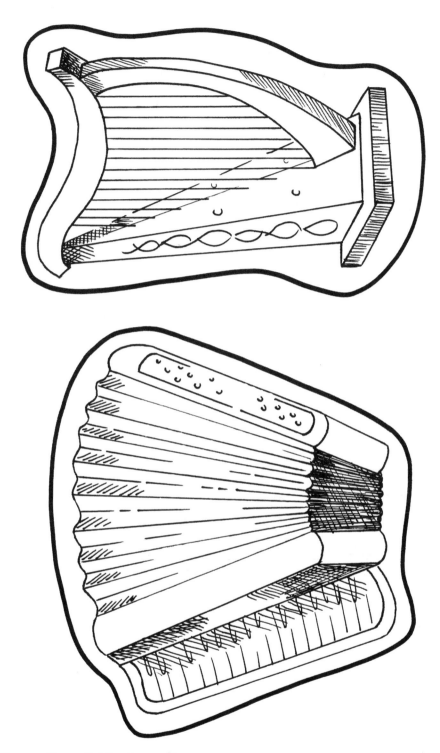

Figure 9.9 **Harp**   Figure 9.10 **Accordian**

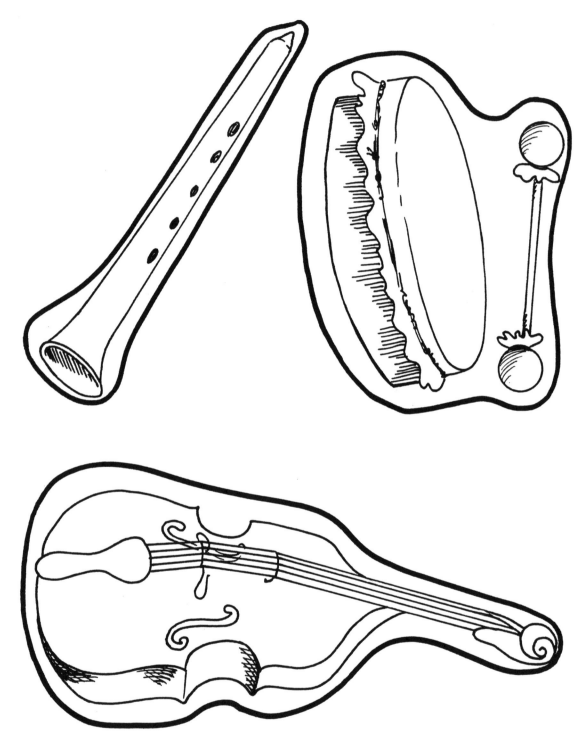

Figure 9.11 **Fiddle (Violin)** Figure 9.12 **Bodhran (Drum)** Figure 9.13 **Penny Whistle (Flute)**

Pirotta, Saviour. "The Giant's Causeway." In *Around the World in 80 Tales*. Illustrated by Richard Johnson. Boston, MA: Kingfisher, 2007. (176 pages)
    This story highlights a challenge between and Irish giant Finn McCool and a Scottish giant Benandonner.

Fingerplays, Songs, Action Rhymes, and Games

A picture of a shillelagh and a description can be found by referring to *Count Your Way through Ireland* by Jim Haskins and Kathleen Benson.

"I'm a Little Leprechaun" Action Rhyme

(sung to "I'm a Little Teapot") by Elaine Harrod

I'm a little leprechaun, bold and wee. *(walk in place)*
Here is my gold and my shillelagh [sha-LAY-lee]. *(hold up one fist, then the other)*
When I hide my pot of precious gold. *(pretend to hold pot)*
Keep your eyes on the Irish rainbows.
(hold hand above eyes as if looking into the sun)

Sources for Fingerplays, Songs Action Rhymes, and Games

Fatus, Sophie and Fred Penner. *Here We Go Round the Mulberry Bush*. Cambridge, MA: Barefoot Books, 2011. (24 pages) Compact disc included.
    This song is known to be used at traditional country Celtic weddings.

MacMillan, Kathy and Christine Kirker. *Storytime Magic: 400 Fingerplays, Flannelboards and Other Activities*. Chicago: American Library Association, 2009.
    Children will enjoy the "Saint Paddy's Day" poem and the "Shamrock Song" found in this outstanding resource.

Putumayo Kids Presents Celtic Dreamland. Putumayo World Music & Crafts. 2008. Compact disc.
    This compact disc contains songs for bedtime that are from Ireland and Scotland. Music can be played during transition times in the library or classroom.

Stewart, Georgiana. *Multicultural Bean Bag Fun*. Kimbo Educational, 2010. Compact disc.
    Kids are given directions on this compact disc to use a bean bag while moving and listening to traditional music from different cultures. "The Irish Leprechaun" is one song that is fun and will add to the theme of Ireland.

Media Choices

Show a DVD as a transition between storytelling activities and crafts.

Hart, Angelina, Nakia Hart, and Chantelle Hart. *Little Travelers. Episode 3: The British Isles*. [s.l.]: dist. by TravelVideoStore.com, 2008. DVD, 40 min.
    Two sisters travel to Ireland, Scotland, and England. They visit the homes of Peter Rabbit and Harry Potter. They also look for the Loch Ness monster.

Holidays for Children: St. Patrick's Day. Wynnewood, PA: Schlessinger, 1996. DVD, 25 min.
Learn how to make a leprechaun puppet. Listen to the story of "Semus and the Leprechaun."

Crafts and Other Activities

Choose a craft suited for the age level of the group and the time allotted for the story time.

Illuminated Manuscript Border

Between the fifth and seventh centuries, monasteries in Ireland were built for monks. Many people in Ireland did not know how to write; however, monks knew how to write in Latin and even developed a written language for Gaelic, which many people spoke (some people still speak Gaelic today). In those days, books were written and copied by hand. This became a large portion of the monks' day-to-day work. They turned their books into wonderful works of art by illustrating the pages. The colors were so bright and beautiful that they seemed to glow. They became known as illuminated manuscripts. Many of these manuscripts are kept in the Trinity College Library in Dublin for the entire world to see.

Storytelling is an important part of Irish culture. The following craft project allows children to combine two aspects of Irish culture: illuminated manuscripts and storytelling. Show children pictures of illuminated manuscripts, which can be found in encyclopedias.

Supplies

Colored pencils   Crayons

Markers   Pencils

Make a copy of Figure 9.15 for each child. Have children write or draw a story inside the illuminated manuscript border. The border pattern allows space for writing and drawing pictures. The border can be enlarged to give the children more space for their art or written tales. If the children are old enough to use the border to write a story, each child may be given two copies. One copy may be used for them to write their story and another copy to draw a picture to accompany their story. Children can also color the border with colored pencils or markers.

Brooches

The Celts were an ancient people who came to Ireland centuries ago. They brought their language, known as Gaelic, which is still used to this day by about 30 percent of Irish people. All school children are taught to read and write Gaelic. The Celts also brought with them a clothing adornment, the brooch, worn by males and females alike. It was used to hold clothes together. It consisted of an open metal disk and a long pin. The clothing was pushed together through the hole; then the pin was stuck through the clothing, holding it in place inside the brooch.

In this craft project, children make brooches similar to those worn by the Celts. Make a sample brooch to show children before beginning the project.

Supplies

Pencils

Scissors

Posterboard

Sequins, buttons, glitter
and beads

Craft knife

Glue (strong-bonding
craft glue)

Safety pin or brooch pin
(available at craft stores)

Use Figures 9.16 and 9.17 to make a brooch.
School-age children can trace the patterns on poster
board and cut out the two pieces. For younger children, an adult will want to precut pieces. Cut two slits
into the brooch where indicated, using a craft knife
(an adult should complete this task). Slide the posterboard brooch pin through the slits (see "Brooch,"
Figure 9.14). Have children glue decorative materials
to the brooch, such as sequins, buttons, and glitter.
Glue a brooch pin (from a craft store) to the back of
the brooch, or pin the brooch to the child's shirt with
a safety pin. Allow the glue to dry completely before wearing.

Figure 9.14   **Brooch Example**

Figure 9.15 **Illuminated Manuscript Border**

cut two slits

Figure 9.16 **Brooch** Figure 9.17 **Brooch Pin**

Sources for Craft Ideas and Activities

Gnojewski, Carol. *St. Patrick's Day Crafts: Fun Holiday Crafts Kids Can Do!* Berkeley Heights, NJ: Enslow Publishers Inc., 2004. (32 pages)
This resource offers many craft ideas such as a bodhran drum, blarney stones, and puppets. In addition to craft projects, the book includes games, websites, and bibliographies.

Speechley, Greta. *World Crafts (Creative Crafts for Kids).* Danbury, CT: Grolier, 2003. (32 pages)
Using black cardboard and colored cellophane, kids can create a beautiful Celtic-inspired stained glass.

Chapter 10

Let's Visit

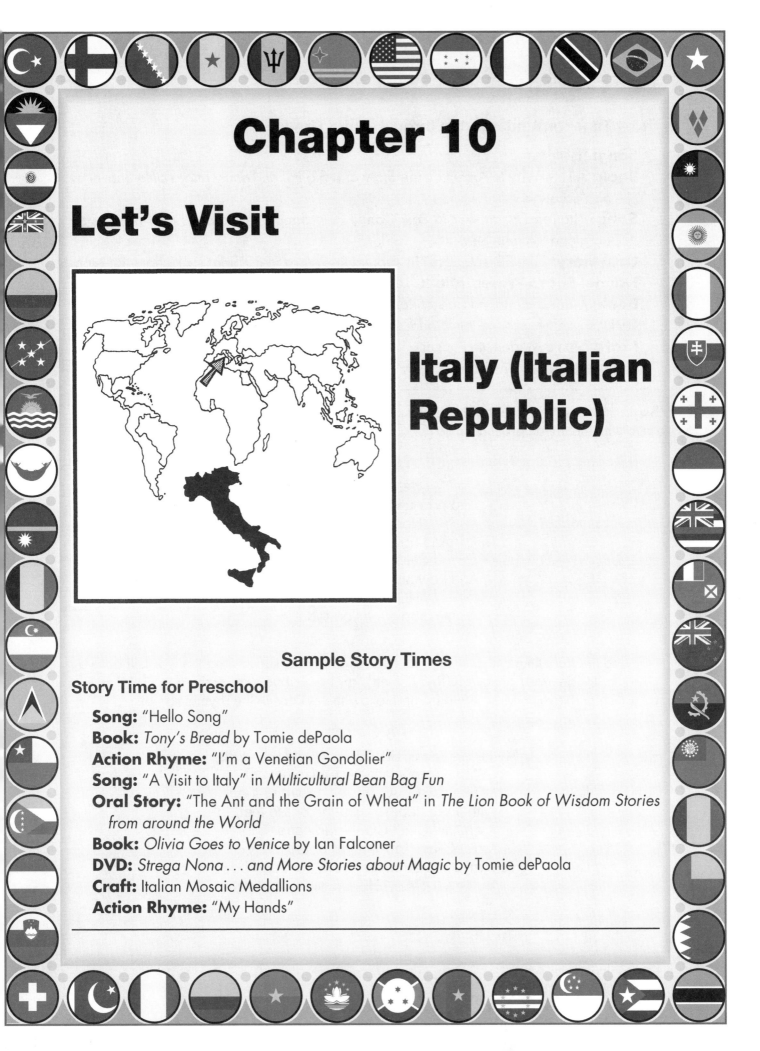

Italy (Italian Republic)

Sample Story Times

Story Time for Preschool

Song: "Hello Song"

Book: *Tony's Bread* by Tomie dePaola

Action Rhyme: "I'm a Venetian Gondolier"

Song: "A Visit to Italy" in *Multicultural Bean Bag Fun*

Oral Story: "The Ant and the Grain of Wheat" in *The Lion Book of Wisdom Stories from around the World*

Book: *Olivia Goes to Venice* by Ian Falconer

DVD: *Strega Nona . . . and More Stories about Magic* by Tomie dePaola

Craft: Italian Mosaic Medallions

Action Rhyme: "My Hands"

Story Time for Kindergarten through Third Grade

Song: "Hello Song"
Book: *All the Way to America: The Story of a Big Italian Family and a Little Shovel* by Dan Yaccarino
Song: "Italian Tarantella" in *Folk Dance Fun: Simple Folk Songs and Dances* by Georgiana Liccione Stewart
Oral Story: "The Silver Goose" in *Around the Word in 80 Tales* by Richard Johnson
Flannel Board Presentation: "Lionbruno"
Book: *Madeline and the Cats of Rome* by John Bemelmans Marciano
DVD: *Countries around the World: Italy*
Craft: Pepitto Marionette Puppet
Action Rhyme: "My Hands"

Begin the story time with the "Hello Song." Then sing the song again, substituting the word *hello* with the Italian greeting *ciao* [CHOW]. (See p. xxix for "Hello Song" music.)

Hello Song

Hello ev'rybody,
And how are you? How are you?
Hello ev'rybody,
And how are you today?
CHOW ev'rybody,
And how are you? How are you?
CHOW everybody,
And how are you today?

End the story time with the "My Hands" action rhyme, substituting the words *thank you* with the Italian word *gratzie* [GRATZEE-eh], and goodbye with *arrivederci* [ah reeveh-DAIRCHEE]. Have children stand up and follow the actions in the rhyme.

My Hands

My hands say GRATZEE-eh. *(hold up hands)*
With a clap, clap, clap. *(clap hands)*
My feet say GRATZEE-eh. *(point to feet)*
With a tap, tap, tap. *(stamp or tap feet)*
Clap! Clap! Clap! *(clap hands)*
Tap! Tap! Tap! *(stamp or tap feet)*
Turn myself around and bow. *(turn and bow)*
Ah reeveh-DAIRCHEE. *(wave goodbye)*

Books to Read Aloud

dePaola, Tomie. *Strega Nona*. USA: Little Simon, 2011. (40 pages).
Strega Nona has a magic pasta pot. When she leaves Big Anthony alone with the pot, he fills the village with pasta.

dePaola, Tomie. *Tony's Bread*. USA: Penguin Group, 1996. (32 pages).
Angelo helps Tony and his daughter Serafina make their dreams come true.

Falconer, Ian. *Olivia Goes to Venice*. New York: Atheneum Books, 2010. (48 pages)
Olivia's family goes on vacation to Venice. Olivia visits the Piazza San Marco, takes a gondola ride, and eats gelato on her vacation.

Gemignani, Tony. *Tony and the Pizza Champions*. Illustrated by Matthew Trueman. San Francisco, CA: Chronicle Books, 2009. (44 pages).
Tony and his team are invited to the world pizza-tossing championship for Italy. This book includes a recipe for pizza and instructions for tossing pizza dough.

Langton, Jane P. *Saint Francis and the Wolf*. Illustrated by Ilse Plume. Jaffrey, NH: David R. Godine, 2007. (32 pages).
When an aggressive wolf threatens the peace in the town of Gubbio, Saint Francis of Assisi finds a way to make peace with the wild wolf.

Marciano, John Bemelmans. *Madeline and the Cats of Rome*. New York: Penguin Group, 2008. (48 pages).
Miss Clavel and all 12 girls, including Madeline, visit Rome in the springtime. This is a continuation of the Madeline stories written and illustrated by Ludwig Bemelmans' grandson John Bemelmans Marciano.

Yaccarino, Dan. *All the Way to America: The Story of a Big Italian Family and a Little Shovel*. New York: Random House for Children, 2011. (40 pages).
The story of an Italian family's many generations as they immigrate to the United States and manage to pass along a small shovel with a large meaning.

Storytelling

"Lionbruno" Flannel Board Presentation

"Lionbruno" is an Italian folktale about a young man and his many adventures. See Figures 10.1 through 10.8 for patterns. Trace the patterns on felt, or photocopy and color them. If photocopying, glue small squares of felt to the backs of the paper figures so they will hold to the flannel board. Place the figures on the flannel board as they are introduced in the story.

Figure 10.1 **Magic Ruby** Figure 10.2 **Fisherman** Figure 10.3 **Lionbruno**

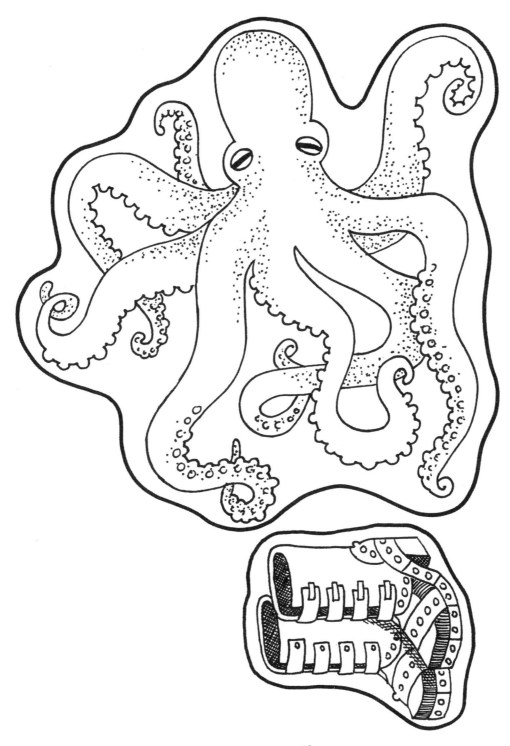

Figure 10.4 **Overgrown Octopus**   Figure 10.5 **Iron Shoes**

Figure 10.6 **Fairy Colina**

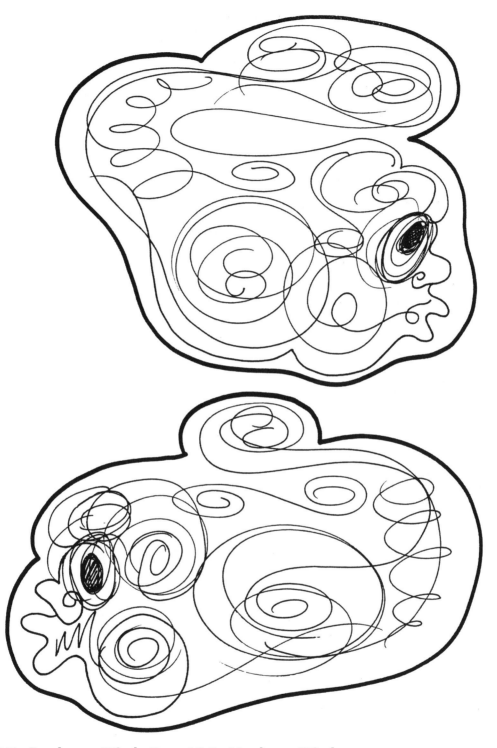

Figure 10.7 **Southwest Wind**   Figure 10.8 **Northeast Wind**

"Lionbruno" retold by Elaine Harrod

Once there was a fisherman who had lost his luck with catching fish. *(place the fisherman on the flannel board)* Every time he pulled in his nets, they were empty. One day, while out in his boat casting his nets, he looked up to see an odd, overgrown octopus. *(place the octopus on the flannel board)*

The octopus said, "I will help you catch fish once again, if you will do something for me." Of course, the fisherman was very interested. "I will make sure that your nets are full of fish every day for the rest of your life. In return however, you must give me you unborn son. You must bring your son to me on his thirteenth birthday."

The fisherman did not like what the octopus said, but he didn't have a son yet. Perhaps he never would! He did, however, have a family to think about now, and he needed to feed them. So the fisherman agreed to the arrangement with the octopus. After the agreement was made, the odd, overgrown octopus disappeared into the sea. *(remove the overgrown octopus from the flannel board)*

The days that followed were very prosperous for the fisherman and his family. Soon, he and his wife were blessed with another child, a son. They named him Lionbruno. The fisherman privately hoped the odd, overgrown octopus would forget their agreement and not come for his son. He loved the boy very much.

Years went by and the son grew. When Lionbruno's thirteenth birthday was near, the odd, overgrown octopus came to the fisherman during one of the fishing trips. *(Place the octopus on the flannel board)* The octopus spoke the words the fisherman had dreaded hearing all these years: "Bring me the boy, tomorrow!" The fisherman was very sad.

The next day, the fisherman took his son to the beach and asked him to wait there. *(place Lionbruno on the flannel board)* Like a good son, Lionbruno sat on the beach waiting for his father. The odd, overgrown octopus swam close to the beach and tried to get Lionbruno to come over to him. Lionbruno kept his distance, for he did not have a good feeling about this sea creature. The odd, overgrown octopus came closer and closer until it grabbed the boy with one of its long tentacles. At that moment, a fairy swooped down from the sky and grabbed Lionbruno away from the octopus. *(place Fairy Colina on the flannel board)* High into the sky she flew with the boy clutched in her arms.

Lionbruno and the fairy traveled a great distance before they landed on the top of a mountain. When the boy looked up at her, he saw the most beautiful creature he had ever seen. The fairy told Lionbruno that her name was Colina. Lionbruno thanked her for saving his life. He stayed on the mountain with Colina and the other fairies who also lived on the mountain. Lionbruno and Colina became great friends. The fairies taught him how to joust and hunt, as well as many other skills that a man might need to know to survive in the wilderness. The fairies also trained Lionbruno to protect himself, for they knew they would not always be around to help him. As the years passed, Lionbruno and Colina grew closer, and when they were grown they were married.

After some time, Lionbruno began to think of his parents more and more often. He missed them more as each day passed. He spoke to Colina about visiting his parents. Colina understood, of course, but she said to Lionbruno, "Please take this magic ruby with you *(place the magic ruby on the flannel board)* and if you need anything on your long journey, you can ask the ruby to grant your wish. I ask only one favor from you, Lionbruno. Please do not tell anyone we are married. The people in your world would not understand that you are married to a fairy!" Lionbruno promised Colina he would not tell, said his goodbyes to all, and began his long journey to his parents' home.

When Lionbruno arrived in his old village, he was excited to see his parents after such a long time. But the grand house he remembered as a child was now old and run-down. His parents were so happy to see Lionbruno that they began to cry. They explained that their lives had little meaning after they lost him. Lionbruno used his magic ruby to make his parents' home grand once again. Before he returned to Colina, Lionbruno promised his parents that he would visit them every year.

Lionbruno began his long journey home. Along the way, he came upon a castle where a jousting tournament was ongoing. Lionbruno decide to use the skills the mountain fairies had taught him and he entered the tournament. To his amazement, he won, but the prize was the king's daughter in marriage.

"I cannot marry the princess. I am already married, and my wife is ten times more beautiful," boasted Lionbruno.

The king was insulted and demanded that Lionbruno produce his wife or be thrown in prison. Lionbruno took his magic ruby and called for Colina to appear. Colina could not reveal her identity; so, she never came. The crowd became angry. They hissed and booed until Lionbruno ran away through the castle's gates.

When Lionbruno reached the road, Colina used her abilities as a fairy to appear before him. "Because you have broken your promise to me, I must leave," said Colina. "To find me, you must travel the world and wear out a pair of iron shoes." *(remove Fairy Colina from the flannel board)* Colina disappeared in a cloud of fairy dust as quickly as she had appeared.

Lionbruno knew that he must find Colina, so he quickly found a blacksmith to make him a pair of iron shoes. *(place the iron shoes on the flannel board)* Once Lionbruno had the shoes, he walked all over the world looking for his wife. He asked everyone he met if they had seen her. After many years, Lionbruno had almost worn out the iron shoes. Still, he had not found Colina and he was very sad. In the distance, he saw a house upon a high hill. He decided to stop and ask for food and a place to sleep.

When he came to the house, he felt the strangest wind. It was warm, hot, cold, and cool—all at one time! He looked into the wind and saw two faces. *(place the southwest and the northeast wind on the flannel board)*

"Who are you?" asked Lionbruno.

"We are the Southwest Wind and the Northeast Wind," they answered. "We live here with our brothers and sisters, who are all the other winds."

Lionbruno told his story to the two brothers.

Puffing excitedly, the Northeast Wind said, "I know where Colina lives! I am the wind that blows through her castle every day. Hop on my back and I will take you to her."

When they arrived at the castle, Colina and Lionbruno hugged each other with joy. Lionbruno promised never to boast, or to break his promises again, and Colina forgave his mistake.

The Northeast Wind took Colina and Lionbruno back to their mountain home, where they have lived happily to this day.

Source for Flannel Board Presentation

Haskins, Jim. *Count Your Way through Italy*. Illustrated by Beth Wright. Minneapolis, MN: Carolrhoda Books, 1991. (24 pages)
　　The book introduces numbers one through ten in Italian, alongside facts and historical information about Italy.

Using Haskin's book, create a flannel board presentation to teach children how to count from one to ten in Italian. The part of the book that shows the number six (*sei*) in Italian also shows gondolas, which are Venetian boats. Make 10 gondolas out of construction paper. Write the Italian words for "one" through "ten" on the gondolas. Next to the Italian words, write the numbers. Glue small pieces of felt to the backs of the figures so they will hold to the flannel board.

Sources for Oral Stories

Pirotta, Savior. "The Silver Goose." In *Around the World in 80 Tales*. Illustrated by Richard Johnson. London: Kingfisher, 2007. (pages 92–93)
　　Count Carlo finds himself in a mess after hanging a sign over his home with the words "Money Can Get You Anything You Want."

Self, David. "The Ant and the Grain of Wheat." In *The Lion Book of Wisdom Stories from around the World*. Illustrated by Christina Balit. Oxford, England: Lion Children's, 2008. (pages 25–26)
　　While the ant is gathering wheat, one of the grains of wheat speaks to the ant. He convinces the ant if some wheat is left on the ground, more wheat will grow in the spring.

Fingerplays, Songs, Action Rhymes, and Games

"I'm a Venetian Gondolier" Action Rhyme

A gondola is a long, narrow, flat-bottomed boat with a high, pointed prow and stern. Gondolas are used on the canals of Venice. The gondola drivers, called gondoliers, do not sit to paddle their boats; instead, they stand at the back and use long poles to push against the bottom of the shallow waterways. Have the children pretend to be Venetian gondoliers as they act out the following rhyme.

I'm a Venetian Gondolier by Sandy Shropshire

I'm a Venetian gondolier. *(stand with hands on hips)*
I paddle my gondola here and there. *(pretend to paddle an oar on
the left and right)*
I transport children, ladies, and men. *(wave like hailing a taxi cab)*
Up the canals and back again. *(paddle again)*
I'm a Venetian gondolier. *(as above)*
I paddle my gondola here and there. *(pretend to paddle an oar
on the left and right)*
I work so hard; so I ask you now—*(shake pointing finger)*
"Please wave to me and call out ciao [CHOW]!" *(wave and say CHOW)*

Sources for Fingerplays, Songs, Action Rhymes, and Games

Stewart, Georgiana Liccione. "Italian Tarantella." In *Folk Dance Fun: Simple Folk Songs and Dances*. Long Branch, NJ: Kimbo Educational, 1984. Compact disc.
Directions for leading the children in the Italian tarantella dance are included.

Stewart, Georgiana Liccione. "A Visit to Italy." In *Multicultural Bean Bag Fun*. Long Branch, NJ: Kimbo Educational, 2010. Compact disc.
Directions for a dance that includes bean bags are included.

Media Choices

Show a DVD or a downloadable movie as a transition between storytelling activities and crafts.

Countries around the World: Italy. Wynnewood, PA: Schlessinger Media, 2007. DVD, 13 min.
Travel to the capital city of Rome to see the cities. Learn about the food, the customs, and the people of Italy.

dePaola, Tomie. *Strega Nona . . . and More Stories about Magic*. Weston, CT: Weston Woods, 2009. DVD, 71 min.
Strega Nona has a magic pasta pot. When she leaves Big Anthony alone with the pot, he fills the village with pasta. ("Strega Nona" segment is 8 min. in length)

Crafts and Other Activities

Choose a craft suited for the age level of the group and the time allotted for the story time.

Pepitto Marionette Puppet

In Italy, large, heavy marionettes were made and used by troupes of puppeteers to tell heroic medieval tales. These troupes traveled through Italy, and even to England, to tell stories using marionette puppets. This art form was first used to create characters for adult productions but later became a popular form used for children's storytelling. One famous Italian marionette puppet all children are familiar with is Pinocchio.

In this craft project, children make their own marionette puppet. This project is best suited for second and third graders. Younger children will need adult assistance.

Figure 10.9   **Marionette Example**

Supplies

Scissors

Yarn

Large paper clips (eight per puppet)

Clear tape

Hole punch

Thick photocopier paper or posterboard

Colored markers

Unsharpened pencils or straws

Photocopy Figures 10.10 through 10.18 for each child. Older children can cut out the pieces. Using markers, the children can add details to the puppet pieces. Using a hole punch, children punch holes on the puppet pieces where marked on the pattern. Please note: The hole for the hat is punched after the hat is constructed. The next step is for the children to roll and tape the arms, legs, hats, and nose pieces. (For arm and leg pieces, roll the paper to form thin, lengthwise tubes; the upper arm and leg tubes will have a hole at each end; the lower arm and leg tubes will have one hole) With tape, attach the hands and feet to the long arm and leg tubes. Tape the head to the body. Tape the nose and hat to the face. Use large paper clips to connect the leg and arm pieces to each other and to the body. Tie a 30-inch piece of yarn to each end of an unsharpened pencil. With tape, attach the other ends of the yarn to the backs of the hands. Tie the 14-inch piece of yarn to the middle of this pencil, and tie the other end to the hole in the top of the hat.

   Note: The pencil and strings that control the puppet's arms are held in front of the pencil and strings that control its body and legs. (Refer to the "Marionette Example," Figure 10.9)

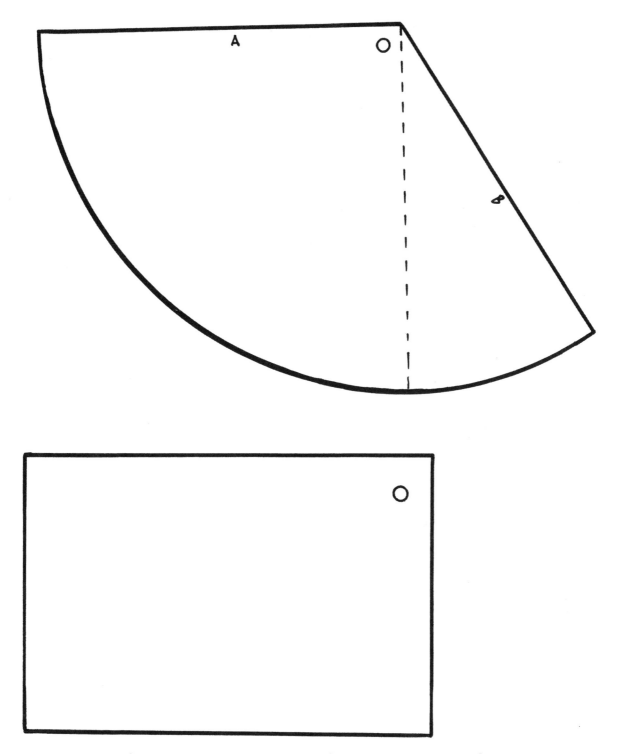

Figure 10.10 **Marionette Hat** Figure 10.11 **Marioneete Lower Arm and Lower Leg**

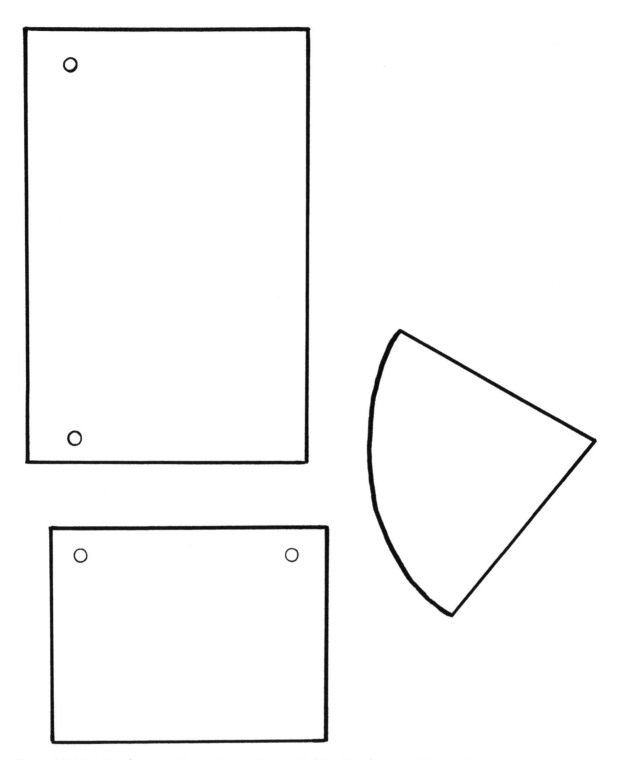

Figure 10.12 **Marionette Upper Leg** Figure 10.13 **Marionette Upper Arm**
Figure 10.14 **Marionette Nose**

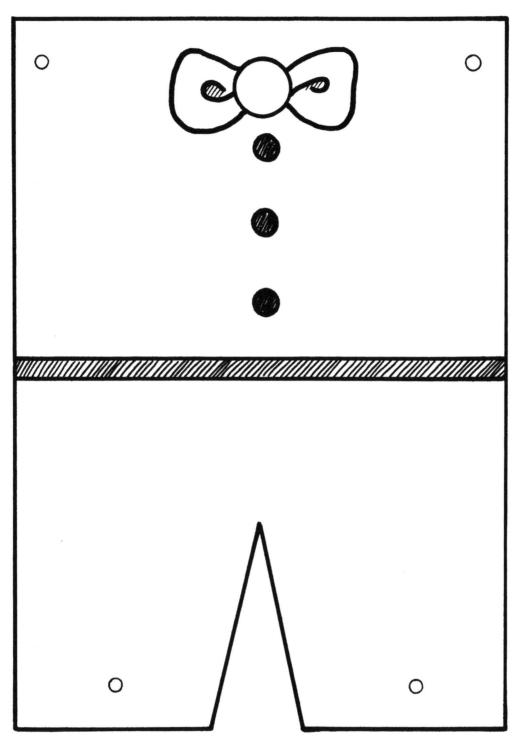

Figure 10.15 **Marionette Body**

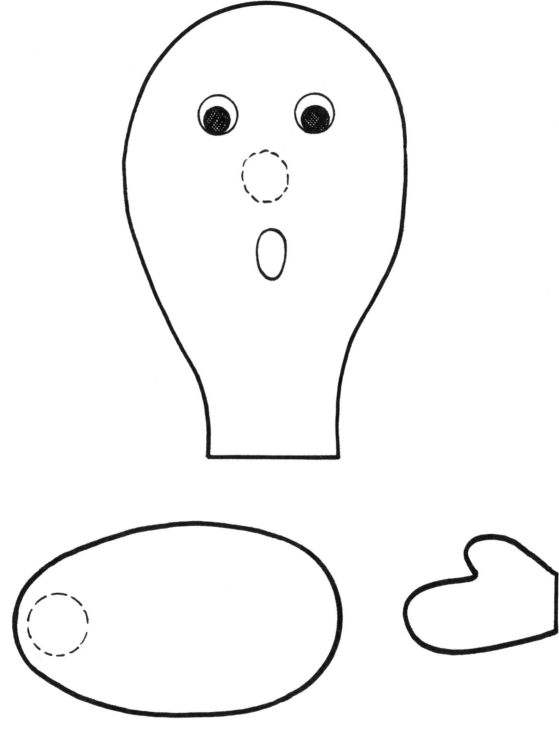

Figure 10.16 **Marionette Foot**   Figure 10.17 **Marionette Hand**
Figure 10.18 **Marionette Head**

Italian Mosaic Medallions

Mosaic designs are made using small pieces of stone, tile, or broken pottery. In Italy, this technique was used for decorative as well as practical purposes. Some mosaics were based on themes, such as hunting, athletic contests, or ocean life. This technique is still used in many places throughout the world.

In this craft project, children make a small mosaic medallion to wear as a necklace.

Supplies

Food coloring

White glue

Rice

Mixing bowl and spoon

Newspaper

Hole punch

Scissors

Posterboard

Cookie sheets

Ribbon or yarn

Before children make the medallions, an adult should prepare the rice. It takes a day or so for the rice to dry. Mix an amount of rice according to the number of children participating in the activity. For each child, use ¼ cup of rice; for every 2 cups of rice, use 5 drops of food coloring. Mix the rice and food coloring in a bowl. Pour the mixture onto a newspaper and let dry. Make several colors of rice (for preschool children, use two colors). After the rice is dry, place each color on a cookie sheet.

Photocopy Figures 10.19 and 10.20 on card stock for each child. There are two designs from which to choose: a butterfly and a flower. Cut out the medallion along the circular edge. Punch a hole at the top of the medallion. Give each child a small bottle of glue. Explain that they should add one color of rice at a time. After they fill the desired spaces with glue, they add one color of rice by sprinkling it onto the medallion. Then repeat the process, filling another space with glue and adding another color of rice.

It's best if an adult can demonstrate this process for children. After children have filled all the spaces with rice, let the medallions dry completely. Attach a length of ribbon or yarn and the medallions are ready to wear.

Figure 10.19 **Butterfly Mosaic Medallion**   Figure 10.20   **Flower Mosaic Medallion**

Sources for Craft Ideas and Activities

Castaldo, Nancy. *Pizza for the Queen.* Illustrated by Melisande Potter. New York: Holiday House, 2005. (32 pages).
  Read this story, which is based on the true history of the first pizza made by Raffaele Esposito for the queen. After reading the story, refer to the recipe for Margherita pizza and share this same pizza for the children to eat.

Wagner, Lisa. *Cool Italian Cooking: Fun and Tasty Recipes for Kids.* Edina, MN: ABDO Publishing, 2011. (pages 28–29).
  The recipe for Tangy Lemon Granita is on pages 28 and 29. One version requires cooking, but there is also a version that requires no cooking. This recipe is fun for kids because they can scrape the mixture with a fork after it is frozen to create the fluffy texture.

Chapter 11

Let's Visit

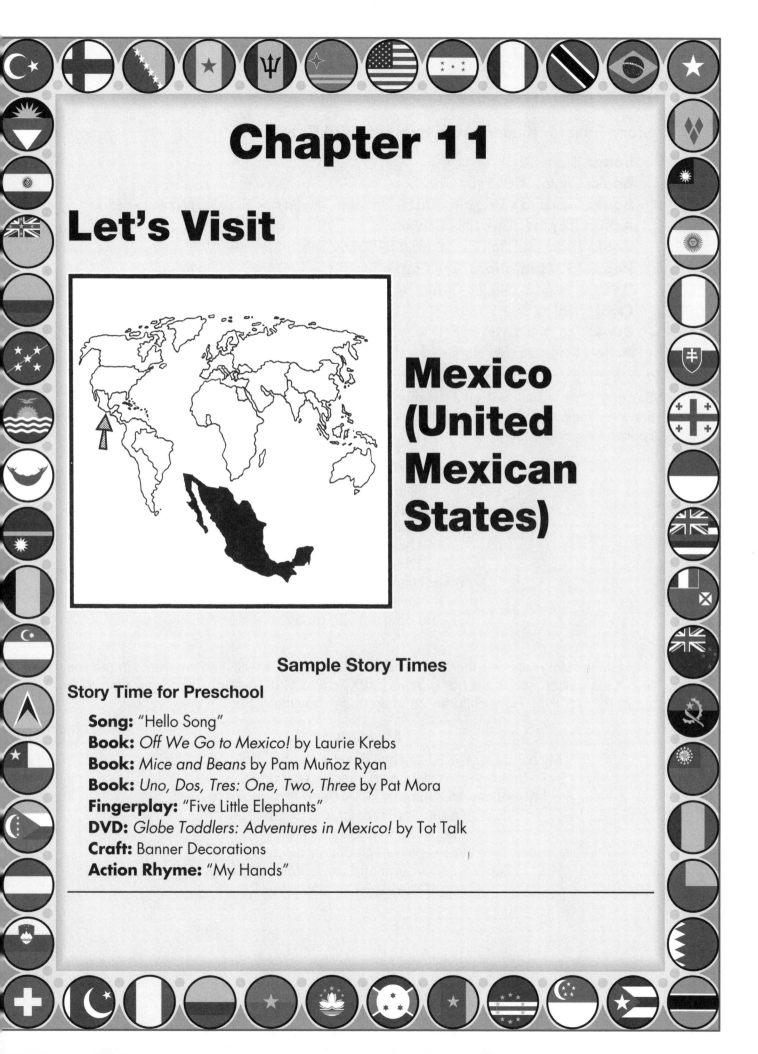

Mexico (United Mexican States)

Sample Story Times

Story Time for Preschool

Song: "Hello Song"
Book: *Off We Go to Mexico!* by Laurie Krebs
Book: *Mice and Beans* by Pam Muñoz Ryan
Book: *Uno, Dos, Tres: One, Two, Three* by Pat Mora
Fingerplay: "Five Little Elephants"
DVD: *Globe Toddlers: Adventures in Mexico!* by Tot Talk
Craft: Banner Decorations
Action Rhyme: "My Hands"

Story Time for Kindergarten through Third Grade

Song: "Hello Song"
Book: *Chato's Kitchen* by Gary Soto
Book: *Grandpa's Magic Tortilla* by Demetria Martin and Rosalee Montoya-Read
Action Rhyme: "Five Little Elephants"
Book: *Pedro and the Coyote* retold by Sandy Sepehri
Puppet Presentation: "The Coyote Scolds His Tail" by Dan Storm
DVD: *Borreguita and the Coyote* by Verna Aardema
Craft: Donkey Sack Piñata
Book: *The Piñata Maker: El Piñatero* by George Ancona
Action Rhyme: "My Hands"

Begin the story time with the "Hello Song." Then sing the song again, substituting the word *hello* with the Spanish greeting *hola* [OH-lah]. (Spanish is the primary language spoken in Mexico; see p. xxix for "Hello Song" music.)

Hello Song

Hello ev'rybody,
And how are you? How are you?
Hello ev'rybody,
And how are you today?
OH-la ev'rybody,
And how are you? How are you?
OH-la ev'rybody,
And how are you today?

End the story time with the "My Hands" action rhyme, substituting the words *thank you* with the Mexican words *muchas gracias* [MOO-chahs GRAH-see-ahs], and *goodbye* with *adiós* [ah-DYOHS]. Have children stand up and follow the actions in the rhyme.

My Hands

My hands say MOO-chahs GRAH-see-ahs. *(hold up hands)*
With a clap, clap, clap. *(clap hands)*
My feet say MOO-chahs GRAH-see-ahs. *(point to feet)*
With a tap, tap, tap. *(stamp or tap feet)*
Clap! Clap! Clap! *(clap hands)*
Tap! Tap! Tap! *(stamp or tap feet)*
Turn myself around and bow. *(turn and bow)*
ah-DYOHS. *(wave goodbye)*

Books to Read Aloud

Ancona, George. *The Piñata Maker: El Piñatero.* Lodi, NJ: Marco Book Co., 2009. (40 pages)
The story of Tio Rico, who for 15 years has created beautiful piñatas, puppets, and masks for the children of his village.

Blackstone, Stella. *My Granny Went to Market: A Round-the-World Counting Rhyme.* Illustrated by Christopher Corr. Cambridge, MA: Barefoot Books, 2005. (22 pages)
Granny flies around the world on a magic carpet to buy things from many different countries, including Mexico. This counting book has colorful, detailed pictures. The end pages show a color-coded map of all the places Granny visits.

Campoy, F. Isabel and Alma Flor Ada. *Celebrate Cinco de Mayo with the Mexican Hat Dance.* Illustrated by Marcela Gomez and David Silva. Doral, FL: Santillana USA Publishing Co., 2006. (31 pages)
Students learn the Mexican hat dance and have to try not to step on the hat. This story of Cinco de Mayo celebrations includes a special section about major holidays.

Cox, Judy. *Cinco de Mouse-O!* Illustrated by Jeffrey Ebbeler. New York, NY: Holiday House, 2010. (32 pages)
Mouse discovers a Mexican tradition when he follows his nose to the Cinco de Mayo celebration.

Dorros, Arthur. *Abuela.* Illustrated by Elisa Kleven. Bridgewater, NJ: Baker & Taylor, 2009. (40 pages)
Abuela tells Rosalba about moving to America from Mexico as they imagine they are flying over New York City.

Gollub, Matthew. *The Twenty-Five Mixtec Cats.* Illustrated by Leovigildo Martinez. Santa Rosa, CA: Tortuga Press, 2004. (27 pages)
The healer in this small village of Oaxaca, Mexico, plays an important role. His cats help save the town butcher to prove their worth to the villagers.

Kimmell, Eric A. *Cactus Soup.* Illustrated by Phil Huling. New York: Marshall Cavendish, 2004. (32 pages)
Set during the Mexican Revolution, soldiers stop at a village and make cactus soup from just one cactus thorn (a version of the "Stone Soup" folktale.)

Krebs, Laurie. *Off We Go to Mexico! An Adventure in the Sun.* Illustrated by Christopher Corr. Cambridge, MA: Barefoot Books, 2006. (32 pages)
Wonderful activities that take place in Mexico are described, along with an introduction of many Spanish-language vocabulary words.

Maldonado, Cristina Falcón. *1, 2, 3 Suddenly in Mexico: The Protective Jaguar.* Illustrated by Marta Fàbrega. Hauppauge, NY: Barron's Educational Series, 2011. (36 pages)
Martin's magic key transports him to Mexico, where he learns about some of the country's customs and traditions.

Meunier, Brian. *Bravo Tavo!* Illustrated by Perky Edgerton. New York, NY: Penguin Group, 2007. (32 pages)
Tavo and his father work together digging a trench to get rain to their corn crops. This story emphasizes overcoming adversity as well as the importance of a strong father-son relationship.

Mora, Pat. *Uno, Dos, Tres: One, Two, Three.* Illustrated by Barbara Lavalle. Bridgewater, NJ: Baker
    & Taylor, 2011. (48 pages)
    Set in a marketplace in Mexico, two sisters shop for their mother's birthday gift while counting
    in English and Spanish.
Ryan, Pam Muñoz. *Mice and Beans.* Illustrated by Joe Cepeda. St. Louis, MO: Turtleback Books,
    2005. (32 pages)
    Grandma Rosa Maria forgets to fill the piñata for Little Catalina's birthday party, but the
    helpful mice that live in her house save the day.
Sepehri, Sandy. *Pedro and the Coyote.* Illustrated by Brian Demeter. Vero Beach, FL: Rourke
    Publishing, 2006. (32 pages)
    Pedro teaches the tricky coyote a valuable lesson after he catches the coyote stealing chickens
    from the chicken coop.
Soto, Gary and Susan Guevara. *Chato's Kitchen.* Lodi, NJ: Marco Book Company, 2009.
    (32 pages)
    Chato, the cat, invites the mice over "for dinner" but is surprised when they bring their own
    guest along with them. Many authentic Mexican dishes are described while Chato is prepar-
    ing the meal.

Storytelling

"The Coyote Scolds His Tail" Puppet Presentation

Storm, Dan. "The Coyote Scolds His Tail." In *Picture Tales from Mexico.* Illustrated by Mark
Storm. Houston, TX: Gulf, 1995. (pages 65–71)

Coyote is a trickster figure from the old lore of many Indian tribes in North America.
Don Coyote is a favorite trickster in Mexican tales. Coyote is known for his capacity to
perform utterly silly acts, as children will see in this puppet presentation.

Use Figures 11.1 through 11.5 to make the body parts for the Coyote hand puppet.
Make a simple cloth or felt hand puppet for the body (see Figure 11.6). The puppet is introduced when Coyote enters the cave. Make the cave using a piece of black felt attached to
round embroidery hoops; cut an X into the corner of the felt to allow the puppet through
(Figure 11.7).

The body parts of Coyote—the feet, ears, eyes, and tail—are attached as they
are introduced in the story. Sew or glue pieces of Velcro to the body parts and to the hand
puppet in the proper places. Attach the nose before beginning the presentation.

"The Coyote Scolds His Tail" by Dan Storm

Señor Coyote had escaped from many different kinds of animals so many times that he must
have begun to think that nothing on two feet or wings could catch him. One day he was
walking along the level valley, between two mountains, when two large dogs, that had
been trying to catch him for a long time, sprang from behind a large stone and almost
caught him before he could jump and run.

Coyote tried to run to the woods, but the dogs had seen to it that he would have to take
to the open country. As he ran around bushes and jumped over rocks and across dry
arroyos, making the dust fly, he thought that he was gaining on the dogs behind. Their

Figure 11.1 **Coyote Tail** Figure 11.2 **Coyote Nose** Figure 11.3 **Coyote Eyes** Figure 11.4 **Coyote Ears** Figure 11.5 **Coyote Feet** Figure 11.6 **Hand Puppet Example**

From *Travel the Globe: Story Times, Activities, and Crafts for Children, Second Edition* by Desiree Webber, Dee Ann Corn, Elaine Harrod, Sandy Shropshire, Shereen Rasor, and Donna Norvell (in memoriam). Santa Barbara, CA: Libraries Unlimited. Copyright © 2013.

yelps of "YO! YO! YO!" were getting a little fainter, he thought as he gasped for his breath and began looking around for the best direction to go.

But while he was trying to make up his mind, two other large, red-and-whited-spotted dogs rose up out of nowhere and made up his mind for him. He was forced to turn back more or less toward the direction he had come. The dogs had planned to take turns racing him back and forth across the desert till he was too tired to go any further. The new pair of dogs were cutting down the distance between themselves and Coyote in a way that made Coyote know he must think fast and act much faster.

Up on the side of the mountain he saw something dark and round that made him take heart. He wished that it were closer. It was a cave that he saw. And now the first pair of dogs had run over slowly and were coming up somewhat rested to join their comrades in the chase.

Figure 11.7　**Coyote Puppet Embroidery-Hoop Cave Example**

He made a sharp turn and raced for the foot of the mountain. Behind him now came all four dogs louder and closer as he reached the mountainside and bolted up toward the cave. The dogs were so close behind him that he could feel their breath upon him as they argued loudly as to which one of them was to get him. He saw the cave close in front of him and a new idea suddenly sent a chill of fear through his body. Was the cave big enough to allow the dogs to enter? Then what? While this cheerless thought haunted his mind, the dogs were now snapping hairs out of the end of the Coyote's tail, *clip-klop, snip-snap.* And with a flying dive, the Coyote sailed into the mouth of the cave. (*hold up "cave" with the left hand—have coyote on the right hand—have coyote puppet enter the cave*)

It was lucky for him that the cave would not allow the dogs to enter. It was barely large enough to let him in. Inside the cave he ran as far back as he could. Outside, the dogs complained and whined and pawed around the cave a while and then he heard no more.

This was easily the worst fright the Coyote ever had; but once safe inside the cave, he began to feel brave again. He began to think he was quite a fellow to be able to get rid of the dogs. As his weary limbs became rested, a desire to boast and brag stole over him. There was no one in the cave to talk to, so he began chatting with the various parts of his body which had had some part in the race against the dogs. (*attach feet*)

"Patos," he said, looking at his four feet one at a time, "what did you do?"

"We carried you away," said the feet. "We kicked up dust to blind the bad dogs. We jumped the rocks, and bushes and brought you here."

"Bueno, bueno," said the Coyote, "good, fine. You feet did very well." Then he spoke to his ears. (*attach ears*)

"Ears, what did you do?"

"We listened to the right and to the left. We listened behind to see how far behind the dogs were, so that the Feet would know how fast to run." (*attach eyes*)

"Splendid!" said the Coyote. "And Eyes, what did you do?"

"We pointed out the road through the rocks and brush and canyons. We were on the lookout for your safety. We saw this cave."

"Marvelous!" said the Coyote with a great laugh. "What a great fellow I am to have such fine eyes, feet, and ears." And so overcome was Coyote with his own self and the great things he had done in his life that he reached over his shoulder to pat himself on the back. And it was then that he saw his tail back there. *(attach tail)*

"Aha, my tail," he said, "I had almost forgotten about you. Come, tell me what you did in this battle with the dogs."

The tail could tell by the tone of Coyote's voice that he did not think too highly of him and so he did not answer.

"About all you did was add extra load," said Coyote. "You held me back, more than anything else. Almost got me caught, too. You let the dogs grab the end of you. But let's hear from you. Speak up!"

"What did I do?" asked the tail. "I motioned to the dogs, like this, telling them to come and get you. While you were running I was back there urging the dogs to come on. Through the dust they could see my whiteness waving." The Coyote's scowl was becoming darker and darker.

"Silencio!" he shouted, stuttering and stammering with anger. "What do you mean?" and he reached back and gave a slap at his tail, and then reached around and bit at it.

"You do not belong here in this cave with the rest of us, you traitor." And Coyote was backing his tail toward the door of the cave. "Out you go," he said. "Outside! There is no room in here for you. You belong outside. You are on the side of the dogs. You tried to help them catch me, and then you brag about it. Outside!"

And Coyote pointed to his tail with one hand, and to the round piece of daylight which was the cave door, he pointed with the other hand. "Get Out!" *(back the coyote puppet out of the cave)*

And the Coyote backed his tail out the door into the open air. The dogs, who had been listening to the talk inside, were waiting hidden outside. When Coyote's tail appeared outside the cave door, the dogs grabbed it. Of course Coyote was jerked out of the cave with his tail. And what the dogs did to him is another story.

Sources for Flannel Board and Audience Participation

Climo, Shirley. *The Little Red Ant and the Great Big Crumb: A Mexican Fable.* Illustrated by Francisco Mora. Boston, MA: Houghton Mifflin Harcourt Trade & Reference Publishers, 2004. (40 pages)
Ant thinks she lacks the strength to move a cake crumb, so she enlists the help of other animals. She finds, however, that she already possesses all the strength she needs.

Sierra, Judy. "The Rattlesnake, the Mouse and the Coyote." In *The Flannel Board Storytelling Book.* 2ⁿᵈ ed. Bronx, NY: H.W. Wilson, 1997. (pages 213–216)
Coyote helps the mouse to outsmart the rattlesnake and saves his life.

Sources for Oral Stories

Climo, Shirley. "The First Monkeys: A Myth from Mexico." In *Monkey Business: Stories from around the World.* Illustrated by Erik Brooks. New York, NY: Henry Holt and Company, 2005. (pages 39–42)
An ancient Mayan myth of how the first stick people became the first monkeys.

Madrigal, Antonio Hernandez. *The Eagle and the Rainbow: Timeless Tales from Mexico*. Illustrated by Tomie dePaola. Golden, CO: Fulcrum Publishing, 2010. (64 pages)
A selection of five legends, one from each of the five indigenous cultures of Mexico. Recommended for school-age children.

Philip, Neil. *Horse Hooves and Chicken Feet: Mexican Folktales*. Illustrated by Jacqueline Mair. Boston, MA: Houghton Mifflin Harcourt Trade & Reference Publishers, 2003. (84 pages)
Fifteen traditional Mexican folktales with classical themes and fairytale elements.

Pirotta, Saviour. "Red Ant, Black Ant: A Story from Mexico" In *Around the World in 80 Tales*. Illustrated by Richard Johnson. Boston, MA: Kingfisher, 2007. (pages 30–31)
The little red ant shows Quetzalcoatl the secret of the mountain, and he takes the seeds to show the humans how to grow corn.

Fingerplays, Songs, Action Rhymes, and Games

"Five Little Elephants" Fingerplay

To make the finger puppets, photocopy Figures 11.8 and 11.9 on white tagboard or construction paper. Use markers to color the elephants and their hats. Laminate and cut out the elephants and finger attachments. Tape together the three flaps of each finger attachment. This will fit over the tip of each finger like a thimble. Tape an elephant to each attachment. Place a puppet on your finger as each elephant is introduced in the rhyme. Substitute the Spanish numbers one through five, and Spanish names for the elephants (Pancho, Pedro, Juan, Maria, and Lolita), when sharing the rhyme.

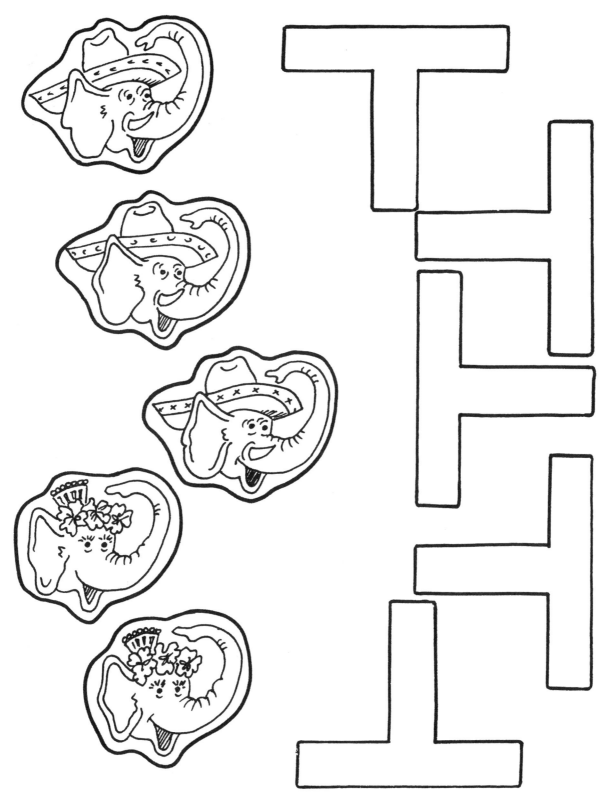

Figure 11.8 **Elephant Finger Puppets**   Figure 11.9 **Finger Puppet Attachments**

Optional: Outline a web with glue in the palm of your hand and then sprinkle on silver glitter to make it sparkle. See Figure 11.10 for a pattern.

1. *uno* [OO-noh]
2. *dos* [DOHS]
3. *tres* [TREHS]
4. *cuatro* [KWAH-tro]
5. *cinco* [SEEN-koh]

Figure 11.10 **Spider Web Example**

Five Little Elephants by Donna Norvell

One (*uno*) little elephant (Pancho) went out to
balance on a spider's web one day. *(show one puppet)*
The web seemed so strong, he called for his friend
(Pedro) to come along and play.
Two (*dos*) little elephants (Pancho and Pedro) went out
to balance on a spider's web one day.
(show two puppets)
The web seemed so strong, they called for their
friend (Juan) to come along and play.
Three (*tres*) little elephants (Pancho, Pedro, and Juan)
went out to balance on a spider's
web one day. *(show three puppets)*
The web seemed so strong, they called for their
friend (Maria) to come along and play.
Four (*cuatro*) little elephants (Pancho, Pedro, Juan, and Maria)
went out to balance on a spider's web one day. *(show four puppets)*
The web seemed so strong they called for their friend (Lolita)
to come along and play. *(show five puppets)*
The spider web swings, and the spider web sways.
Snap! went the spider web, and blew away.
Five (*cinco*) little elephants can no longer play on the spider
web today. *(remove puppets)*

Sources for Fingerplays, Songs, Action Rhymes, and Games

Barbarash, Lorriane. *Multicultural Games.* Champaign, IL: Human Kinetics, 1997.
Older children will enjoy choosing partners to play "Bolan Maldecida" (poison ball), found on page 66.

Stewart, Georgiana. "Hola Amigos" In *Multicultural Bean Bag Fun.* Long Branch, NJ: Kimbo Educational, 2009. Compact disc and guide.

The movement concepts of high, low, shake, and twirl are covered in this song, which features Mexican mariachi music and the celebration of Cinco de Mayo.

Stewart, Georgiana. "La Cucaracha." In *Multicultural Rhythm Stick Fun*. Long Branch, NJ: Kimbo Educational, 1992. Compact disc.
    Children shake sticks to the left and to the right while counting in Spanish.

Media Choices

Show a DVD or downloadable movie as a transition between storytelling activities and crafts.

Aardema, Verna. *Borreguita and the Coyote*. Lincoln, NE: Reading Rainbow, 2003. DVD, 30 min.
    A charming retelling of a Mexican folktale in which a little lamb uses her wits to gain the upper hand and outsmart a hungry coyote.

Countries around the World: Mexico. Wynnewood, PA: Schlessinger Media, 2007. DVD, 13 min. Available digitally on Safari Montage.
    Children are given a tour of Mexico City and take in some of the capital's most famous sites. Audience also listens to a mariachi band play the traditional folksong "La Cucaracha."

Globe Toddlers: Adventures in Mexico! Tot Talk, 2008. DVD, 39 min. Available as an MP3 download.
    Young children will enjoy the musical rhythms. Presentation uses a combination of both animation and live scenes featuring children and puppets.

Crafts and Other Activities

Choose a craft suited for the age level of the group and the time allotted for the story time.

Fiestas

Fiestas (celebrations) are observed daily throughout Mexico. Individual towns and villages have fiestas to celebrate their patron saint or to celebrate national and civic holidays. People dress in colorful traditional costumes, dance, enjoy lively music, have parades, and enjoy lots of spicy food. Rodeos, bullfights, and fireworks are common events in most fiestas.

Donkey Sack Piñata

An important part of Mexican fiestas is the piñata, a decorated container filled with candy, gum, sweets, and small toys. Traditionally, the breaking of the piñata goes back almost 400 years to the time when the Spaniards came to Mexico. The stick used to break the piñata is called "the stick of goodness." Symbolically, when the piñata is broken, the love of worldly goods is destroyed and blessings are showered upon the one who breaks the piñata and also upon those who are celebrating.

    In this craft project, children make their own piñatas. For more information about piñatas, share the book *The Piñata Maker: El Piñatero* by George Ancona (Lodi, NJ: Marco Book Company, 2009) (see "Books to Read Aloud").

Supplies

Lunch-size paper bags	Glue sticks
Colored tissue paper	Colored markers
Wrapped pieces of candy (optional)	Stapler
	Hole punch
Brown tagboard	Scissors
Twine, heavy yarn, or macramé cord	

Figure 11.11   **Paper Bag Donkey Piñata Example**

Photocopy Figures 11.13 and 11.14 on brown tagboard and cut out the patterns (precut for younger children). Children can stuff a paper bag about two-thirds full of tissue paper and add candy. Fold the top of the bag two times and staple. Punch a hole in the center of the fold. Tie a loop of twine or heavy yarn through the hole to make a hanger (see Figure 11.11). Cut some of the tissue paper into 1-inch strips and cut to make a fringe (cut every inch). Glue the strips of tissue paper around the bag, starting at the bottom and overlapping the fringe towards the top of the bag. (For younger children, precut the fringed pieces of tissue paper.) Glue the head and legs to the bag and make a tail of yarn or macramé cord.

Banner Decorations

Banners are hung in the areas where a fiesta is to be held. In this craft project, children make simple banner decorations.

Supplies

Brightly colored pieces of 18- by 24-inch tissue paper	Scissors
	Tape
	Heavy yarn

Figure 11.12   **Fiesta Banners Example**

Fold a piece of the tissue paper in half four or five times. (The pattern becomes more elaborate each time the paper is folded. However, too many folds will make the paper more difficult to cut for younger children.) Cut out small pieces (designs) around the folded edges (See Figure 11.12). Carefully unfold the paper, tape it to heavy yarn, and hang it in the room.

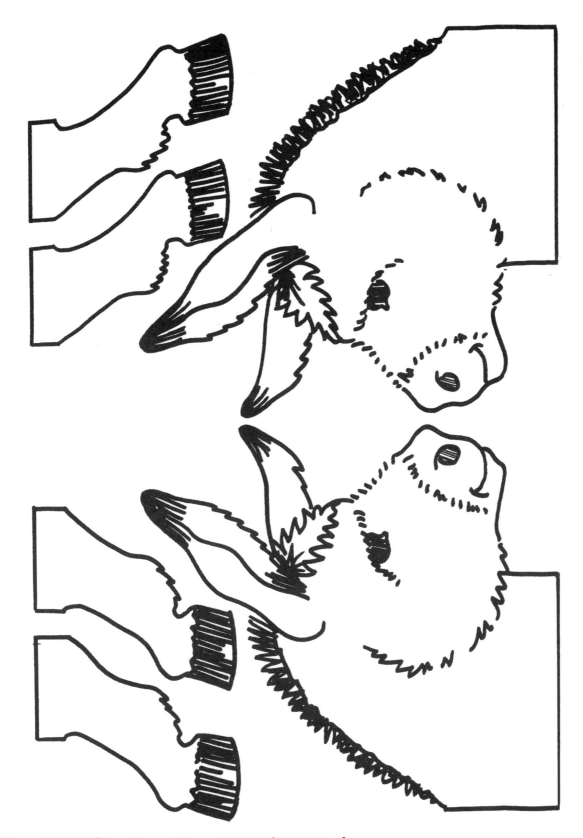

Figure 11.13 **Piñata Legs**   Figure 11.14 **Piñata Head**

Mexican Hat Dance

Clear a space in the room and place a sombrero on the floor for children to dance around. Alternating feet, children jump, putting one heel forward and then the other. When the music changes, children join hands and move toward the sombrero with their hands raised, then lower their hands as they move back. Repeat until the music ends. Suggested music: "Hola Amigos," from the CD *Multicultural Bean Bag Fun* (see "Sources for Fingerplays, Songs, Action Rhymes, and Games").

Sources for Craft Ideas and Activities

McGill, Jordan. *Cinco de Mayo.* New York, NY: Weigl Publishers, 2011. (24 pages)
   Includes arts, crafts, and music activities.

Michaels, Alexandra. *The Kids' Multicultural Art Book.* Nashville, TN: Williamson Books, 2007. (157 pages)
   Activities include a section titled "Hispanics: Mexico and Central America" on pages 46 through 66.

Nicholson, Sue. *World Art.* Laguna Hills, CA: QEB Publishing, 2005. (32 pages)
   Create amazing art from felt, foam, and feathers. "Mexican Metapec Sun" is on pages 22 and 23.

Speechley, Greta. "Mexican Armadillo." In *Creative Crafts for Kids Crafts: World Crafts.* New York: Gareth Stevens Publishing, 2010. (pages 20–21)
   Kids can make and paint an armadillo with a wobbling head using air-drying clay.

Wagner, Lisa. *Cool Mexican Cooking: Fun and Tasty Recipes for Kids.* Minneapolis, MN: ABDO Publishing Company, 2011. (32 pages)
   This book provides easy Mexican food cooking activities for children.

Chapter 12

Let's Visit

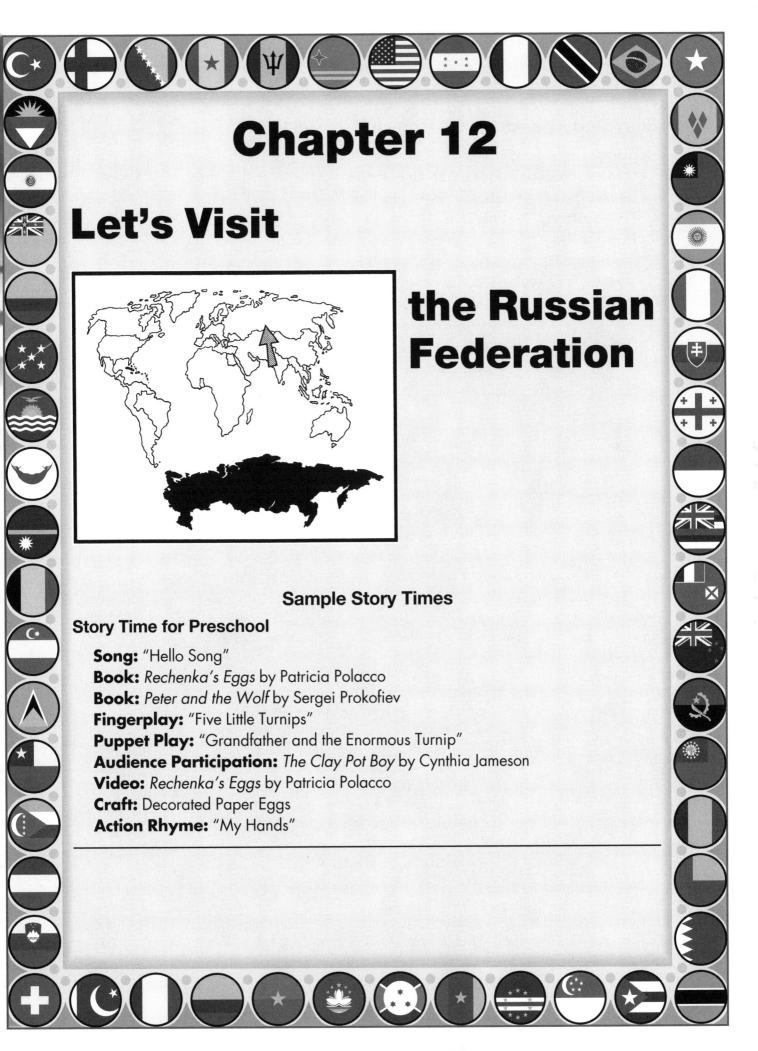

the Russian Federation

Sample Story Times

Story Time for Preschool

Song: "Hello Song"
Book: *Rechenka's Eggs* by Patricia Polacco
Book: *Peter and the Wolf* by Sergei Prokofiev
Fingerplay: "Five Little Turnips"
Puppet Play: "Grandfather and the Enormous Turnip"
Audience Participation: *The Clay Pot Boy* by Cynthia Jameson
Video: *Rechenka's Eggs* by Patricia Polacco
Craft: Decorated Paper Eggs
Action Rhyme: "My Hands"

Story Time for Kindergarten through Third Grade

Song: "Hello Song"
Book: *Babushka's Doll* by Patricia Polacco
Book: *The Magic Babushka* by Phyllis Tildes
Fingerplay: "Five Little Turnips"
Puppet Play: "Grandfather and the Enormous Turnip"
Audience Participation: *The Clay Pot Boy* by Cynthia Jameson
Video: *The Keeping Quilt* by Patricia Polacco
Craft: Matryoshka Dolls (Stacking Dolls)

Begin the story time with the "Hello Song." Then sing the song again, substituting the word *hello* with the Russian greeting pronounced "ZDRA-hst-voo-yti." (See p. xxix for "Hello Song" music.)

Hello Song

Hello ev'rybody
And how are you? How are you?
Hello ev'rybody,
And how are you today?
ZDRA-hst-voo-yti ev'rybody,
And how are you? How are you?
ZDRA-hst-voo-yti ev'rybody, and how are you today?

End the story time with the "My Hands" action rhyme, substituting the words *thank you* with the Russian word pronounced "spa-si-ba," and *goodbye* pronounced "DAS-fidá-hniya." Have children stand up and follow the actions in the rhyme.

My Hands

My hands say spa-si-ba. *(hold up hands)*
With a clap, clap, clap. *(clap hands)*
My feet say spa-si-ba. *(point to feet)*
With a tap, tap, tap. *(stamp or tap feet)*
Clap! Clap! Clap! *(clap hands)*
Tap! Tap! Tap! *(stamp or tap feet)*
Turn myself around and bow. *(turn and bow)*
DAS-fidá-hniya. *(wave goodbye)*

Books to Read Aloud

Buyske, Gail. *How the Russian Snow Maiden Helped Santa Claus*. Illustrated by Natasha Voronina. Vernissage Press, 2005. (32 pages)
A Christmas tale with a valuable lesson to be yourself and do the best you can. Includes an introduction to Russian folk characters, traditions, and a few easy Russian words with a pronunciation guide.

Frost, Helen. *A Look at Russia*. Mankato, MN: Capstone Press, 2002. (24 pages)
   A beginning reading nonfiction title with many interesting facts about Russia.

Kabakov, Vladimir. *R is for Russia*. Photographs by Prodeepta Das. London, UK: Frances Lincoln
   Children's Books, 2011. (24 pages)
   Each letter of the alphabet represents something from or about Russia.

Muth, Jon J. *The Three Questions*. New York: Scholastic, 2002. (32 pages)
   Based on a story by Leo Tolstoy of a young boy asking important questions about life.

Polacco, Patricia. *The Keeping Quilt*. Logan, IA: Perfection Learning Corporation, 2007.
   (32 pages)
   A homemade quilt ties together four generations of an immigrant Jewish family from Russia.

Polacco, Patricia. *Luba and the Wren*. New York: Penguin Group, 2002. (40 pages)
   A Russian version of "The Fisherman and His Wife" where a young girl finds a frightened wren
   that promises to grant her wishes, but her parents' greed cannot be satisfied as each wish
   increases in size.

Polacco, Patricia. *Rechenka's Eggs*. New York: Learning Links, 2002. (32 pages)
   Babushka becomes very attached to the injured goose she rescues and cares for. When the
   goose, named Rechenka, joins her own kind, she leaves behind a miracle egg.

Polacco, Patricia. *Thunder Cake*. Lodi, NJ: Marco Book Company, 2009. (32 pages)
   Babushka (Grandmother) helps her granddaughter overcome her fear of thunderstorms.

Polacco, Patricia. *Uncle Vova's Tree*. New York: Penguin Group, 2009. (32 pages)
   Many traditions are celebrated in a Midwestern home during the Russian Orthodox holiday of
   Epiphany.

Prokofiev, Sergei. *Peter and the Wolf*. Retold and illustrated by Chris Raschka. New York: Simon &
   Schuster Children's Publishing, 2008. (40 pages)
   An artistic interpretation of Sergei Prokofiev's *Peter and the Wolf*, best read after the original
   story like the ones written by Vladimir Vagin or Janet Schulman.

Prokofiev, Sergei. *Peter and the Wolf*. Retold and illustrated by Vladimir Vagin. New York:
   Scholastic Press, 2000. (26 pages)
   A beautifully illustrated version of the classic *Peter and the Wolf* story from the symphony by
   Sergei Prokofiev.

Prokofiev, Sergei. *Sergei Prokofiev's Peter and the Wolf*. Retold by Janet Schulman, Illustrated by
   Peter Malone. New York: Random House, 2004. (32 pages plus compact disc)
   The classic Russian version of *Peter and the Wolf* with a fully orchestrated and narrated com-
   pact disc, which includes the story and music by Sergei Prokofiev. *Peter and the Wolf* is a musi-
   cal fairytale in which each character is played by a different instrument of the orchestra.
   (Length of full story on compact disc is 23 min.)

Shepard, Aaron. *The Sea King's Daughter: A Russian Legend*, 15th Anniversary Edition. Illustrated
   by Gennady Spirin. Friday Harbor, WA: Shepard Publications, 2011. (36 pages)
   A poor musician named Sadko is invited to play at the Sea King's underwater palace.

Spirin, Gennady. *The Tale of the Firebird*. Translated and illustrated by Tatiana Popova. New York:
   Penguin Group, 2002. (32 pages)
   Ivan Tsarevitch, the youngest son of the tsar, goes in search of the beautiful and amazing Firebird. He must confront a wicked Baba Yaga to rescue an enchanted princess from Koshchei
   the Immortal.

Yolen, Jane. *Firebird*. Illustrated by Vladimir Vagin. New York: Harper Collins Publishers, 2002.
   (32 pages)

Prince Ivan saves the princess and her nine maidens from the evil wizard, Koshchei the Deathless, with help from the Firebird.

Ziefert, Harriet. *The Snow Child*. Illustrated by Julia Zanes. New York: Penguin Group, 2000. (32 pages)
An old, childless Russian couple builds a little girl out of snow to bring them happiness, but she can only stay when the weather is cold.

Stories about Baba Yaga, a Russian Witch

Lurie, Alison. *Baba Yaga and the Stolen Baby*. Illustrated by Jessica Souhami. London, UK: Frances Lincoln Limited, 2008. (32 pages)
The forest animals give Elena what she needs to help rescue her baby brother from Baba Yaga.

Yolen, Jane. *The Flying Witch*. Illustrated by Vladimir Vagin. New York: Harper Collins Publishers, 2003. (40 pages)
The famed Russian witch flies all over the countryside searching for plump children to put in her thin, watery stew. Then she gets outsmarted by a feisty young girl who falls off her father's turnip truck.

Stories about Babushka and Matryoshka Dolls

Bliss, Corinne Demas. *The Littlest Matryoshka*. Illustrated by Kathryn Brown. New York: Hyperion Press, 1999. (32 pages)
Nina, the smallest of her group of *matryoshkas*, or Russian nesting dolls, is separated from her sisters and ends up on a dangerous journey.

Horn, Sandra A. *Babushka*. Illustrated by Cinzia Ratto. Cambridge, MA: Barefoot Books, 2002. (32 pages)
Babushka journeys to find a special baby and learns that the more you give, the more you will receive.

Ogburn, Jacqueline K. *The Magic Nesting Doll*. Illustrated by Laurel Long. New York: Penguin Group, 2000. (32 pages)
Katya's grandmother gives her a magic matryoshka that she may only use three times. Katya finds she needs it most to save the prince and his land.

Polacco, Patricia. *Babushka's Doll*. Boston, MA: Houghton Mifflin Harcourt School Publishers, 1999. (32 pages)
Natasha plays with her grandmother's babushka doll while grandmother is shopping. The doll comes to life—and it is even more rambunctious than Natasha.

Polacco, Patricia. *Babushka's Mother Goose*. New York: Penguin Group, 2000. (64 pages)
Russian characters and scenes are shared in traditional rhymes. The poem "Matroishka" is included.

Tildes, Phyllis Limbacher. *The Magic Babushka*. Watertown, MA: Charlesbridge Publishing, 2009. (32 pages)
When Nadia rescues a magical old woman, she is rewarded with a handkerchief that makes her designs for the colorful patterned eggs called pysanky become possible.

Storytelling

"Grandfather and the Enormous Turnip" Puppet Presentation

"Grandfather and the Enormous Turnip" is a retelling of a well-known Russian folktale about a giant turnip. Use Figures 12.1 through 12.7 to make the figures for the puppet

Figure 12.1 **Mouse** Figure 12.2 **Cat** Figure 12.3 **Dog** Figure 12.4 **Granddaughter**

Figure 12.5 **Grandmother**   Figure 12.6   **Grandfather**

Figure 12.7 **Giant Turnip**

play. Photocopy the patterns on white card stock and color them with bright oranges, reds, and yellows, in the old Russian tradition. Cut them out and attach paint sticks to the backs.

The storyteller might have children from the group hold the stick puppets, or the storyteller might hold the puppets while telling the story. For larger groups, enlarge the puppet patterns for better visibility. Introduce the play by showing children a real turnip. Ask, "Has anyone ever eaten a turnip? Can you tell us what it tastes like?" Then tell children, "I know a Russian grandfather who loved to grow turnips. He had a problem, though—sometimes they grew too big!"

The following Russian words are used for the characters in the play. Introduce the words to children as the story is told:

grandfather	*diadushka*	[DYEH-doosh-kah]
grandmother	*babushka*	[BAH-bush-kah]
granddaughter	*dyevachka*	[DYE-VUS-kah]
dog	*sobaka*	[sah-BAH-kah]
cat	*kot*	[KAWT]
mouse	*mwishka*	[mwihsh-kah]

"Grandfather and the Enormous Turnip" retold by Donna Norvell

Out in his garden, Grandfather (Diadushka) spent a lot of time growing vegetables: green cabbages, cucumbers, peas, carrots, onions, beets, and potatoes. Of all the vegetables he grew, however, his favorite was the turnip. *(hold up the grandfather puppet)* From tiny seeds, the vegetables grew and grew. Grandfather (Diadushka) was anxious to harvest them and make a fine stew. Then one day he saw an incredible sight. One turnip had grown to a wondrous height, and its leafy top rose high into the sky.

Grandfather (Diadushka) pulled and pulled and then gave a great sigh. Help was needed, so he called for Grandmother (Babushka) to come quick and see this strange sight—an enormous turnip holding tight. *(hold up the grandmother puppet)* Grandmother (Babushka) grabbed Grandfather (Diadushka) by his belt, and they pulled and pulled, while chanting (children may chant the verse with the storyteller):

> "Pull and tug as hard as you can.
> This turnip is as stubborn as stubborn can be.
> But so are we, so are we!"

But the enormous turnip held on tight.

However, Grandmother (Babushka) was not ready to give up the fight. She called for Granddaughter (Dyevachka) to come quick and see this strange sight—an enormous turnip holding tight. *(hold up the granddaughter puppet)* Granddaughter (Dyevachka) grabbed

Grandmother (Babushka) by her waist, Grandmother (Babushka) grabbed Grandfather (Diadushka) by the belt, and they pulled and pulled while chanting:

[repeat verse]

But the enormous turnip held on tight.

However, Granddaughter (Dyevachka) was not ready to give up the fight. She called for Dog (Sobaka) to come quick and see this strange sight—an enormous turnip holding tight. *(hold up the dog puppet)* Dog (Sobaka) grabbed Granddaughter (Duevachka) by her skirt. Granddaughter (Dyevachka) grabbed Grandmother (Babushka) by her waist. Grandmother (Babushka) grabbed Grandfather (Diadushka) by his belt, and they pulled and pulled while chanting:

[repeat verse]

But the enormous turnip held on tight.

However, Dog (Sobaka) was not ready to give up the fight. He called for Cat (Kot) to come quick and see this strange sight—an enormous turnip holding tight. *(hold up the cat puppet)* Cat (Kot) grabbed Dog (Sobaka) by his tail, Dog (Sobaka) grabbed Granddaughter (Dyevachka) by her skirt, Granddaughter (Dyevachka) grabbed Grandmother (Babushka) by her waist, Grandmother (Babushka) grabbed Grandfather (Diadushka) by his belt, and they pulled and pulled while chanting:

[repeat verse]

But the enormous turnip held on tight.

However, Cat (Kot) was not ready to give up the fight. He called for Mouse (Mwishka) to come quick and see this strange sight—an enormous turnip holding tight. *(hold up the mouse puppet)* Mouse (Mwishka) grabbed Cat (Kot) by his back paw, Cat (Kot) grabbed Dog (Sobaka) by his tail, Dog (Sobaka) grabbed Granddaughter (Dyevachka) by her skirt, Granddaughter (Dyevachka) grabbed Grandmother (Babushka) by her waist, Grandmother (Babushka) grabbed Grandfather (Diadushka) by his belt, and they pulled and pulled while chanting:

[repeat verse]

Then, much to their surprise, the enormous turnip no longer held on tight. It was lying there, in plain sight. *(hold up the giant turnip puppet)* They had won the final fight!

Other Versions of the Story "The Turnip"

Fearnley, Jan. *Mr. Wolf and the Enormous Turnip.* London, UK: Egmont Books Limited, 2005. (40 pages)
> Mr. Wolf needs help pulling the enormous turnip he found so he can make spicy turnip stew.

Sierra, Judy. *The Flannel Board Storytelling Book.* 2nd ed. New York: H.W. Wilson, 1997.
> "The Turnip: A Russian Folktale" is a good audience participation version of "The Turnip" story with a repetitive "Fee, fie, foe, fout, this turnip won't come out!" Story and pictures are on pages 123 through 127.

Tolstoy, Aleksei. *The Gigantic Turnip.* Illustrated by Niamh Sharkey. Cambridge, MA: Barefoot Books Inc., 2009. (40 pages)
> The little mouse makes all the difference in pulling up a gigantic turnip so everyone can enjoy a hearty turnip supper.

Zunshine, Tatiana. *A Little Story about a Big Turnip.* Illustrated by Evgeny Antonenkov. Colombus, OH: Pumpkin House Limited, 2004. (32 pages)

An adaptation of a Russian children's folktale about a family that must work together to help the grandfather pull the turnip from his garden.

"The Clay Pot Boy" Audience Participation Story

Jameson, Cynthia. *The Clay Pot Boy*. Illustrated by Arnold Lobel. New York: Coward, McCann & Geoghegan, 1973. (64 pages)

This story is about an old man and woman who never had any children. They make a clay pot in the shape of a boy. When they remove him from the oven, he begins asking for things to eat. He eats a number of characters whole before a billy goat saves the day.

This story is appropriate for audience participation. The storyteller narrates the story while playing the part of the Clay Pot Boy. Children selected from the audience play the characters that are swallowed whole by the Clay Pot Boy.

To give a visual appearance of swallowing characters, the storyteller wears a floor-length robe constructed of two sheets sewn together. As the Clay Pot Boy swallows the story's characters, the children duck through the opening and underneath the sheets. As more characters enter through the opening, the larger the Clay Pot Boy grows—with hilarious results. In the end, the billy goat bumps the Clay Pot Boy and all the characters tumble out through the side slit.

To create the robe, sew two full-size sheets together at the top. Leave an opening in the middle for the head. For the best results, sew in elastic or a drawstring at the neck. This will gather the material around the neck and shoulders, making it easier for the storyteller to move about. The robe should be long enough to reach the floor. Next, sew along one side, leaving an opening for the hand and arm to come through. The other side is left open.

Using colored construction paper, make a replica of the Clay Pot Boy for a mask (refer to the illustrations in *The Clay Pot Boy* by Cynthia Jameson). Attach a paint stick or craft stick to the back of the mask. The storyteller holds the mask to his or her face when the Clay Pot Boy speaks and away from the face when narrating the remainder of the story.

Sources for Oral Stories

Feldman, Jean. "The Great, Big, Enormous Turnip." In *Puppets & Storytime*. New York: Teaching Resources, 2005. (page 43)
    This participation story has children act out the story as it is told and encourages them to join in on the repetitive chorus.

Lupton, Hugh. "Little Lord Feather-Frock." In *The Story Tree: Tales to Read Aloud*. Illustrated by Sophie Fatus. Cambridge, MA: Barefoot Books, 2001. (pages 32–39)
    A retelling of "The Cat, the Cock, and the Fox" from Aleksandr Afanasiev's *Russian Fairy Tales* with a much happier ending.

Milord, Susan. "The Clever Maiden." In *Tales Alive! Ten Multicultural Folktales with Activities*. Illustrated by Michael A. Donato. Nashville, TN: Ideals Publications, 2007. (pages 25–29)
    The daughter of a poor farmer impresses the czar with her clever wisdom. Four story extension activities follow the story on pages 30 through 35, including a puzzle using beans or pebbles and "Egg-ceptional Eggs."

Pellowski, Anne. "Naughty Marysia." In *The Story Vine: A Source Book of Unusual and Easy-to-Tell Stories from around the World*. Illustrated by Lynn Sweat. New York: Simon & Schuster/Paula Wiseman Books, 2008. (pages 80–83)

The story "Naughty Marysia" might be told using a set of matryoshka nesting dolls. During this story the dolls are taken apart as they are introduced.

Fingerplays, Songs, Action Rhymes, and Games

"Five Little Turnips" Fingerplay

Teach children the Russian numbers one through five and substitute them in the following fingerplay.

1	*odin*	[ah-DEEN]
2	*dva*	[DVAH]
3	*tri*	[TREE]
4	*chetire*	[cheh-TI-ree]
5	*pyaht*	[PYAHT]

For this fingerplay, begin with five turnip puppets, one on each finger. Remove a puppet each time a turnip is pulled by Babushka. Photocopy "Turnip Finger Puppets" and "Finger Puppet Attachment's (Figures 12.8 and 12.9) on white tagboard or construction paper. Use markers to color the turnip tops green and the bodies of the turnips white and purple. Laminate and cut out the turnips and finger attachments. Tape together the three flaps of each finger attachment. This will fit over the tip of each finger like a thimble. Tape a turnip to each attachment.

Five Little Turnips by Donna Norvell

Five (*pyaht*) little turnips planted in a row.
Water them a lot, and watch them grow.
Along comes Babushka ready to make stew.
Pulled up a turnip, now only four (*chetire*) grew.
Four (*chetire*) little turnips planted in a row.
Water them a lot, and watch them grow.
Along comes Babushka ready to make stew.
Pulled up a turnip, now only three (*tri*) grew.
Three (*tri*) little turnips planted in a row.
Water them a lot, and watch them grow.
Along comes Babushka ready to make stew.
Pulled up a turnip, now only two (*dva*) grew.
Two (*dva*) little turnips planted in a row.
Water them a lot, and watch them grow.
Along comes Babushka ready to make stew.
Pulled up a turnip, now only one (*odin*) grew.
One (*odin*) little turnip growing in the row.
Water it good, and watch it grow.
Along comes Babushka ready to make stew.
Pulled the last turnip, and finished her stew.
Yum, yum, it's ready for me and you.

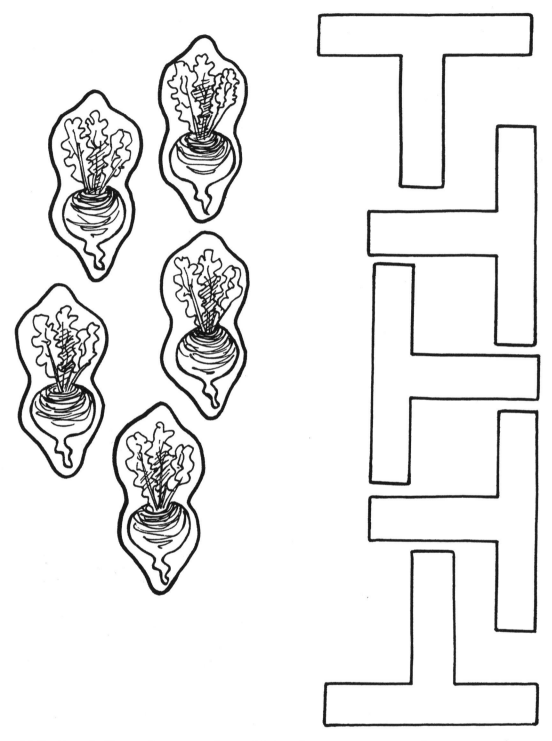

Figure 12.8 **Turnip Finger Puppets**   Figure 12.9   **Finger Puppet Attachments**

Sources for Fingerplays, Songs, Action Rhymes, and Games

Barbarash, Lorriane. *Multicultural Games.* Champaign, IL: Human Kinetics, 1997.
   Children will enjoy playing "Goellki" from page 48. "Ribaki," found on page 49, or "Square Pull" from page 50, which are intended for larger groups and older primary-aged children, are also fun Russian culture games.

Disney Baby Einstein. *World Music.* Burbank, CA: Walt Disney Records, 2009. Compact disc.
   Children will enjoy the lively tune of "Trepak," Tchaikovsky's Russian Dance from *The Nutcracker Suite* (selection 11).

Scott, Anne. *The Laughing Baby: Remembering Nursery Rhymes and Reasons.* South Hadley, MA: Bergin & Garvey, 1987. (125 pages)
   Includes the fingerplays and action rhymes "Bliny" (Pat-a-Cake), "Edu-Edu" (Here I Go), "Zaika Belen kii sidit" (Little White Rabbit Sits), and "Pal chik-mal chik" (Little Boy-Finger).

Stewart, Georgiana. "Trepak (Nutcracker Suite)." In *Multicultural Rhythm Stick Fun.* Long Branch, NJ: Kimbo Educational, 2001. Compact disc.
   Children tap rhythm sticks (or clap hands) and move side-to-side to the beat of this song.

Stewart, Georgiana. "A Visit to My Friend." In *Children of the World: Multicultural Rhythmic Activities.* Long Branch, NJ: Kimbo Educational, 1998. Compact disc.
   Children move in a circle while they clap, wave, and hop to this song. The lyrics tell of visiting friends in Mexico, Russia, and Greece.

Warren, Jean and Elizabeth McKinnon. *Small World Celebrations: Multi-Cultural Holidays to Celebrate with Young Children.* Illustrated by Marion Hopping Ekberg. Everett, WA: Warren, 1988. (157 pages)
   "Dancing Bears," "Troika, Troika," and "Dance, Little Snow Girl" are a few of the songs and action rhymes included in the chapter about Russia.

Weissman, Jackie. "Sasha and Natasha." In *Joining Hands with Other Lands: Multicultural Songs and Games.* Long Branch, NJ: Kimbo Educational, 2011, 1993. Compact disc, 2 min.
   "Sasha and Natasha" inspires movement. Have children clap their hands and stomp. This song is played on the *balalaika,* a popular Russian stringed instrument.

Media Choices

Show a DVD or downloadable movie as a transition between storytelling activities and crafts.

Brett, Jan. *The Mitten.* New York: Spoken Arts, 2000. DVD, 8 min.
   A Ukrainian folktale in which a little boy loses his mitten, and, magically, wild animals crowd into it for shelter.

Cultural Kaleidoscope. *Matryoshka Doll . . . A Symbol of Russian Folk Art: The Story from Tree to Finished Doll.* Kansas City, MO: Cultural Kaleidoscope, 2006. Compact disc, 42 min.
   Visit a Russian factory where matryoshka dolls are made and the home of an artist who paints them. The making of the doll segment is 24 minutes and the "Visit with Zhanna," the artist, is 18 minutes. Adobe PDF teaching resource guide is included.

Polacco, Patricia. *Rechenka's Eggs.* Lincoln, NE: GPN Educational Media, 2003. DVD, 30 min.
   A Reading Rainbow program featuring *Rechenka's Eggs* by Patricia Polacco is a 6- minute segment. Other segments include "Art from an Egg," "Meet Patricia Polacco," and "Egg Strength."

Prokofiev, Sergei. *Peter and the Wolf*. New York: BMG Entertainment, 1995. DVD, 49 min.
    The classic *Peter and the Wolf* story features Prokofiev's musical score that introduces the
    instruments of the orchestra to young children. Peter's adventure in outsmarting the wolf is a
    combination of a live-action and animated story.

Templeton, Suzie. *Peter and the Wolf*. New York: Magnolia Home Entertainment, 2008. DVD, 34 min.
    This adaptation of Peter and the Wolf features stop-motion animation that takes place in a
    more modern Russian setting.

Crafts and Other Activities

Choose a craft suited for the age level of the group and the time allotted for the story time.

Matryoshka Dolls (Stacking Dolls)

Begin this craft project by introducing author and illustrator Patricia Polacco. Patricia
Polacco was born to parents of Russian heritage; many of her stories reflect this heritage
and convey Russian traditions. Show or read one of the following works by Polacco:
Babushka's Doll or the poem "Matroishka" in *Babushka's Mother Goose* (see "Books to
Read Aloud"). Matryoshka [MAH-trohsh-kah] dolls—a sequence of brightly colored
wooden dolls that fit inside of one another—are a favorite toy of Russian children. Some
matryoshka dolls have as many as 20 dolls, the tiniest one being a wooden bead with eyes.

In this craft project, children each make a set of matryoshka dolls. For younger children, adapt this craft project as a coloring activity: Photocopy the largest doll, "Matryoshka
Dolls A" (Figure 12.10), and have children create their own designs.

Supplies

White tagboard paper (card stock or
construction paper)
Colored markers, colored pencils, or crayons

Stapler or clear tape
Scissors

Photocopy "Matryoshka Dolls A–E" and "Pockets A–D" (Figure 12.10 through 12.18) on
white tagboard or other paper. The children color the dolls using markers, colored pencils,
or crayons. (Suggested colors: scarf—orange; hair—yellow; cheeks—pink; eyes—blue;
mouth—red; flower petals—red; flower center—yellow; leaves—green; dress—blue.) Cut
out the dolls and the pockets. With help from an adult, children staple the pockets onto
the backs of the dolls, matching sizes. Staple as close to the edges as possible so the dolls
fit inside the pockets. For younger children, adults should do the stapling or taping.

Figure 12.10 **Matroshka Doll A**

Figure 12.11 **Matroshka Doll B**

Figure 12.12 **Matroshka Doll C**

Figure 12.13 **Matroshka Doll D**   Figure 12.14 **Matryoshka Doll E**   Figure 12.15 **Pocket A**

From *Travel the Globe: Story Times, Activities, and Crafts for Children, Second Edition* by Desiree Webber,
Dee Ann Corn, Elaine Harrod, Sandy Shropshire, Shereen Rasor, and Donna Norvell (in memoriam).
Santa Barbara, CA: Libraries Unlimited. Copyright © 2013.

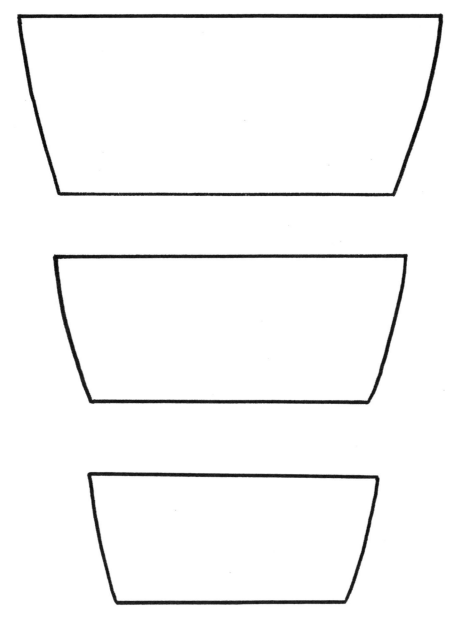

Figure 12.16 **Pocket B**   Figure 12.17 **Pocket C**   Figure 12.18 **Pocket D**

Decorated Paper Eggs

To introduce this craft project, have available a basket of colored eggs to show children. Share the story *Rechenka's Eggs* by Patricia Polacco (see "Books to Read Aloud"), and discuss the Ukrainian-style eggs that Babushka paints for the Easter Festival in Moskava (Moscow). Have available samples of eggs that have been "blown" to show children how fragile they are. (Blown eggs have small holes at each end through which the whites and yolks have been blown out).

Decorated Easter Eggs are created by *pysanky*, a beautiful form of folk art that originated in the Ukraine and spread east into Russia. (Ukraine borders the Russian Federation.) A pysanky egg is created using a *kistka* (a small tool), a lighted candle, shavings of beeswax, and several brilliant dyes. Pysanky eggs may take several hours to complete and have several layers of wax and dyes.

There are many books available that show full-color photographs of beautifully decorated eggs from many countries; for example, *Decorative Eggs* by Candace Ord Manroe (New York: Crescent Books, 1992). Share the photographs with children, as well as information about Fabergé eggs. Karl Fabergé was the jeweler to the imperial family of prerevolutionary Russia and created beautiful jeweled eggs.

Supplies

Crayons or brightly colored markers

White tagboard, card stock, or construction paper

Scissors

White glue

Photocopy the "Pysanky Egg" (Figure 12.20) on white tagboard, card stock, or construction paper. The designs and colors of decorated pysanky eggs are based on symbols. Divide the egg into geometric shapes (see "Pysanky Egg Geometric Design Examples," Figure 12.19), and then decorate with borders and designs (see "Pysanky Egg Symbols, Patterns, and Border Examples," Figure 12.21). Before coloring the eggs, refer to

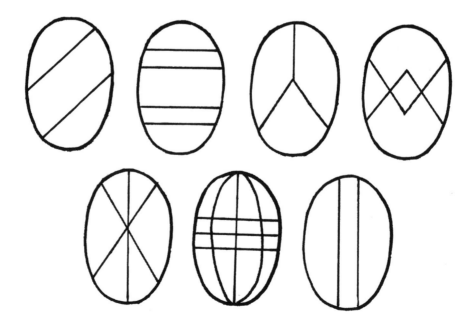

Figure 12.19 **Pysanky Egg Geometric Designs Example**

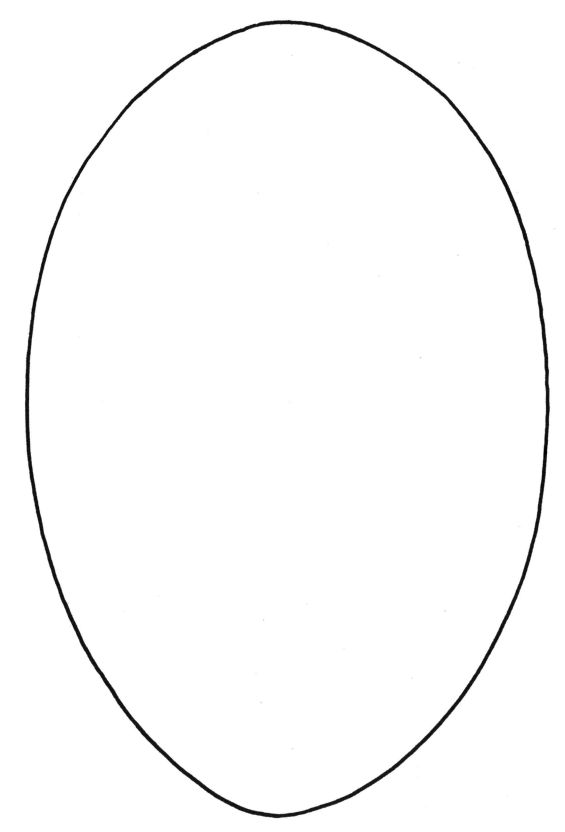

Figure 12.20 **Pysanky Egg**

the "Symbols" list on p. 211, which notes the meanings for symbols and colors. Encourage children to create original borders and designs. For younger children, simplify this activity by having them glue pieces of fabric and yarn, sequins, and rickrack to their eggs.

Symbols

Animal: Prosperity; wealth
Bee: Hard work; pleasantness
Bird: Fulfillment of wishes; protection; a good harvest
Flower: Beauty; children; wisdom; love; charity; goodwill
Fruit: Knowledge; health; wisdom; a good life
Spider: Good fortune
Star: Success
Sun: Growth; good fortune
Tree: Long life; good health; strength; youthfulness
Water: Health
Waves and ribbons: Closed circle around the egg symbolizes eternity
Wheat: Bountiful harvest

Colors

Blue: Good health; sky; air
Brown: Prosperity
Green: Hope; wealth; happiness
Orange: Power; endurance
Pink: Success
Purple: Faith; trust
Red: Love; happiness; hope; life
White: Purity
Yellow: Spirituality; wisdom

Russian Ballet

Russia takes special pride in the ballet, and many Russian cities have their own ballet troupes. Share with children Kate Castle's book *Ballet* (see "Sources for Crafts and Other Activities"). Invite someone from the community to demonstrate for children the basic ballet movements. Ask the dancers to wear their ballet costumes. After the presentation, play Russian ballet music; for example, Peter Tchaikovsky's "Swan Lake," "The Sleeping Beauty," or "The Nutcracker." Invite children to dance on their tiptoes, moving their arms and bodies gracefully to the music.

Figure 12.21 **Pysanky Egg Symbols, Patterns, and Borders Examples**

Sources for Crafts Ideas and Activities

Gomez, Aurelia. *Crafts of Many Cultures: 30 Authentic Craft Projects from around the World*. New York: Scholastic, 1999.
  Craft projects include instructions for making flax dolls, a popular craft from western Russia, found on pages 96 and 97.

Gould, Roberta. *The Kids' Multicultural Craft Book: 35 Crafts from around the World*. Illustrated by Sarah Rakitin. Charlotte, VT: Williamson Publishers, 2004.
  Children will enjoy making nesting dolls of their own family, a project found on pages 51 and 52. Also included is a brief history of the Russian nesting doll. There are instructions for making a "Golden Khokhloma Bowl" on pages 53 and 54. These activities are well suited to older primary-aged children.

Speechley, Greta. "Dancing Bear" in *Creative Crafts for Kids: World Crafts*. New York: Gareth Stevens Publishing, 2010. (pages 24–25)
  This "Russian Dancing Bear" is modeled after the traditional toy with a thread attached to the arms and legs that make the bear dance when pulled.

Chapter 13

Let's Visit the

United States of America (Native Americans)

Sample Story Times

Story Time for Preschool

Song: "Hello Song"

Book: *Turtle's Race with Beaver* by Joseph and James Bruchac

Flannel Board Presentation: "Baby Rattlesnake" retold by Lynn Moroney

Action Rhyme: "Going on a Buffalo Hunt" by Desiree Webber

Fingerplay: "Bears in a Cave" in *Big Book of Animal Rhymes, Fingerplays and Songs* by Elizabeth Cothen Low.

Book or Puppet Presentation: *How Chipmunk Got His Stripes* by Joseph Bruchac and James Bruchac.

DVD: *If You're Happy and You Know It!* by Anna McQuinn, adapter.

Craft: Baby Rattlesnake Hand Puppet

Action Rhyme: "My Hands"

Story Time for Kindergarten through Third Grade

Song: "Hello Song"

Book: *How the Rabbit Lost His Tail: A Traditional Cherokee Legend* by Deborah Duvall

Flannel Board Presentation: *"Baby Rattlesnake"* retold by Lynn Moroney

Action Rhyme: "Going on a Buffalo Hunt" by Desiree Webber

Book: *The Christmas Coat: Memories of My Sioux Childhood* by Virginia Hawk Sneve

DVD: *Hiawatha* by Henry Wadsworth Longfellow

Game: "Firewood" in *Native American Games and Stories* by James Bruchac and Joseph Bruchac

Action Rhyme: "My Hands"

Begin the story time with the "Hello Song." Then sing the song again, substituting the word *hello* with the Cherokee greeting pronounced "O-see-Yo." (See p. xxix for "Hello Song" music.)

Hello Song

Hello ev'rybody,
And how are you? How are you?
Hello ev'rybody,
And how are you today?
O-see-Yo ev'rybody,
And how are you? How are you?
O-see-Yo ev'rybody,
And how are you today?

End the story time with the "My Hands" action rhyme, substituting the words *thank you* with the Cherokee word pronounced "wa-DO," and goodbye with the Cherokee word pronounced "DO-dada-GO-huh-E." (This is how one says goodbye to several others. When saying goodbye to one person, the word is pronounced "do-na-DA-go-huh-E.") Have children stand up and follow the actions in the rhyme.

My Hands

My hands say wa-DO. (*hold up hands*)
With a clap, clap, clap. (*clap hands*)
My feet say wa-DO. (*point to feet*)
With a tap, tap, tap. (*stamp or tap feet*)
Clap! Clap! Clap! (*clap hands*)
Tap! Tap! Tap! (*stamp or tap feet*)
Turn myself around and bow. (*turn and bow*)
DO-dada-GO-huh-E. (*wave goodbye*)

Books to Read Aloud

Bruchac, Joseph and James Bruchac. *How Chipmunk Got His Stripes*. Illustrated by Jose Aruego and Ariane Dewey. New York: Puffin Books, 2003. (32 pages)
Bear brags that he can keep the sun from rising, but Brown Squirrel says Bear is not that powerful. When the sun rises the next morning, Brown Squirrel learns a lesson in humility when he teases Bear about being wrong.

Bruchac, Joseph and James Bruchac. *Turtle's Race with Beaver: A Traditional Seneca Story*. Illustrated by Jose Aruego and Ariane Dewey. New York: Puffin Books, 2005. (32 pages)
Beaver builds a dam that floods the pond where turtles live. Beaver proposes a race where whoever wins can stay at the pond while the others have to move.

Duvall, Deborah L. *How the Rabbit Lost His Tail: A Traditional Cherokee Legend*. Illustrated by Murv Jacob. Albuquerque, NM: University of New Mexico Press, 2003. (32 pages)
Duvall and Jacob have collaborated on several Cherokee legends called "Grandmother Stories." Rabbit is a trickster character and often brags and boasts about how smart and handsome he is. In this story, Rabbit's bragging causes him to lose his long, beautiful tail. Recommended for school-age children.

Duvall, Deborah L. *Rabbit and the Well*. Illustrated by Murv Jacob. Albuquerque, NM: University of New Mexico Press, 2008. (32 pages)
Librarians and teachers will recognize similarities to "The Tar Baby" by Joel Chandler Harris. Harris collected his stories from African folk legends. Artist Murv Jacob states that the origins of "The Tar Baby" are with the Cherokees. In this tale, Rabbit finds himself in trouble with the other animals through his selfish and arrogant actions. Recommended for school-age children.

French, Fiona. *Lord of the Animals: A Native American Creation Myth*. 1997; repr., London: Frances Lincoln Children's Books, 2009. (28 pages)
A great read-aloud story on how crafty Coyote created man. Share the details of the fun illustrations by award-winning illustrator Fiona French. For example, when the animals make their idea of the "Lord of the Animals" out of mud, Mouse constructs a tiny mouse figure. (Mouse is located in the upper left-hand corner of the two-page spread.)

Napoli, Donna Jo. *The Crossing*. Illustrated by Jim Madsen. New York: Atheneum Books for Young Readers, 2011. (42 pages)
Lush paintings in picture-book format are the backdrop for the telling of Lewis and Clark's famous adventure to find a passage to the West Coast. Napoli writes in brief, picturesque, poetic language, making this true story accessible to young and elementary-age children. The travels are told through the eyes of Sacagawea's young son Jean Baptiste.

Perrow, Angeli. *Many Hands: Penobscot Indian Story*. Illustrated by Heather Austin. Down East Books, 2011. (32 pages)
Lily is proud of the basket she has woven, but none of her family members give her the attention she deserves. Instead they tell her that it takes many hands to make a basket. Introduces a few Penobscot words. Recommended for school-age children.

Sneve, Virginia Driving Hawk. *The Christmas Coat: Memories of My Sioux Childhood*. Illustrated by Ellen Beier. New York: Holiday House, 2011. (32 pages)
Every winter, boxes of donated clothes arrive at the South Dakota reservation where Virginia and her family live. Virginia needs a new winter coat, but her mother asks her to pick last from the boxes. Her father is the Episcopal priest for the village and her mother says, "The others need it more than we do." It is hard for Virginia to watch as the other girls find coats they like and leave unattractive coats from which Virginia must select. Recommended for school-age children.

StJohn, Amanda. *Coyote Rides the Sun: A Native American Folktale.* Illustrated by Durga Yael Bern-
hard. Mankato, MN: Child's World, 2012. (24 pages)
This Paiute tale explains why the tip of Coyote's tail is black and why coyotes seek shade
during the day and only hunt at night.

Storytelling

"Baby Rattlesnake" Flannel Board Presentation

Te Ata. *Baby Rattlesnake.* Adapted by Lynn Moroney. Illustrated by Veg Reisberg. San
Francisco: Children's Book Press, 1989. (30 pages) Reprinted with permission from Children's Book Press, San Francisco, CA.

The following story is a teaching tale from the book *Baby Rattlesnake.* Te Ata was a
Chickasaw storyteller who died October 26, 1995, at the age of 99. She was born in
1895 in what was then Oklahoma Territory. Her name means "Bearer of the Morning."
Te Ata traveled the nation, sharing Native American stories, songs and poetry; she performed several times for the Roosevelts at the White House. Lynn Moroney, an Oklahoma
storyteller and author, received permission from Te Ata to retell "Baby Rattlesnake." Like
Te Ata, Moroney travels the United States, telling this and other stories.

See Figures 13.1 through 13.8 for patterns. Trace the figures on felt, or photocopy
and color them. If photocopying, glue small pieces of felt to the backs of the paper figures
so they will hold to the flannel board. Place the figures on the flannel board as they are
introduced in the story. When Baby Rattlesnake receives his rattle, the storyteller should
manipulate one of his arms like Baby Rattlesnake's tail: Bend the arm at the elbow
with the palm of the hand facing the audience. Shake or quiver the hand while saying,
"Ch-Ch-Ch! Ch-Ch-Ch!" The storyteller can also use a small plastic container that fits in the
palm of his hand. Fill the plastic container with a teaspoon of rice. This will make a lively
sound effect of a rattlesnake shaking his tail.

"Baby Rattlesnake" by Te Ata; adapted by Lynn Moroney

Out in the place where the rattlesnakes lived, there was a little baby rattlesnake who cried
all the time because he did not have a rattle. *(place Baby Rattlesnake on the flannel board)*

He said to his mother, "I don't know why I don't have a rattle. I'm made just like my
brother and sister. How can I be a rattlesnake if I don't have a rattle?" *(place Mother and
Father Rattlesnake on the flannel board)*

Mother and Father Rattlesnake said, "You are too young to have a rattle. When you
get to be as old as your brother and sister, you will have a rattle, too."

But Baby Rattlesnake did not want to wait. So he just cried and cried. He shook his tail
and when he couldn't hear a rattle sound, he cried even louder.

Mother and Father said, "Shhh! Shhh! Shhhhh!"

Brother and Sister said, "Shhh! Shhh! Shhhhh!"

But Baby Rattlesnake wouldn't stop crying. He kept the Rattlesnake People awake all night.

The next morning, the Rattlesnake People called a big council. *(remove Mother and
Father Rattlesnake from the flannel board)* They talked and they talked just like people do,
but they couldn't decide how to make that little baby rattlesnake happy. He didn't want
anything else but a rattle.

At last one of the elders said, "Go ahead, give him a rattle. He's too young and he'll get into trouble. But let him learn a lesson. I just want to get some sleep."

So they gave Baby Rattlesnake a rattle. *(add the rattle to the end of Baby Rattlesnake's tail)* Baby Rattlesnake loved his rattle. He shook his tail and for the first time he heard, "Ch-Ch-Ch! Ch-Ch-Ch!" He was so excited!

He sang a little rattle song, "Ch-Ch-Ch! Ch-Ch-Ch!"

He danced a rattle dance, "Ch-Ch-Ch! Ch-Ch-Ch!"

Soon Baby Rattlesnake learned to play tricks with his rattle. He hid in the rocks and when the small animals came by, he darted out rattling, "Ch-Ch-Ch! Ch-Ch-Ch!"

He made Jack Rabbit jump. *(place Jack Rabbit on the flannel board)*

He made Old Man Turtle jump. *(place Old Man Turtle on the flannel board)*

He made Prairie Dog jump. *(place Prairie Dog on the flannel board)*

Each time Baby Rattlesnake laughed and laughed. He thought it was fun to scare the animal people.

Mother and Father warned Baby Rattlesnake. "You must not use your rattle in such a way." *(place Mother and Father Rattlesnake on the flannel board)*

Each time Baby Rattlesnake laughed and laughed. He thought it was fun to scare the animal people.

Big Brother and Big Sister said, "You are not being careful with your rattle."

The Rattlesnake People told Baby Rattlesnake to stop acting so foolish with his rattle. Baby Rattlesnake did not listen.

One day, Baby Rattlesnake said to his mother and father, "How will I know a chief's daughter when I see her?"

"Well, she's usually very beautiful and walks with her head held high," said Father.

"And she's very neat in her dress," added Mother.

"Why do you want to know?" asked Father.

"Because I want to scare her!" said Baby Rattlesnake. And he started right off down the path before his mother and father could warn him never to do such a thing like that. *(remove all characters from the flannel board except Baby Rattlesnake)*

The little fellow reached the place where the Indians traveled. He curled himself up on a log and he started rattling, "Ch-Ch-Ch! Ch-Ch-Ch!" He was having a wonderful time.

All of a sudden he saw a beautiful maiden coming toward him from a long way off. She walked with her head held high, and she was very neat in her dress. *(place the chief's daughter on the flannel board)*

"Ah," thought Baby Rattlesnake. "She must be the chief's daughter."

Baby Rattlesnake hid in the rocks. He was excited. This was going to be his best trick.

He waited and waited. The chief's daughter came closer and closer. When she was in just the right spot, he darted out of the rocks.

"Ch-Ch-Ch! Ch-Ch-Ch!"

"Ho!" cried the chief's daughter. She whirled around, stepping on Baby Rattlesnake's rattle and crushing it to pieces. *(remove the rattle from Baby Rattlesnake's tail and remove the chief's daughter)*

Baby Rattlesnake looked at his beautiful rattle scattered all over the trail. He didn't know what to do. He took off for home as fast as he could. *(place Mother and Father Rattlesnake on the flannel board)*

With great sobs, he told Mother and Father what had happened. They wiped his tears and gave him big rattlesnake hugs.

For the rest of that day, Baby Rattlesnake stayed safe and snug, close by his rattlesnake family.

Puppet Presentation

Bruchac, Joseph and James Bruchac. *How Chipmunk Got His Stripes.* Illustrated by Jose Aruego and Ariane Dewey. New York: Puffin Books, 2003. (32 pages)

Bear becomes angry at Brown Squirrel for teasing and embarrassing him. Brown Squirrel escapes with his life but not before Bear scrapes his claw down Brown Squirrel's back creating "Chipmunk."

Use stick puppets to tell this entertaining story. Make a bear's face using brown or black construction paper; glue a craft or paint stick to the back of the face. Create a double-sided squirrel/chipmunk using brown construction paper; glue a craft stick between the sides. Draw stripes on one side of the squirrel/chipmunk (the other side is plain brown).

Begin the story using the bear puppet and the plain-sided squirrel. As the bear scratches the squirrel's back, flip to the other side showing the chipmunk with his stripes.

Sources for Oral Stories

Larson, Jeanette and Adrienne Yorinks. "Why the Hummingbird Has No Song." In *Hummingbirds: Facts and Folklore from the Americas.* Watertown, MA: Charlesbridge, 2011. (p. 47–49)
This Navajo legend says that when the world was new all the birds were alike in size, color and song. Each day Hummingbird would greedily ate up all the seeds and berries, so the other birds decided to make a change.

Larson, Jeanette and Adrienne Yorinks. "Why the Hummingbird's Throat Is Red." In *Hummingbirds: Facts and Folklore from the Americas.* Watertown, MA: Charlesbridge, 2011. (p. 11–13)
The Ohlone, indigenous people on the central California coast, tell how Hummingbird took fire from the Badger people, who refused to share fire with the other animals. While taking a small ember from a hidden stash, the ember flared up and turned Hummingbird's throat red.

MacDonald, Margaret Read. "Coyote's Crying Song." In *Twenty Tellable Tales: Audience Participation for the Beginning Storyteller.* Illustrated by Roxane Murphy. Chicago: American Library Association, 2005. (pages 10–19)
Inspired by a Hopi tale in which Coyote insists that Dove is not crying but singing. Children will enjoy this humorous tale, which is appropriate for audience participation.

MacDonald, Margaret Read. "Coyote's Rain Song." In *Twenty Tellable Tales: Audience Participation for the Beginning Storyteller.* Illustrated by Roxane Murphy. Chicago: American Library Association, 2005. (pages 20–23)
MacDonald states that she has used this audience participation tale in preschool story times with children as young as two and a half. Versions of this story have been found in Navajo folklore.

Moroney, Lynn. "Rooster Crows Up the Sun." In *The Feather Moon.* Native American flute music composed and played by Michael Graham Allen. Oklahoma City: Lynn Moroney, 1988. Compact disc.
Coyote hears beautiful music and finds that it is Rooster singing. The two enter a competition as to who can sing the sun awake. Rooster wins at the cost of his melodic voice. Storytellers will enjoy the sound effects in telling this humorous tale. Compact disc is available from Moroney's website at http://www.lynnmoroney.com.

Figure 13.1 **Baby Rattlesnake**   Figure 13.2 **Chief's Daughter**   Figure 13.3 **Rattle**

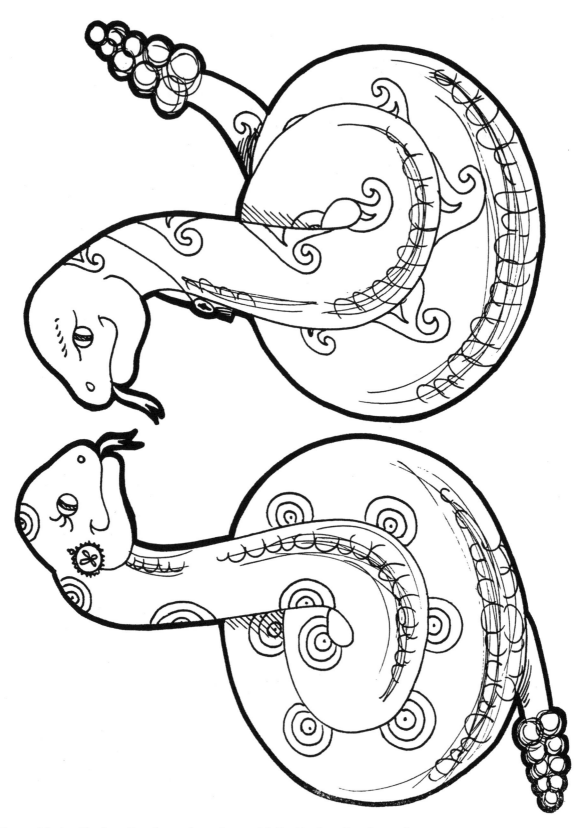

Figure 13.4 **Mother Rattlesnake** Figure 13.5 **Father Rattlesnake**

Figure 13.6 **Jack Rabbit**   Figure 13.7 **Old Man Turtle**   Figure 13.8 **Prairie Dog**

Fingerplays, Songs, Action Rhymes, and Games

The Comanches, Crow, Kiowas, and other Native Americans living on the Plains prior to the 1900s hunted buffalo. The buffalo not only provided meat for food and hides for tipis, but other parts were also used to make tools, cooking utensils, and even baby powder. In this action rhyme, children go in search for buffalo and meet other animals who live on the Plains.

"Going on a Buffalo Hunt" Action Rhyme

by Desiree Webber and Sandy Shropshire

We're going on a buffalo hunt, *(walk in place)*
Ok? Are you ready?
Let's go!
Look high, look low, *(shade eyes with one hand)*
Look out for buffalo.
Oh, here's Grandfather Owl.
Grandfather Owl, have you seen any buffalo?
Whooo, Whooo, Whooo. *(hoot like an owl)*
Not here, not I,
May you find some,
Bye and bye.
Look high, look low, *(walk in place and shade eyes with one hand)*
Look out for buffalo.
Oh, here's Sister Snake.
Sister Snake, have you seen any buffalo?
Hisssss, Hisssss, Hisssss. *(hiss like a snake)*
Not here, not I,
May you find some,
Bye and bye.
Look high, look low, *(walk in place and shade eyes with one hand)*
Look out for buffalo.
Oh, here's Cousin Coyote.
Cousin Coyote, have you seen any buffalo?
Yip, Yip, Oooouuuuuuu. *(yip and then howl like a coyote)*
Not here, not I,
May you find some,
Bye and bye.
Look high, look low, *(walk in place and shade eyes with one hand)*
Look out for buffalo.
Oh, here's Papa Prairie Dog.
Papa Prairie Dog, have you seen any buffalo?
Bark, bark, yip, *(make a short bark and yip)*
Not here, not I,
May you find some,
Bye and bye.

Wait . . . listen . . . *(pause between words)*
Shhhhh, a thunder low *(whisper)*
The ground is pounding *(stomp in place)*
Why, it's buffalo!
Bark, bark
Ooouuuuu
Hisssss, hisssss
Whoooo, whooo.

Sources for Fingerplays, Songs, Action Rhymes and Games

Bruchac, James and Joseph Bruchac. *Native American Games and Stories.* Illustrated by Kayeri Akweks. Golden, CO: Fulcrum Publishing, 2008. (116 pages)
   Each chapter begins with a story that introduces some type of skill. The last chapter covers "awareness." The game titled "Firewood" (pages 102–103) can be played inside or outside and is a great extending activity for teachers. Players sit in a circle with one player wearing a blindfold. The blindfolded child is called the "fire-keeper" and has several pieces of wood in front of him or her. The other children in the circle quietly try to take one piece of wood without the fire-keeper hearing.

Dennis, Yvonne Wakim and Arlene Hirschfelder. *A Kid's Guide to Native American History: More Than 50 Activities.* Chicago: Chicago Review Press, 2010. (226 pages)
   The foot-toss game, on page 146, is simple enough for children ages five and older to play. Children place a lightweight stone on one foot to toss (similar to the "hacky sack" game). Create competitions to toss stones the farthest, highest, closest to a target, and so on. According to the authors of this book, the Apaches of the Southwest United States played a similar game.

Low, Elizabeth Cothen. *Big Book of Animal Rhymes, Fingerplays and Songs.* Westport, CT: Libraries Unlimited, 2009. (324 pages)
   Animals played important roles in the daily lives of indigenous people across the United States. Meat provided food, fur and hides provided clothing and housing, and bones provided tools. Share "Bear Hunt" action rhyme on page 7 and "Bears in a Cave" fingerplay on page 8.

Media Choices

Show a DVD as a transition between storytelling activities and crafts.

Longfellow, Henry Wadsworth. *Hiawatha.* Illustrations by Susan Jeffers. Weston Woods, 2005. DVD, 7 min.
   Introduction tells how Longfellow's epic poem came to be published in 1855. *The Song of Hiawatha* was based on an Ojibwa/Chippewa legend. Susan Jeffers's picture book version focuses the part of Longfellow's poem in which Hiawatha is a young boy.

McQuinn, Anna, adapter. *If You're Happy and You Know It!* Illustrated by Sophie Fatus. Sung by Susan Reed. Cambridge, MA: Barefoot Books, 2009. Enhanced CD-ROM, 3 min. (22 pages with CD-ROM)
   To view the video, play the CD-ROM in a PC or Mac computer. It shows children from countries around the world singing "If You're Happy and You Know It!" It also introduces "hello" in several languages. This is a great way to start or end a "Travel the Globe" story time series.

Crafts and Other Activities

Choose a craft suited for the age level of the group and the time allotted for the story time.

Baby Rattlesnake Hand Puppet

This craft is an effective extending activity for children. Introduce the story "Baby Rattle-snake" (see *Baby Rattlesnake* by Te Ata, retold by Lynn Moroney, under "Flannel Board Presentations") and follow with this hand puppet activity. Encourage children to take their snake puppets home and retell "Baby Rattlesnake" to a friend or member of their family.

Supplies

Green, black, yellow, red, and orange construction paper
White glue

Rice
Scissors
Pencils
Stapler or clear tape

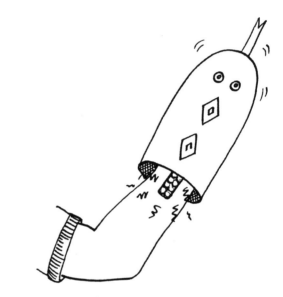

Figure 13.9   **Rattlesnake Puppet Example**

See Figures 13.10 through 13.16 for patterns. The teacher or librarian should make the snake's rattle prior to beginning the craft project with children. This allows the glue to dry thoroughly before the children connect the rattles to their snakes. Using orange construction paper, trace and cut out the rattle pattern. Fold in half on the dashed line. Glue the bottom and side edges. Do not glue the top edge (the end with the dashed line). Allow the glue to dry.

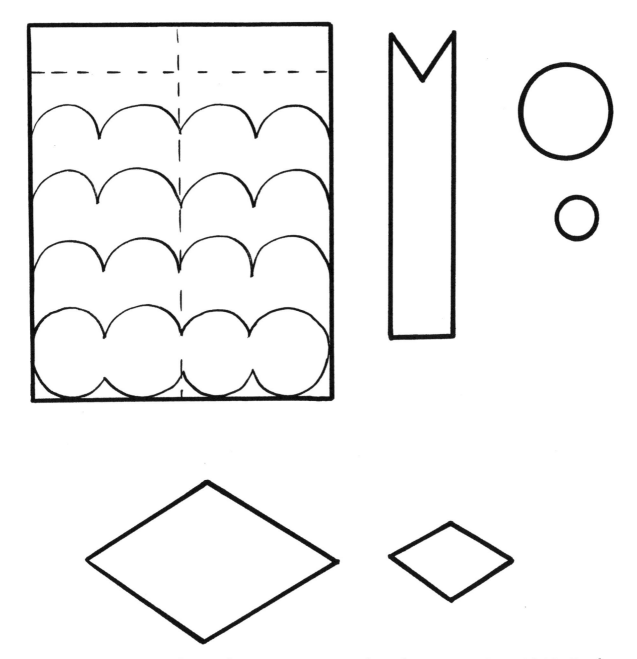

Figure 13.10 **Rattlesnake Rattle** Figure 13.11 **Rattlesnake Tongue** Figure 13.12 **Rattlesnake Eye** Figure 13.13 **Rattlesnake Eye Pupil** Figure 13.14 **Rattlesnake Large Diamond** Figure 13.15 **Rattlesnake Small Diamond**

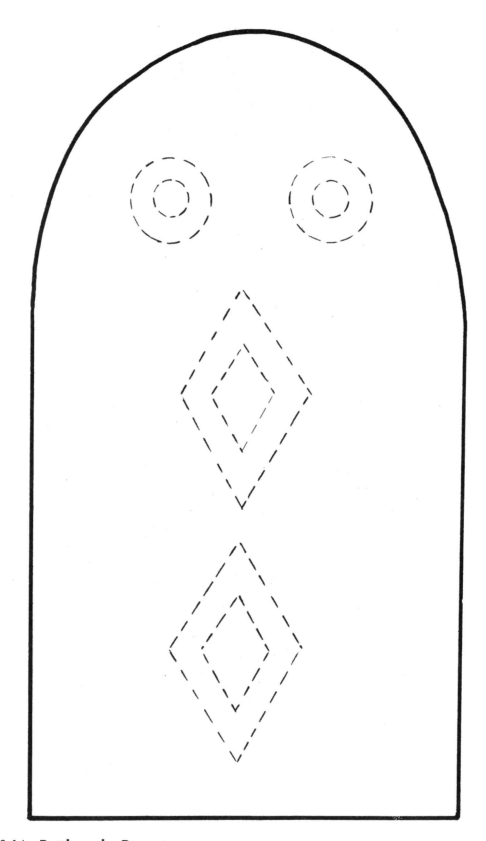

Figure 13.16 **Rattlesnake Puppet**

After the glue has dried, pour approximately two teaspoons of rice through the opening at the top of the rattle. Glue the top edge. Allow the glue to dry completely.

For preschool children or if time is limited, precut all the pieces. Using green construction paper, trace and cut out two hand puppet patterns. One pattern will be the bottom of the snake and the other pattern the top of the snake. Using red construction paper, trace and cut out the tongue. Glue the tongue to the inside of the bottom pattern piece where the mouth would be located. Glue only about ½ inch of the tongue to the puppet, leaving the forked end sticking out from the mouth. Next, glue the top pattern to the bottom pattern along the sides and head.

Leave the bottom end open for the hand to enter. Tell the children not to insert their hands until the glue has dried. (For quicker construction, staple or tape the two puppet pieces together instead of gluing.) Have the children decorate their snakes. Using orange construction paper, trace and cut out two large diamonds (Figure 13.14); using yellow construction paper, trace and cut out two small diamonds (Figure 13.15). Glue these into place (see Figure 13.9). With yellow construction paper, trace and cut out two eyes (Figure 13.12) and, with black construction paper, trace and cut out two pupils. Glue into place. The last step is to tape the end of the rattle with the dashed line to the inside of the top pattern piece of the puppet. Align the dashed line on the rattle with the bottom edge of the puppet piece. The rattle will hang down and rest on the top of the child's arm. As the child moves his or her hand up and down, the rattle will hit against the child's arm, making a rattling noise.

Plains Indian Breastplate

The breastplate was worn mainly for decoration. It was first used by American Indians living on the Plains, although other tribes, such as the Utes, adopted this chest ornament. A breastplate typically included hair-pipes, which were long, thin bones held into place by leather strips. Seashells, beads, feathers, horsehair danglers, and colorful ribbons were sometimes used to decorate the front of the breastplate.

In this craft project, children make a breastplate using cardboard or posterboard and straws, yarn, and pony beads. The straw represents hair pipes; the yarn represents the leather strips; and the pony beads represent either seashells or beads.

Supplies

Cardboard or posterboard	White glue
Straws	Hole punch
Yarn	Scissors
Pony beads	

Use Figure 13.18 (half-pattern) and prepare a breastplate for each child. An adult should precut a breastplate from cardboard or heavy-ply posterboard.

Figure 13.17   **Breastplate Example**

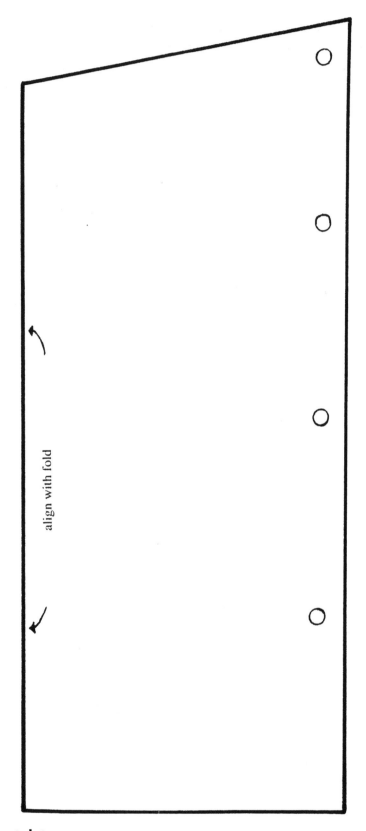

align with fold

Figure 13.18 **Breastplate**

Using a single-hole punch, the adult should punch a hole near the top right and top left corners, plus the three holes along each side of the breastplate.

Next, cut one piece of yarn 24 inches long and eight pieces of yarn 5 inches long for each child. Also, cut several straws into 3-inch pieces. Each breastplate needs approximately 28 pieces, depending upon how close the children want to glue the straws next to each other.

The children can now decorate their breastplates. First, tie the 24-inch piece of yarn to the two holes punched at the top. There should be enough room for the child to slip the yarn over his or her head and allow the breastplate to lie flat on the chest.

The next step is to tie the eight 5-inch pieces of yarn to the holes punched along each side of the breastplate, including the holes at the top. Thread one or several colorful pony beads onto each piece of yarn and knot each end. Finally, glue the straws into place horizontally as shown in Figure 13.17

Sources for Craft Ideas and Activities

Dennis, Yvonne Wakim and Arlene Hirschfelder. *A Kid's Guide to Native American History: More Than 50 Activities.* Chicago: Chicago Review Press, 2010. (226 pages)
Make a simple "Delaware Storyteller Bag" (page 31) or a "Delaware Gorget" (page 32). The storyteller bag is constructed of felt or other fabric and is designed with fabric paints or markers. The children place "memory items" inside their bags. When they retrieve the memory item, they tell a story. The gorget is a piece of jewelry worn by both boys and girls around the neck, wrist, or on a piece of clothing as a button. The gorget is made with self-hardening clay. Designs are etched into the clay with toothpicks.

Fullman, Joe. *Native North Americans: Dress, Eat, Write, and Play Just Like the Native Americans.* Irvine, CA: QEB Publishing, 2009. (32 pages)
This is a quality, well-made book with a variety of child-oriented crafts reflective of various tribes across North America. There is a sand painting craft using colored sand (page 7), wampum bead bracelet using pasta (page 5), along with a dream catcher, warrior headdress, rattle, Kachina doll, and more.

Michaels, Alexandra. *The Kids' Multicultural Art Book: Art & Craft Experiences from around the World.* Nashville, TN: Williamson Books, 2007. (157 pages)
Several pages are devoted to crafts reflecting Native American culture in North America. Pages 16 through 22 focus on Plains Indian culture; pages 26 through 28 have "Inuit Finger Masks" and "Eskimo Laughing Mask" crafts; pages 30 through 34 focus on the Northwest area, followed by the Southwest on pages 36 through 38. The section ends with sponge painting cut-outs and a "Chippewa Dream Catcher" (pages 40–44) from the Northwest and Woodland areas.

Speechley, Greta. *World Crafts.* New York: Gareth Stevens Publishing, 2010. (pages 16–17)
Children can create a beautiful Native American dream catcher. The web design allows bad dreams to slip through but catches happy dreams. Supplies include a metal ring, gold thread, ribbon, beads and feathers. Craft can be simplified with inexpensive cardboard cut into a ring and yarn instead of thread and ribbons. Adult assistance is needed with younger children.

Chapter 14

Let's Visit

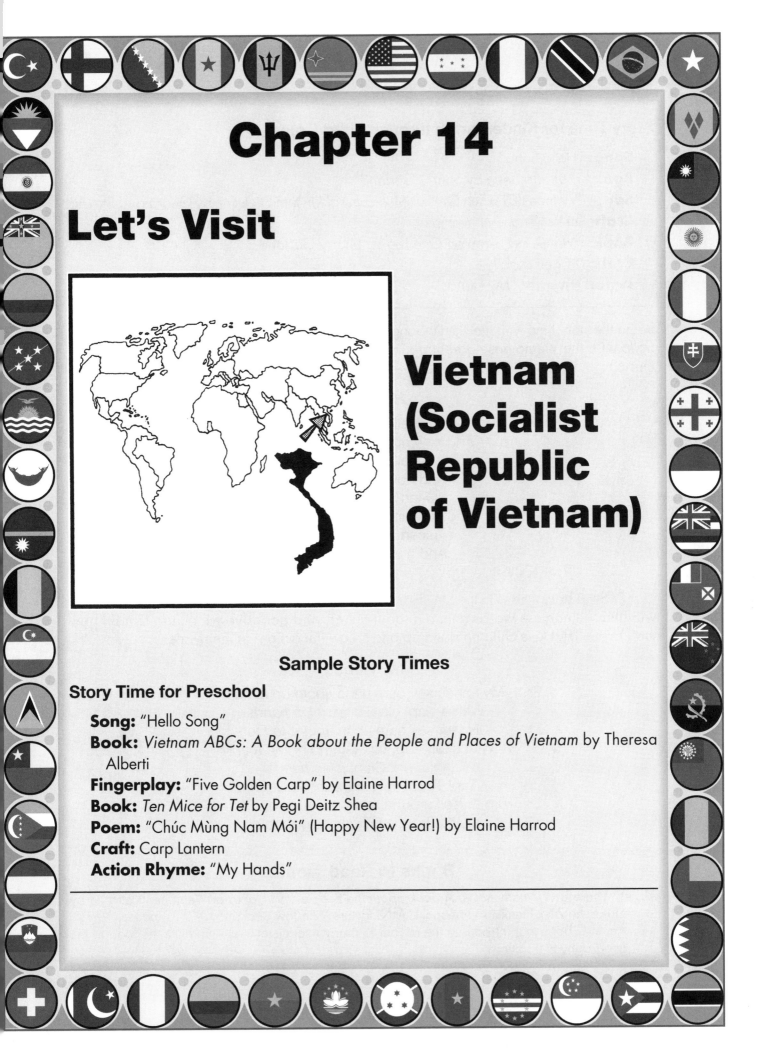

Vietnam (Socialist Republic of Vietnam)

Sample Story Times

Story Time for Preschool

Song: "Hello Song"

Book: *Vietnam ABCs: A Book about the People and Places of Vietnam* by Theresa Alberti

Fingerplay: "Five Golden Carp" by Elaine Harrod

Book: *Ten Mice for Tet* by Pegi Deitz Shea

Poem: "Chúc Mùng Nam Mói" (Happy New Year!) by Elaine Harrod

Craft: Carp Lantern

Action Rhyme: "My Hands"

Story Time for Kindergarten through Third Grade

Song: "Hello Song"
Book: *The Lotus Seed* by Sherry Garland
Song: "Vietnam (Chu Ech On)" in *Multicultural Rhythm Stick Fun* by Georgiana Stewart
Craft: Tet Red Money Envelopes
Book: *Why Ducks Sleep on One Leg* by Sherry Garland
Craft: Dragon Mobile
Action Rhyme: "My Hands"

Begin the story time with the "Hello Song." Then sing the song again, substituting the word *hello* with the Vietnamese greeting *xin chào* [seen jow]. (See p. xxix for "Hello Song" music.)

Hello Song

Hello everybody,
And how are you? How are you?
Hello everybody,
And how are you today?
(seen jow) everybody,
And how are you? How are you?
(seen jow) everybody,
And how are you today?

End the story time with the "My Hands" action rhyme, substituting the words *thank you* with the Vietnamese words *cám o'n* [gam uhhn], and goodbye with *chào têm bit* [jow tha'hm bee'IT], Have children stand up and follow the actions in the rhyme.

My Hands

My hands say gam uhhn. *(hold up hands)*
With a clap, clap, clap. *(clap hands)*
My feet say gam uhhn. *(point to feet)*
With a tap, tap, tap. *(stamp or tap feet)*
Clap! Clap! Clap! *(clap hands)*
Tap! Tap! Tap! *(stamp or tap feet)*
Turn myself around and bow. *(turn and bow)*
jow tha'hm bee'IT. *(wave goodbye)*

Books to Read Aloud

Alberti, Theresa. *Vietnam ABCs: A Book about the People and Places of Vietnam.* Illustrated by Natascha Alex Blanks. Minneapolis, MN: Picture Window Books, 2007. (32 pages)
An ABC book that introduces the reader to many aspects of Vietnam, from the food to the geography to traditions.

Garland, Sherry. *The Lotus Seed*. Illustrated by Tatsuro Kiuchi. New York: Harcourt Brace Jovanovich, 1993. (26 pages)

A Vietnamese girl keeps a special seed for many years. When she becomes a grandmother, something wonderful happens to the seed.

Garland, Sherry. *Why Ducks Sleep on One Leg*. Illustrated by Jean Tseng and Mou-sien Tseng. New York: Scholastic, 1993. (30 pages)

This Vietnamese folktale explains why ducks sleep on one leg.

Jules, Jacqueline. *Duck for Turkey Day*. Illustrated by Kathryn Mitter. Morton Grove, IL: Albert Whitman, 2009. (32 pages)

Tuyet is worried that her family is preparing duck, instead of turkey, for Thanksgiving. Then she learns that some of her other classmates enjoy many different types of food for the Thanksgiving holiday.

Shea, Pegi Deitz. *Ten Mice for Tet*. Illustrated by To Ngọc Trang. Embroidery by Phạm Viết Dinh. San Francisco: Chronicle Books, 2003. (36 pages)

A simple counting book sharing highlights about the important holiday of Tet. More details about Tet are included at the end of the book.

Sugarman, Brynn Olenberg. *Rebecca's Journey Home*. Illustrated by Michelle Shapiro. Minneapolis: Kar-Ben Pub, 2006. (32 pages)

A couple, with two little boys, decides to adopt a young daughter from Vietnam.

Thong, Roseanne. *Fly Free!* Illustrated by Eujin Kim Neilan. Honesdale, PA: Boyds Mills Press, 2010. (32 pages)

Mai believes that when you do a good deed, it will come back to you.

Zee, Ruth Vander. *Always with You*. Illustrated by Ronald Himler. Grand Rapids, MI: Eerdmans Books for Young Readers, 2008. (32 pages)

Kim is four years old when she loses her mother in an attack during the Vietnam War. During the same attack, Kim also loses her eyesight. This book is based on a real-life story.

Storytelling

"How the Tiger Got His Stripes" Flannel Board Presentation

This Vietnamese legend is a common folktale of how a farmer uses his wisdom to outwit the tiger, and the tiger escapes with a new appearance. See Figures 14.1 through 14.4 for patterns. Trace the patterns on felt, or photocopy and color them. If photocopying, glue small pieces of felt to the backs of the paper figures so they will hold to the flannel board.

Place the figures on the flannel board as they are introduced in the following story. When in the story the farmer uses a rope to tie up the tiger, wrap a piece of black yarn around the tiger (without stripes) at the appropriate time in the story. After the tiger is untied, place the tiger with stripes on the flannel board.

"How the Tiger Got His Stripes" retold by Elaine Harrod

One day long ago in Vietnam, a water buffalo pulled a farmer's plow. *(place the water buffalo and the farmer on the flannel board)* The labor was hard and the weather was hot, but the farmer's buffalo always worked hard, and this day was no different than any other. The two strove very hard all morning. Lunch time finally came, and the man watered and fed his buffalo, then left to go to his hut to eat his noon meal. *(remove the farmer from the flannel board)*

After the man left, a tiger came out of the forest. *(place the tiger without stripes on the flannel board)* The buffalo felt nervous with the tiger so close, and just as he thought about running away, the tiger spoke to the buffalo. "Please don't leave," the tiger said. "I am not here to hurt you. I only want to ask you a question."

"When I was in the forest this morning," said the tiger, "I couldn't help but come closer and watch you work for the man. I wonder, why does a powerful beast, such as yourself, work for man? He is obviously weaker than you are."

The buffalo spoke to the tiger with much pride. "Yes, you are correct. I am a powerful beast and have much strength, but the man has a powerful mind. He has powerful wisdom, more wisdom than all the animals of the forest!"

The tiger flicked his tail with interest. He wished to have man's wisdom. *(place the farmer on the flannel board)*

When the man returned from his noon meal, he was very upset to see a tiger near his buffalo. As he approached, he picked up a large rock to use against the tiger. The tiger spoke to the man, repeating what he had said to the buffalo. I only wish to ask you a question."

"Yes?" the man said, still holding the rock and approaching very cautiously. "My question is about your wisdom." said the tiger. "I can see you have power over creatures stronger than you. What is this wisdom the water buffalo speaks about?"

"Tiger, I don't carry my wisdom with me," the man answered. "It is back at my hut."

"Could I see your wisdom?" requested the tiger.

"I cannot just leave you here with my water buffalo while I am gone."

"I promise not to do anything to harm the water buffalo," said the tiger.

"I will go to the hut and get my wisdom if you let me tie you to that tree stump."

The tiger agreed to let the man tie him to the tree stump. *(wrap the black yarn around the tiger)* Then the man left for his hut.

When the tiger saw the man returning, he realized he was carrying something. That must be his wisdom that he is carrying, thought the tiger. As the man came closer, the tiger saw that it was not wisdom at all, but a bow and arrow. The tiger knew these weapons very well, for he had seen animals in the forest killed with them.

The tiger then realized that the man was going to kill him. He began to struggle to free himself from the ropes. He worked and pulled and tugged, but it seemed he would never be able to escape the tight knots of the rope. The tiger used strength he did not even know he possessed, and tigers are very strong, as you all know. Just as the man raised his bow and arrow to kill the tiger, the tiger broke free from the ropes and ran as fast as his legs could carry him, back into the forest, never to return! *(remove the tiger without stripes and place the tiger with stripes on the flannel board)*

When the tiger was a safe distance from the farm, he looked down at himself. He saw that he was changed: He was a new tiger, one with stripes! The ropes had cut through his fur and left black marks. To this day, the tiger still has stripes.

Figure 14.1 **Tiger without Stripes** Figure 14.2 **Water Buffalo**

Figure 14.3 **Tiger with Stripes**   Figure 14.4 **Farmer**

Source for Oral Stories

Pirotta, Saviour. *Around the World in 80 Tales.* Illustrated by Richard Johnson. Boston, MA: Kingfisher, 2007. (pages 157–158)
    In the story "Food for the Emperor," three brothers compete to become the next emperor by
    preparing a meal for their father.

Fingerplays, Songs, Action Rhymes, and Games

"Five Golden Carp" Fingerplay

For this fingerplay, add a carp puppet each time a carp is added in the poem. The storyteller wears the finger puppets. Children hold up five fingers and follow along. To make finger puppets, photocopy Figures 14.5 through 14.6 on white card stock. Use markers to
color the carp. Laminate and cut out the carp and finger attachments. Tape together the
three flaps of each finger attachment. This will fit over the tip of each finger like a thimble.
Tape a carp to each finger attachment.

Five Golden Carp by Elaine Harrod

The pond was beautiful and had a bridge,
And one golden carp who lived past the ridge. *(add carp puppet)*
Two golden carp wanted to swim in the sea; *(add carp puppet)*
When those two carp turned around there were three. *(add carp puppet)*
Three golden carp who knew there could be more
Saw one under the bridge, and that made four. *(add carp puppet)*
Four golden carp learning how to dive,
Looked up and saw another; that made five. *(add carp)*
Five golden carp eating bugs in the pond.
Spent many years together they had formed a bond.

"Chúc Mùng Nam Mói" Rhyme

This poem helps children imagine the Vietnamese New Year holiday, Tet. This poem
might be shared before the craft project "Tet Red Money Envelopes" (see "Crafts and Other
Activities").

Chúc Mùng Nam Mói (Happy New Year!) by Elaine Harrod

In Vietnam the New Year holiday is Tet.
On New Year's Eve we dance the dragon dance.
We make very loud sounds with our fire crackers.
One thing we like about Tet is the red envelopes.
Our parents put money in them for us.
They are red with the words Chúc Mùng Nam Mói written on them.
This means "Happy New Year!"

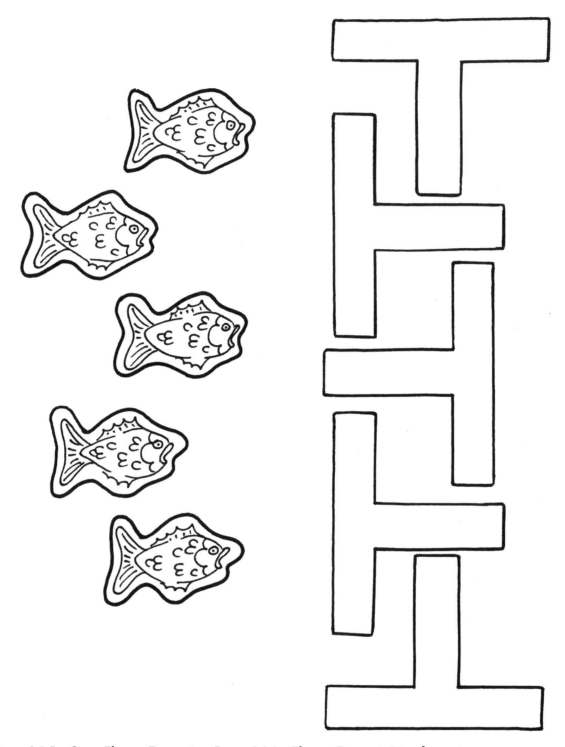

Figure 14.5 **Carp Finger Puppets**   Figure 14.6   **Finger Puppet Attachments**

Sources for Fingerplays, Songs, Action Rhymes, and Games

Stewart, Georgiana. "Chu Ech On." In *Multicultural Rhythm Stick Fun*. Long Branch, NJ: Kimbo Educational, 1992. Compact disc.
Kids use rhythm sticks and follow the directions for tapping and other movements during the song.

Media Choices

Show a DVD or downloadable movie as a transition between storytelling activities and crafts.

Rashad, Phylicia. *Vietnamese-American Heritage: American Cultures for Children*. Wynnewood, PA: Schlessinger Media, 2006. DVD, 25 min.
See how people in Vietnam live, work, and play. Count to 10 in Vietnamese and find out about the food and music in this country.

Sussard, Becca. *Families of Vietnam*. Arden Films: Master Communications: United States. 2009. DVD, 30 min.
Learn about the lives of two children who live in Vietnam.

Crafts and Other Activities

Choose a craft suited for the age level of the group and the time allotted for the story time.

Tet Red Money Envelopes

To celebrate Tet, the Vietnamese New Year, children receive red envelopes with money inside. Even babies receive envelopes. The envelope pattern provided in this book has the Vietnamese words "Chúc Mùng Nam Mói" written on one side. Before beginning this craft project, perhaps share with children the poem "Chúc Mùng Nam Mói." (see "Fingerplays, Songs, Action Rhymes, and Games").

Supplies

Red photocopier paper
Yellow yarn or ribbon

Gold star stickers
Scissors

Figure 14.7 **Money Envelope Example**

On red photocopier paper, duplicate a copy of Figure 14.8 for each child. Cut out the envelopes and have children fold them. (see Figure 14.7). Use yellow yarn or ribbon to tie the envelopes and gold star stickers to decorate them.

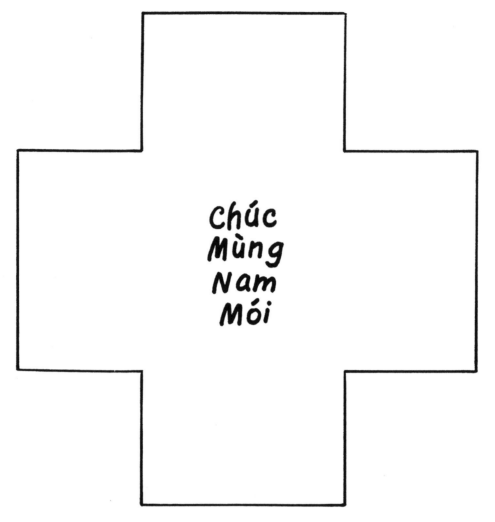

Figure 14.8   **Tet Red Money Envelope**

Carp Lantern

In Vietnam, children make lanterns for the mid-autumn festival Tết Trung Thu, which is held in honor of the moon. The lanterns are constructed using rice paper and bamboo poles. When evening comes, children light a candle in their lanterns and march in a parade. Not every child makes it to the end of the parade with his or her lantern. Sometimes the candle burns out or the lantern burn up! Children spend a lot of time creating the most attractive lanterns they can. When they get home, they hang their lanterns where everyone can see and admire them.

In this craft project, children make carp lanterns similar to those used in Tết Trung Thu. After children have completed their lanterns, play music and have children participate in a lantern parade.

Supplies

Three sheets of orange or yellow paper (per lantern)

Colored markers

Hole punch

Three 12-inch lengths of yarn (per lantern)

Pencil or straw (one per lantern)

Photocopy Figure 14.10. Have children cut out the carp lantern and use marker to decorate them. Attach the first two sides together by placing them back to back and stapling one side. Add the third pattern by stapling its sides to the open sides of the other two patterns (the lantern will be three-sided; see Figure 14.9). Punch holes near the mouth of each fish where indicated by the dots on the patterns. Tie a 12-inch piece of yarn to each hole, and tie all the yarn pieces together at the ends. Attach the yarn to an unsharpened pencil or a plastic straw.

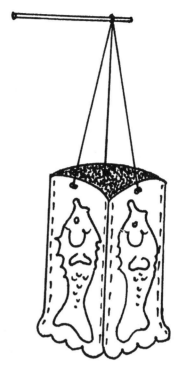

Figure 14.9 **Carp Lantern Example**

Figure 14.10 **Carp Lantern**

Dragon Mobile

During Tet, the Vietnamese New Year's holiday, many dragon dances are performed. The people of Vietnam gather in the streets to watch the dragon dances. The dragons are large puppets worn by many people together. The lead individual wears the large papier-mâché head; many others support the long body and tail. Music is played as the dragon makes his way down the streets.

Figure 14.11 **Dragon Mobile Example**

In this craft project, children make their own dragon mobiles. They might hang the mobiles in their rooms at home and imagine that they are watching a dragon dance in Vietnam on Tet.

Supplies

Yellow photocopier paper (or any bright color)
Hole punch
Metal hanger (one per mobile)
Seven 5-inch pieces of yarn

Four 3-inch pieces of yarn
White glue
Clear tape
Scissors
Dragon patterns

Copy Figures 14.12 through 14.16 onto yellow photocopier paper for each child. Have children cut out their dragon mobile parts. Roll the head and tail parts into cone shapes and secure with tape. Punch holes in each section of the dragon—the head, tail, and body circles. Glue the body circles together, matching up the holes, to make three body circles. (The body circles will be two-sided after they are glued together.)

Each body section will have three holes punched in it. Use the four 3-inch pieces of yarn to attach the head to the first circle, the first circle to the second, and so on. Use the 5-inch pieces of yarn to attach the dragon to the hanger (see Figure 14.11). Tape the "Dragon Mouth Fire" piece (Figure 14.15) to the dragon's mouth and the "Dragon Tail Spike" (Figure 14.14) to the end of the dragon's tail. After the dragon is tied to the hanger, wind currents will make the dragon move like the dragons in the Tet dragon dance.

Figure 14.12 **Dragon Body Circles**

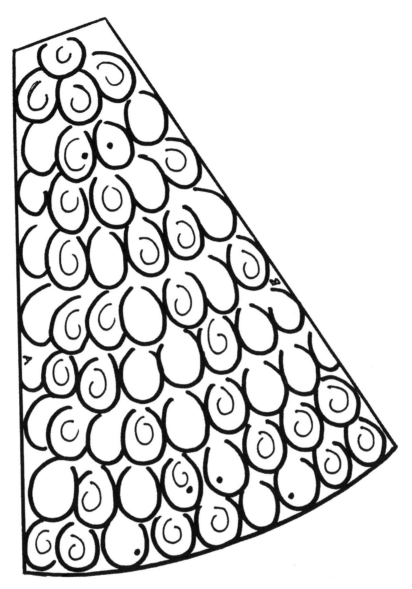

Figure 14.13 **Dragon Tail**

Figure 14.14 **Dragon Tail Spike**   Figure 14.15 **Dragon Mouth Fire**
Figure 14.16 **Dragon Head**

Sources for Craft Ideas and Activities

Michaels, Alexandra. *The Kids' Multicultural Art Book: Ages 3–9*. Nashville, TN: Williamson Books, 2007. (157 pages)
Make the "Vietnamese Dancing Dragon Cup" using a cup, straw, and construction paper to create a simple dragon craft (page 150).

Press, Judy. *Around-the-World Art & Activities; Visiting the 7 Continents through Craft Fun*. Charlotte, VT: Williamson, 2001. (128 pages)
Make a lotus flower using an egg carton and construction paper and paint to create a lotus flower craft (page 54–55).

Multicultural Series Bibliography

Bilingual Picture Dictionaries Series

Mankato, MN: Capstone Press

The Bilingual Picture Dictionaries Series has simple text paired with themed photos that invite the reader to learn new words and phrases.

Kudela, Katy R. *My First Book of Arabic Words.* 2011.
Kudela, Katy R. *My First Book of French Words.* 2009.
Kudela, Katy R. *My First Book of German Words.* 2011.
Kudela, Katy R. *My First Book of Greek Words.* 2011.
Kudela, Katy R. *My First Book of Hindi Words.* 2011.
Kudela, Katy R. *My First Book of Italian Words.* 2011.
Kudela, Katy R. *My First Book of Japanese Words.* 2011.
Kudela, Katy R. *My First Book of Korean Words.* 2011.
Kudela, Katy R. *My First Book of Mandarin Chinese Words.* 2009.
Kudela, Katy R. *My First Book of Polish Words.* 2011.
Kudela, Katy R. *My First Book of Portuguese Words.* 2011.
Kudela, Katy R. *My First Book of Russian Words.* 2011.
Kudela, Katy R. *My First Book of Spanish Words.* 2009.
Kudela, Katy R. *My First Book of Vietnamese Words.* 2011.

Countries Around the World DVD Series

Wynnewood, PA: Schlessinger Media

The *Countries Around the World* series includes 52 volumes that introduce the daily life and physical characteristics of different regions of the world. Video segments are 13 minutes in length and are intended for grades 2 through 5. These videos are also available digitally on Safari Montage. The segments listed here are a selection of the countries featured in *Travel the Globe.*

Australia
Brazil
China

Greece
India
Ireland

Italy

Mexico

Russia

United States

Vietnam

Discover the World Alphabet Series

Chelsea, MI: Sleeping Bear Press

This alphabet book series invites young readers to explore each country's rich history, diverse geography, and many traditions.

Bajaj, Varsha. *T Is for Taj Mahal: An India Alphabet.* 2011.
Crane, Carol. *D Is for Dancing Dragon: A China Alphabet.* 2009.
Grodin, Elissa. *C Is for Ciao: An Italy Alphabet.* 2008.
Johnston, Tony. *P Is for Piñata: A Mexico Alphabet.* 2008.
Scillian, Devin. *D Is for Down Under: An Australia Alphabet.* 2010.

Flat Stanley's Worldwide Adventures

New York: HarperCollins Children's Books

Flat Stanley is a popular children's book character. His adventures continue in this chapter book series as he travels around the world. This series would be ideal for classroom teachers to read aloud as an extending activity to "Travel the Globe" story times. Book illustrations by Macky Pamintuan. Travel to www.flatstanleybooks.com for games, global facts, and more activities for kids, parents, and classrooms.

Brown, Jeff and Josh Greenhut. *Flat Stanley's Worldwide Adventures #1: The Mount Rushmore Calamity.* 2009.
Brown, Jeff and Josh Greenhut. *Flat Stanley's Worldwide Adventures #2: The Great Egyptian Grave Robbery.* 2009.
Brown, Jeff and Josh Greenhut. *Flat Stanley's Worldwide Adventures #3: The Japanese Ninja Surprise.* 2009.
Brown, Jeff and Josh Greenhut. *Flat Stanley's Worldwide Adventures #4: The Intrepid Canadian Expedition.* 2009.
Brown, Jeff and Josh Greenhut. *Flat Stanley's Worldwide Adventures #5: The Amazing Mexican Secret.* 2010.
Brown, Jeff and Josh Greenhut. *Flat Stanley's Worldwide Adventures #6: The African Safari Discovery.* 2010.
Brown, Jeff and Josh Greenhut. *Flat Stanley's Worldwide Adventures #7: The Flying Chinese Wonders.* 2011.
Brown, Jeff and Josh Greenhut. *Flat Stanley's Worldwide Adventures #8: The Australian Boomerang Bonanza.* 2011.
Brown, Jeff and Josh Greenhut. *Flat Stanley's Worldwide Adventures #9: The U.S. Capital Commotion.* 2011.

Our World Series

Mankato, MN: Pebble Books

Pebble Books's *Our World* series describes and illustrates the land, animals, and people of different countries.

Frost, Helen. *A Look at Australia*. 2002.
Frost, Helen. *A Look at Canada*. 2006.
Frost, Helen. *A Look at China*. 2006.
Frost, Helen. *A Look at Cuba*. 2009.
Frost, Helen. *A Look at Egypt*. 2003.
Frost, Helen. *A Look at France*. 2002.
Frost, Helen. *A Look at Germany*. 2009.
Frost, Helen. *A Look at Japan*. 2002.
Frost, Helen. *A Look at Kenya*. 2002.
Frost, Helen. *A Look at Mexico*. 2002.
Frost, Helen. *A Look at Russia*. 2006.
Frost, Helen. *A Look at Vietnam*. 2003.

Questions and Answers: Countries Series

Mankato, MN: Capstone Press

Bauer, Brandy. *Brazil*. 2005.
Hodgkins, Fran. *Mexico*. 2005.
Olson, Nathan. *Australia*. 2007.
Olson, Nathan. *Canada*. 2007.
Olson, Nathan. *China*. 2005.
Olson, Nathan. *India*. 2005.
Olson, Nathan. *Italy*. 2007.
Preszler, June. *Haiti*. 2006.
Spengler, Kremena. *France*. 2005.
Spengler, Kremena. *Germany*. 2005.
Spengler, Kremena. *Greece*. 2007.
Spengler, Kremena. *Russia*. 2005.
Spengler, Kremena. *The United States*. 2007.
Webster, Christine. *Egypt*. 2005.

Secret Agent Jack Stalwart Series

New York: Weinstein Books

Jack Stalwart, a nine-year-old secret agent, goes on many adventures and travels the globe trying to find and rescue his brother, Max. This chapter-book series introduces the location and culture of many countries. Classroom teachers can read aloud as an extending activity to a "Travel the Globe" story time. Illustrations by Brian Williamson. Great games, puzzles, free downloads, activities, competitions, and much more may be found at www.jack stalwart.com. Recommended for school-age children.

Hunt, Elizabeth Singer. *The Escape of the Deadly Dinosaur: USA Book #1*. 2007.
Hunt, Elizabeth Singer. *The Search for the Sunken Treasure: Australia Book #2*. 2007.
Hunt, Elizabeth Singer. *The Mystery of the Mona Lisa: France Book #3*. 2007.
Hunt, Elizabeth Singer. *The Caper of the Crown Jewels: England Book #4*. 2008.
Hunt, Elizabeth Singer. *The Secret of the Sacred Temple: Cambodia Book #5*. 2008.
Hunt, Elizabeth Singer. *The Pursuit of the Ivory Poachers: Kenya Book #6*. 2008.
Hunt, Elizabeth Singer. *The Puzzle of the Missing Panda: China Book #7*. 2008.
Hunt, Elizabeth Singer. *Peril at the Grand Prix: Italy Book #8*. 2009.
Hunt, Elizabeth Singer. *The Deadly Race to Space: Russia Book #9*. 2009.
Hunt, Elizabeth Singer. *The Quest for the Aztec Gold: Mexico Book #10*. 2009.
Hunt, Elizabeth Singer. *Theft of the Samurai Sword: Japan Book #11*. 2009.
Hunt, Elizabeth Singer. *Fight for the Frozen Land: The Arctic Book #12*. 2009.
Hunt, Elizabeth Singer. *The Hunt for the Yeti Skull: Nepal Book #13*. 2011.
Hunt, Elizabeth Singer. *The Mission to Find Max: Egypt Book #14*. 2011.

World Alphabet Series

London: Frances Lincoln Children's Books

A photographic journey of the people, culture, food, and scenery of many interesting countries. Photography contributions by Prodeepta Das.

Abate, Betelhem. *E Is for Ethiopia*. 2010.
Cave, Kathryn. *W Is for World*. 2000.
Cave, Kathryn. *W Is for World Big Book*. 2004.
Cheung, Hyechong. *K Is for Korea*. 2008.
Cordero, Flor de Maria. *M Is for Mexico*. 2008.
Das, Prodeepta. *I Is for India*. 2004.
Das, Prodeepta. *K Is for Korea*. 2010.
Kabakov, Vladimir. *R Is for Russia*. 2011.
Mrówczyska, Agnieska. *P Is for Poland*. 2008.
Naidoo, Beverley. *S Is for South Africa*. 2010.
Rahman, Urmi. *B Is for Bangladesh*. 2009.
Razzak, Shazia. *P Is for Pakistan*. 2011.
So, Sungwan. *C Is for China*. 2000.
Tossuon, Nevin. *T Is for Turkey*. 2010.
Zephaniah, Benjamin. *J Is for Jamaica*. 2006.

Author/Title Index

Activity Index

About the Authors

DESIREE WEBBER is director of Mustang Public Library in Mustang, Oklahoma. A former children's librarian, she received her master's degree in library and information studies from the University of Oklahoma and her bachelor's degree in communications from the University of California, San Diego. Her published works include Libraries Unlimited's *Travel the Globe: Multicultural Story Times; The Kids' Book Club: Lively Reading and Activities for Grades 1–3*; and *Integrated Library Systems: Planning, Selecting and Implementing*, as well as *The Buffalo Train Ride* and *Bone Head: Story of the Longhorn*.

DEE ANN CORN has served as children's library assistant in the Children's Department at the Moore Public Library in the Pioneer Library System of Norman, Oklahoma, for over 20 years. Corn has presented numerous trainings and workshops for professional organizations and schools on children's literature and story times. Her published works include the first edition of *Travel the Globe: Multicultural Story Times*. Corn received her bachelor's degree in business administration from the University of Oklahoma.

ELAINE HARROD has served as children's library assistant with the Moore Public Library, Moore, Oklahoma, for 17 years. A former kindergarten teacher, her published works include *Travel the Globe: Multicultural Story Times*. Harrod holds a bachelor's degree in early childhood education from the University of Science and Arts of Oklahoma.

SHEREEN RASOR, MLIS, is library media director at Mustang Creek Elementary School, Mustang, Oklahoma. A classroom teacher for 17 years, she earned a bachelor's degree from the University of Central Oklahoma and a master's degree in library and information studies from the University of Oklahoma. Rasor is the oldest daughter of Donna Norvell, original author from the first edition of Libraries Unlimited's *Travel the Globe: Multicultural Story Times*.

SANDY SHROPSHIRE is materials selection specialist with the Children's Readers Center, Pioneer Library System, Norman, Oklahoma. She was a children's librarian assistant for over 20 years at the Moore Public Library in Moore, Oklahoma. Her published works include Libraries Unlimited's *Travel the Globe: Multicultural Story Times* and *The Kids' Book Club: Lively Reading and Activities for Grades 1–3*. In addition, she illustrated *The Buffalo Train Ride* and *Bone Head: Story of a Longhorn*. Shropshire holds a degree in professional art from the University of Science and Arts of Oklahoma.